W0111763

Computer Communications and Networks

Series editors

A. J. Sammes, Cyber Security Centre, Faculty of Technology,
De Montfort University, Leicester, UK

Jacek Rak, Department of Computer Communications, Faculty of Electronics,
Telecommunications and Informatics, Gdansk University of Technology,
Gdansk, Poland

The **Computer Communications and Networks** series is a range of textbooks, monographs and handbooks. It sets out to provide students, researchers, and non-specialists alike with a sure grounding in current knowledge, together with comprehensible access to the latest developments in computer communications and networking.

Emphasis is placed on clear and explanatory styles that support a tutorial approach, so that even the most complex of topics is presented in a lucid and intelligible manner.

More information about this series at http://www.springer.com/series/4198

Pethuru Raj · Anupama Raman

Software-Defined Cloud Centers

Operational and Management Technologies and Tools

 Springer

Pethuru Raj
Reliance Jio Cloud Services
Bangalore
India

Anupama Raman
Flipkart Internet India Pvt. Ltd.
Bangalore
India

ISSN 1617-7975   ISSN 2197-8433   (electronic)
Computer Communications and Networks
ISBN 978-3-030-08752-4   ISBN 978-3-319-78637-7   (eBook)
https://doi.org/10.1007/978-3-319-78637-7

Foreword

The Present-Day IT Landscape is abuzz with the new concept of the "Software-Defined Data Center," or SDCC. SDCC supports all cloud capabilities which are required for enterprises. The key differentiator between SDDC and traditional data center is the replacement of physical assets with virtualized components which will lead to several types of optimization like cost optimization, space optimization, power optimization, performance optimization to name a few top of the mind items. SDDC opens avenues for several new use cases which include managing, deploying, storing, computing, and networking a plethora of business applications in a cloud environment. It is a huge leap in the IT world as it marks the transition of computing to an era where data center components are abstracted from the underlying hardware. There is virtualization in every aspect starting from compute to network to storage. This had led to a new dimension in infrastructure components like software-defined compute, software-defined network, and software-defined storage. All these software-defined infrastructure components form the basis of software-defined data center.

By 2020, Gartner predicts that the programmatic capabilities of an SDDC will be considered a core requirement for 75 percent of Global 2000 enterprises that have plans to either implement a DevOps approach or a hybrid cloud model. This prediction throws light on the importance of SDDC in the years to come. Authors of this book have undoubtedly chosen a topic which is the need of the day to write a book. I have gone through this book and it beautifully articulates the various components of SDDC like:

- Software-Defined Compute
- Software-Defined Network
- Software-Defined Storage

Some aspects which are critical for any SDDC are orchestration and service management as these are the core aspects pertaining to cloud capabilities. It is vital to ensure that there is seamless management of components within an SDDC to deliver upon the agreed terms of quality of service and service-level agreement.

Authors have beautifully articulated these concepts, and they have given in-depth coverage of orchestration and cloud service management in an SDDC.

Last but not least, security is the most important concern when it comes to any form of cloud capability and the same applies to SDDC as well. The diverse types of security concerns and the steps that could be taken to protect the SDDC from those security threats are articulated well in this book.

My concluding remarks the book is "This book provides a bird's eye view of SDDC and is a must to read for any practitioner, architect or engineer who wants to setup or use a SDDC."

Bangalore, India   R. Murali Krishnan
General Manager, Pre-sales Head—Engineering and
R&D Services, Vertical Mid-Market HCL
Technologies Ltd.

Preface

Without an iota of doubt, it has been an incredible and inspiring journey for the cloud phenomenon thus far. Worldwide institutions, innovators, and individuals are showing unprecedented interest and involvement in consciously absorbing and adopting various proven and potential cloud technologies and tools to be ahead of their competitors and to retain the edge gained. The cloud concept is bringing in a variety of delectable advancements toward highly optimized and organized IT. Further on, the cloud paradigm opens up hitherto unknown possibilities and opportunities for solid innovations and improvisations in IT operations and delivery. There are a bevy of cloud-induced automation, acceleration, and augmentation, and these are being meticulously imbibed and imbedded to set up and sustain lean, green, and clean IT. The cloud-empowered IT, in turn, fervently lays down a stimulating and sustainable foundation for envisioning and ensuring better and bigger business capabilities with less IT investment and infrastructures. The IT wastage is being carefully pinpointed and plugged. New deployment and service models are being thought through and implemented in the IT landscape to cater emerging and evolving business needs. And the resulting savings are being routed back to bring forth fresh competencies in IT and business. The business agility, autonomy, adaptability, and affordability are being easily and quickly realized with the real-ization of cloud-enabled IT efficiency and elegance.

New business models are being framed to simplify and streamline various business offerings. The business productivity goes up significantly while the business operations are extremely and elegantly automated. The scores of cloud-sponsored advancements and accomplishments in the IT domain have direct and decisive impacts on business verticals. The mesmerizing implications of the cloud paradigm on IT and subsequently on business enterprises are to continue relentlessly in the days ahead due to the innate wherewithal of the cloud idea. Precisely speaking, the cloud conundrum has been making waves and penetrating into newer territories. The cloudification is being touted as the most overwhelming and game-changing process that has definitely and deftly disrupted and transformed the struggling IT field. As IT is the direct and greatest enabler of businesses, the cloud-inspired IT is to result in radical business enablement. This book is produced in order to tell all that are silently happening in the cloud space and how they are succulently and smartly utilized to bring pioneering and people-centric IT.

Chapter 1 illustrates the various trends and transitions happening in the IT space. This chapter explains how the incarnation of cloud-attached IT is to be the cynosure of IT experts, evangelists, and exponents for hosting and running analytical, operational, and transactional workloads. This chapter also details how the ensuing era of IoT, blockchain, and cognitive analytics is to be achieved through the bunch of evolutionary and revolutionary technologies in the cloud IT space.

Chapter 2 is describing the cloud 2.0 version. That is, how the new innovation of software-defined cloud environments is bringing in the right and relevant automation in traditional cloud centers. I have talked about software-defined compute, storage, and networking and how these three transitions collectively work in unison to produce the next-generation cloud centers, which are more tuned toward modern enterprises.

Chapter 3 is software-defined storage (SDC) for storage virtualization. Data center of present-day organization is facing lot of challenges to accommodate the huge amounts of unstructured data which is created from various sources. So it is the need of the day to devise techniques which will help them to optimize storage device usage. This is where storage virtualization technique comes into picture. The various aspects of storage virtualization which form a part of software-defined storage like cloud storage, storage tiering, deduplication are covered in detail in this chapter. Some of the technological advancements in the field of big data storage which are used extensively in data centers like Google File System, HDFS are also covered in this chapter.

Chapter 4 is software-defined networking (SDN) for network virtualization. This chapter focuses exclusively on techniques which are used for network optimization in data center. The core technological foundation of all these technologies is net-work virtualization. Hence, the concept of network virtualization is covered in detail in this chapter. The other network virtualization topics which are covered in detail in this chapter are software-defined networking and network functions virtualization.

Chapter 5 is about the hybrid cloud formation. Typically, bridging private and public clouds results in hybrid clouds. There are certain requirements, scenarios, and use cases mandating for hybrid clouds. This chapter is specially allocated for digging deep and describing about the various qualities and benefits of hybrid clouds. How some of the concerns and challenges of public and private clouds are being surmounted by establishing a beneficial synchronization between private and public cloud environments are explained in this chapter.

Chapter 6 is security management of a software-defined data center. The software-defined data center infrastructure in its entirety contains a wide gamut of technologies like cloud, big data, mobile devices, and Internet of things. Each of these technological components is susceptible to several types of security vul-nerabilities and threats which can render them ineffective. It is very important to ensure that the infrastructure components are adequately safeguarded from various security breaches. The crux of the lesson is the techniques to be adopted for securing the platforms and technologies which form a part of the software-defined data center ecosystem.

Chapter 7 is cloud service management. Organizations across the world are now moving toward a model in which they are using a combination of on-premise and cloud-based services to manage their infrastructure and application components. This has led to evolution of a new paradigm which is called hybrid IT. In this chapter, we propose a framework which can be used by organizations for managing their hybrid IT infrastructure components. Some of the key characteristics which need to be kept in mind while designing such frameworks are also discussed in this chapter. We also cover the various aspects of cloud management platforms (CMPs) and some leading cloud management platforms which are available in the market.

Chapter 8 details about multi-cloud environments and how they are being managed through automated tools. Having understood the strategic significance of multi-cloud strategy and projects, enterprises across the world are jumping into the multi-cloud bandwagon. However, the multi-cloud management is a tough affair. There are a few cloud management platforms being presented as the best-in-class solution for multi-cloud management and maintenance. This chapter has a lot of useful details for our esteemed readers to gather and gain immeasurably.

Chapter 9 is for describing the new software product in the growing cloud landscape. The cloud ecosystem continuously expands with multiple and different services. The cloud service and resource providers are journeying in their own ways utilizing heterogeneous technologies and tools. The cloud service registry and repository is growing steadily. The service charges are also varying hugely. For cloud consumers, clients, customers, and consultants, the tasks of minutely and dynamically gathering and visualizing consolidated information and other decision-enabling and value-adding details such as service quality, the compliance, the costs from cloud and communication service providers are tough and time-consuming job. The emergence of cloud broker, a highly smart and sophisticated software solution and organizations providing cloud brokerage services, comes handy for cloud users toward simplified and streamlined cloud access, use, and composition.

Chapter 10 is for expressing the latest advancements and accomplishments in cloud orchestration, which is a hard nut to crack with traditional methods and tools. We need state-of-the-art solutions and platforms for automating most of the cloud operations. This chapter tells the importance of cloud and container orchestration in order to automate the end-to-end application integration, testing, infrastructure provisioning, software deployment, configuration, and delivery.

Bangalore, India   Pethuru Raj
                                                                      Anupama Raman

Acknowledgements

I express my sincere gratitude to Mr. Simon Rees, Springer, Associate Editor, Computer Science, for immensely helping us from the conceptualization to the completion of this book. I thank my managers (Mr. Anish Shah and Mr. Kiran Thomas) from Reliance Jio Infocomm. Ltd, India, for extending their moral support in finishing this book. I thank my co-author (Anupama Raman) for her consistent cooperation in completing this book.

I, at this point in time, recollect and reflect on the selfless sacrifices made by my parents in shaping up to me to this level. I would expressly like to thank my wife (Sweetlin Reena) and sons (Darren Samuel and Darresh Bernie) for their perseverance as I have taken the tremendous and tedious challenge of putting the book chapters together. I thank all the readers for their overwhelming support for our previous books. I give all the glory and honor to my Lord and Savior Jesus Christ for His abundant grace and guidance.

Anupama Raman
I take this opportunity to express my heartfelt thanks to Mr. Simon from Springer publications for this constant support for the completion of this book. I also express my sincere thanks to the reviewing and publishing teams of Springer Verlag and wholehearted thanks to Dr. Pethuru Raj for this constant support, guidance, and insights that helped me craft this book.

I also want to sincerely acknowledge the support extended by my parents, husband, and daughter (Aparna). I would also like to thank my friends and other relatives who have constantly motivated me to complete this book. Nothing in this world is possible without the blessings of the Almighty. At this point, I would like to thank the Almighty for giving me an opportunity to work on this book.

Contents

Chapter 1
The Distinct Trends and Transitions in the Information Technology (IT) Space

1.1 Introduction

There are competent technologies and tools that intrinsically empower IT infrastructures. That is the reason why we often hear, read, and even sometimes experience the buzzwords such as infrastructure as a service (IaaS), infrastructure programming, infrastructure as code. Especially, the impacts of Cloud technologies are really mesmerizing. That is, the Cloud idea is a blessing and boon for IT to do more with less. A variety of novel and noble things are being worked out with the application of the highly popular Cloud concepts. This chapter is specially prepared for enumerating and explaining the various dimensions of IT and how all these advances facilitate a better world for the society.

1.2 The Software-Defined IT

Due to the heterogeneity and multiplicity of software technologies such as programming languages, development models, data formats, and protocols, the software development, operational, and management complexities are growing continuously. Especially, enterprise-grade application development, deployment, and delivery are beset with real challenges. In the recent past, there are several breakthrough mechanisms to develop and run enterprise-grade software in an agile and adroit fashion. There came a number of complexity-mitigation and rapid development techniques for producing production-grade software in a swift and smart manner. The leverage of "divide and conquer" and "the separation of crosscutting concerns" techniques are being consistently experimented and encouraged to develop flexible and futuristic software solutions. The potential concepts of abstraction, encapsulation, virtualization, and other compartmentalization methods are being copiously invoked to reduce the software production pain. In addition, there are performance engineering and enhancement aspects getting utmost consideration from software architects, testing professionals, DevOps folks, and site reliability engineers (SREs). Thus software development processes, best practices, design patterns, evaluation metrics, key

© Springer International Publishing AG, part of Springer Nature 2018
P. Raj and A. Raman, *Software-Defined Cloud Centers*,
Computer Communications and Networks,
https://doi.org/10.1007/978-3-319-78637-7_1

guidelines, integrated platforms, enabling frameworks, simplifying templates, programming models, etc., are gaining immense significance in this software-defined world.

On the other hand, the software suites are being proclaimed as the most significant factor in bringing in the real automation for businesses as well as individuals. Automating the various business tasks gets nicely and neatly fulfilled through the leverage of powerful software products and packages. Originally, software was being touted as the business enabler. Now the trend is remarkably changing for a better world. That is, every individual is being lustrously enabled through software innovations, disruptions, and transformations. In other words, software is becoming the most appropriate tool for people empowerment. The contributions of the enigmatic software field are consistently on the rise. The software has been penetrative, participative, and pervasive. We already hear, read, and even experience software-defined Cloud environments. Every tangible thing is being continuously upgraded to be software-defined. Even the security domain got a name change. That is, the paradigm of software-defined security is becoming popular.

Digitized Objects through Software enablement—All kinds of common, cheap, and casual things in our everyday environments are software-enabled to be digitized. All the digitized entities and elements are capable of joining in the mainstream computing. Digital objects in the vicinity are inherently capable of getting connected with one another and can interact with remotely held enabled things, Web site contents, Cloud services, data sources, etc. Implantables, wearables, handhelds, instruments, equipment, machines, wares, consumer electronics, utensils, and other embedded systems (resource-constrained or intensive) are getting systematically digitized and networked in order to be remotely monitored, measured, managed, and maintained. Precisely speaking, any physical, mechanical, and electrical systems are software-enabled through an arsenal of edge technologies (sensors, microcontrollers, stickers, RFID tags, bar codes, beacons and LEDs, smart dust, specks, etc.). Even robots, drones, and our everyday items are precisely software-enabled to be distinct in their operations, outputs, and offerings. When sentient materials become digitized, then they are able to form a kind of ad hoc network in order to bring forth better and bigger accomplishments for humans. Everything is becoming smart, every device becomes smarter, and human beings are being empowered by the IoT and cyber-physical systems (CPSs) to be the smartest in their everyday decisions, deals, and deeds.

As per the market analysis and research reports, there will be millions of software services, billions of connected devices, and trillions of digitized entities in the years ahead. The challenge is to how to produce production-grade, highly integrated, and reliable software suites that draw its data from different and distributed devices. The software field has to grow along with all the other advancements happening in the business and IT spaces.

1.3 The Agile IT

The development and release cycles are becoming shorter and shorter. Delivering the right business value is what the software development is now all about. Traditionally, a software development project was structured in long cycles containing different well-defined phases like "requirements gathering and analysis," "systems architecture and design," "system development," "system test" and "system release" containing the entire scope of a system. The brewing trend is to bring in the desired agility in software engineering. As a result, software development and release cycles have become shorter. It is important to release a small scope of functionality quickly so immediate feedback can be received from the users. The evolution of a system becomes a more gradual approach.

There are agile methods being rolled out to speed up the process of bringing software solutions and services to the market. Pair programming, extreme programming, Scrum, behavior-driven development (BDD), and test-driven development (TDD) are the prominent and dominant ways and means of achieving the goals of agile programming. That is, software gets constructed quickly but the story does not end there. After the development activity, the unit, integration, and regression tests happen to validate the software. Thereafter, the software is handed over to the administration and operational team to deploy the production-grade software in production environments to be subscribed and used by many.

Now the operational team also has to equally cooperate with the development team to set up the reliable operational environment to deploy and run applications. The speed with which the runtime environments and the ICT infrastructures are being established and supplied plays a very vital role in shaping up the agile delivery of software applications to their users. Precisely speaking, for ensuring business agility, besides the proven agile programming techniques, the operational efficiency is bound to play a very critical role. That is, the need of leveraging a wider variety of automated tools for enabling the distinct goals of DevOps is being widely recognized and hence the DevOps movement is gaining a lot of traction these days.

1.4 The Hybrid IT

The worldwide institutions, individuals, and innovators are keenly embracing the Cloud technology with all the clarity and confidence. With the faster maturity and stability of Cloud environments, there is a distinct growth in building and delivering cloud-native applications and there are viable articulations and approaches to readily make cloud-native software. Traditional and legacy software applications are being meticulously modernized and moved to Cloud environments to reap the originally envisaged benefits of the Cloud idea. Cloud software engineering is one hot area drawing the attention of many software engineers across the globe. There are public, private, and hybrid Clouds. Recently, we hear more about edge/fog Clouds. Still, there are traditional IT environments and it is going to be the hybrid world.

1.5 The Distributed IT

Software applications are increasingly complicated yet sophisticated. Highly integrated systems are the new normal these days. Enterprise-grade applications ought to be seamlessly integrated with several third-party software components running in distributed and disparate systems. Increasingly software applications are made out of a number of interactive, transformative, and disruptive services in an ad hoc manner on a need basis. Multi-channel, multimedia, multi-modal, multi-device, and multi-tenant applications are becoming pervasive and persuasive. Further on, there are enterprise, Cloud, Web, mobile, IoT, Blockchain, and embedded applications in plenty hosted in virtual and containerized environments. Then there are industry-specific and vertical applications (energy, retail, government, telecommunication, supply chain, utility, healthcare, banking and insurance, automobiles, avionics, robotics, etc.) which are being designed and delivered via Cloud infrastructures.

There are software packages, homegrown software, turnkey solutions, scientific and technical computing services, customizable and configurable software applications, etc., to meet up distinct business requirements. In short, there are operational, transactional, and analytical applications running on private, public, and hybrid Clouds. With the exponential growth of connected devices, smart sensors and actuators, fog gateways, smartphones, microcontrollers, single-board computers (SBCs), the software-enabled data analytics and proximate moves to edge devices to accomplish real-time data capture, processing, decision-making, and action. We are destined toward real-time analytics and applications. Thus, it is clear that software is purposefully participative and productive. Largely, it is going to be the software-intensive world.

Development teams are geographically distributed and are working on multiple time zones. Due to the diversity and multiplicity of IT systems and business applications, distributed applications are being touted as the way forward. That is, the various components of any software application are being distributed across multiple locations for enabling redundancy-enabled high availability. Fault tolerance, less latency, independent software development, no vendor lock-in, etc., are being given as the reason for the realm of distributed applications. Accordingly, software programming models are being adroitly tweaked in order to do justice for the era of distributed and decentralized applications. Multiple development teams working on multiple time zones across the globe have become the new normal in this hybrid world of the onshore and offshore development model.

With big data era is all set in, the most usable and unique distributed computing paradigm is to flourish through the dynamic pool of commoditized servers and inexpensive computers. With the exponential growth of connected devices, the days of device Clouds are not too far away. That is, distributed and decentralized devices are bound to be clubbed together in large numbers to form ad hoc and application-specific Cloud environments for data capture, ingestion, preprocessing, and analytics. Thus, it is no doubt that the future belongs to distributed computing. The fully matured and stabilized centralized computing is unsustainable due to the need for Web-scale applications. Also, the next-generation Internet is the Internet of digitized things, connected devices, and microservices.

1.6   The Service IT

Mission-critical and versatile applications are to be built using the highly popular MSA pattern. Monolithic applications are being consciously dismantled using the MSA paradigm to be immensely right and relevant for their users and owners. Microservices are the new building block for constructing next-generation applications. Microservices are easily manageable, independently deployable, horizontally scalable, relatively simple services. Microservices are publicly discoverable, network-accessible, interoperable, API-driven, composed, replaceable, and highly isolated. The future software development is primarily finding appropriate microservices. Here are few advantages of the microservices architecture (MSA) style.

- **Scalability**—An application typically uses three types of scaling. The X-axis scaling is for horizontally cloning the application, the Y-axis scaling is for splitting the various application functionalities, and the Z-axis scaling is for partitioning or sharding the data. When the Y-axis scaling is applied to monolithic applications, the application is being broken into many and easily manageable units (microservices). Each unit fulfills one responsibility.
- **Availability**—Multiple instances of microservices are deployed in different containers (Docker) in order to guarantee high availability. Through this redundancy, the service and application availability is ensured. The service-level load balancing can be utilized to achieve high availability while the circuit breaker pattern can be utilized to achieve fault tolerance. And service configuration and discovery can enable the discovery of new services to communicate and collaborate toward the business goals.
- **Continuous deployment**—Microservices are independently deployable, horizontally scalable, and self-defined. Microservices are decoupled/lightly coupled, and cohesive fulfilling the elusive mandate of modularity. The dependency-imposed issues get nullified by embracing this architectural style. This leads to the deployment of any service independent of each other for faster and more continuous deployment.
- **Loose coupling**—As indicated above, microservices are autonomous and independent by innately providing the much-needed loose coupling. Every microservice has its own layered architecture at the service level and its own database at the backend.

- **Polyglot Microservices**—Microservices can be implemented through a variety of programming languages. As such, there is no technology lock-in. Any technology can be used to realize microservices. Similarly, there is no compulsion for using certain databases. Microservices work with any file system SQL databases, NoSQL and NewSQL databases, search engines, etc.
- **Performance**—There are performance engineering and enhancement techniques and tips in the microservices arena. For example, high-blocking call services are implemented in the single-threaded technology stack, whereas high CPU usage services are implemented using multiple threads.

There are other benefits for business and IT teams by employing the fast-maturing and stabilizing microservices architecture. The tool ecosystem is on the climb, and hence, implementing and involving microservices gets simplified and streamlined. Automated tools ease and speed up building and operationalizing microservices. You can find more about microservices in the subsequent sections.

1.7   The Containerized IT

The Docker idea has literally shaken the software world. A bevy of hitherto unknown advancements is being realized through the containerization. The software portability requirement, which has been lingering for a long time, gets solved through the open-source Docker platform. The real-time elasticity of Docker containers hosting a variety of microservices enabling the real-time scalability of business-critical software applications is being touted as the key factor and facet for the surging popularity of containerization. The intersection of microservices and Docker containers domains has brought in paradigm shifts for software developers as well as system administrators. The lightweight nature of Docker containers along with the standardized packaging format in association with the Docker platform goes a long way in stabilizing and speeding up software deployment.

   The container is a way to package software along with configuration files, dependencies, and binaries required to enable the software in any operating environment. There are a number of crucial advantages as enlisted below.

- **Environment consistency**—Applications/processes/microservices running on containers behave consistently in different environments (development, testing, staging, replica, and production). This eliminates any kind of environmental inconsistencies and makes testing and debugging less cumbersome and time-consuming.
- **Faster deployment**—A container is lightweight and starts and stops in a few seconds as it is not required to boot any OS image. This eventually helps to achieve faster creation, deployment, and high availability.
- **Isolation**—Containers running on the same machine using the same resources are isolated from each other. When we start a container with Docker run, behind the scenes, Docker creates a set of namespaces and control groups for the container. Namespaces provide the first and most straightforward form of isolation. That is,

processes running within a container cannot see and affect processes running in another container, or in the host system. Each container also gets its own network stack meaning that a container does not get privileged access to the sockets or interfaces of another container. If the host system is set up accordingly, then containers can interact with each other through their respective network interfaces. When we specify public ports for your containers or use links, then the IP traffic is allowed between containers. They can ping each other, send/receive UDP packets, and establish TCP connections, etc. Typically, all containers on a given Docker host are sitting on bridge interfaces. This means that they are just like physical machines connected through a common Ethernet switch.

All containers running on a specific host share the host kernel. While this is fine for a large number of use cases, for certain security-focused use cases, this is not acceptable. That is, there is a need for a stronger isolation. This is where the newly emerging concept of isolated containers is picking up. In the isolated containers approach, the containers have their own kernel and leverage isolation provided by virtualization mechanism; while retaining the usage, packaging, and deployment benefits of a container. There are multiple works happening in the area of providing stronger isolation to a container by leveraging virtual machine technology. Intel's clear containers approach and hyper from HyperHQ are few notable approaches.

1.8 The High-Quality IT

We have been developing software and hardware systems fulfilling the various functional requirements. But the challenge ahead is to guarantee the systems' non-functional requirements (NFRs). The much-maligned quality of service (QoS)/experience (QoE) attributes of IT systems and business applications ought to be ensured through a host of path-breaking technological solutions. Software development organizations, IT product vendors, research laboratories, academic institutions have to consciously strategize to devise ways and means of leveraging the latest advancements happening in the IT field. Business houses have to embark on a series of activities in order to embolden their IT with all the right and relevant capabilities in order to be ready for the ensuring era of knowledge. The current process steps have to be refined sharply; powerful architectural design and integration patterns have to be unearthed and popularized; infrastructure optimization through cloudification has to be sustained through a series of innovations, disruptions, and transformations; the distribution and decentralization computing models have to be consistently encouraged for the increasingly digitized world; the compartmentalization techniques (virtualization and containerization) have to be employed very frequently along with other automation methods, etc. Thus, realizing highly reliable software and hardware systems for the digital era have to be kick-started with care, clarity, and confidence.

1.9 The Cloud IT

Cloud centers are being positioned as the one-stop IT solution for deploying and delivering all kinds of software applications. Cloud storages are for stocking corporate, customer, and confidential data. Cloud platforms are accelerating the Cloud setup and sustenance. Cloud infrastructures are highly optimized and organized for hosting IT platforms and business applications. Distributed and different Cloud environments are being connected with one another in order to build federated Clouds. The standardization being incorporated in Cloud environments is to result in open Clouds by eliminating all sorts of persisting issues such as vendor lock-in. Massive and monolithic applications are being dismantled to be a growing collection of microservices and being taken to Cloud environments to be subscribed and used by many. The legacy applications are, through the leverage of microservices architecture and containerization, being modernized and migrated to Clouds. With the Cloud emerging as the centralized, consolidated, compartmentalized, automated, and shared IT infrastructure, the enterprise IT is veering toward the Cloud IT.

The popularity of the Cloud paradigm is surging, and it is overwhelmingly accepted as the disruptive, transformative, and innovative technology for the entire IT field. The direct benefits include IT agility through rationalization, simplification, heightened utilization, and optimization. This section explores the tectonic and seismic shifts of IT through the raging and rewarding Cloud concepts.

Adaptive IT—There is a number of cloud-inspired innovations in the form of service-oriented deployment, delivery, pricing, and consumption models in order to sustain the IT value for businesses. With IT agility setting in seamlessly, the much-insisted business agility, autonomy, affordability, and adaptivity are being guaranteed with the conscious adoption and adaption of Cloud idea.

People IT—Clouds support centralized yet federated working model. It operates at a global level. For example, today there are hundreds of thousands of smartphone applications and services accumulated in Cloud environments. There are specific Clouds for delivering mobile applications. There are powerful smartphones and other wearables to access Cloud resources and applications. With ultra-high broadband communication infrastructures networking advanced compute and storage infrastructures in place, the days of the Internet of devices, services, and things are to see a neat and nice reality. Self-, surroundings-, and situation-aware services will become common, plentiful, and cheap, thereby ITs are to see a grandiose transition to fulfill peoples' needs precisely. Personal IT will thrive and bring forth innumerable advantages and automation in humans individually as well as collectively in the days ahead.

Green IT—The whole world is becoming conscious about the power energy consumption and the heat getting dissipated into our living environment. There are calculated campaigns at different levels for arresting the catastrophic climate change and for the sustainable environment through less greenhouse-gas emission. IT data centers and server farms are also contributing to the environmental degradation. IT is being approached for arriving at workable green solutions. The grid and Cloud computing concepts are the leading concepts for establishing green IT environments. Besides, IT-based solutions are being worked out for closely monitoring, measuring, analyzing, and moderating power consumption and to lessen heat dissipation in non-IT environments. Especially, the smart energy grid and the Internet of Energy (IoE) disciplines are gaining a lot of ground in order to contribute decisively to the global goal of sustainability. The much-published and proclaimed Cloud paradigm leads to lean compute, communication, and storage infrastructures, which significantly enhance power conservation.

Optimal IT—There are a number of worthwhile optimizations happening in the business-enabling IT space. "More with less" has become the buzzword for IT managers as business executives mandate IT, teams, to embark on optimization tasks. Cloud-enablement has become the mandatory thing for IT divisions as there are several distinct benefits getting accrued out of this empowerment. Cloud certainly has the wherewithal for the goals behind the IT optimization drive.

With a number of delectable advancements in the wireless and wired broadband communication space, the future Internet is being positioned as the central tenet in conceiving and concretizing people-centric applications. With Cloud emerging as the new-generation IT infrastructure, we will have connected, cognizant, and cognitive IT that offers more influential and inferential capability to humans in their everyday deals, deeds, and decisions.

Converged, Collaborative, and Shared IT—The Cloud idea is fast penetrating into every tangible domain. Cloud's platforms are famous for not only software deployment and delivery but also for service design, development, debugging, and management. Further on, Clouds, being the consolidated, converged, and centralized infrastructure, are being prescribed and presented as the best bet for enabling seamless and spontaneous service integration, orchestration, and collaboration. With everything (application, platform, and infrastructure) are termed and touted as publicly discoverable, network-accessible, self-describing, autonomous, and multi-tenant services, Clouds will soon become the collaboration hub. Especially, composable businesses can be easily realized with the cloud-based collaboration platform.

Real-time and Real-world IT—Data's variety, volume, and velocity are on the climb. With the mass appeal of Hadoop implementations such as MapR, Cloudera, Hortonworks, Apache Hadoop, squeezing out usable insights out of big data is becoming common. The parallelization approaches, algorithms, architectures, and applications go a long way in extracting useful information out of data heaps. Similarly, there are real-time systems and databases emerging and evolving fast in order to spit out real-time insights in order to enable men and machines to initiate the countermeasures in time with all the clarity and confidence. The traditional IT systems find it difficult for the era of big data. Another trend is to discover pragmatic insights out of big data in real time. There are in-memory computing and in-database systems along with clusters of commodity hardware elements. Thus, all kinds of data (big, fast, streaming, and IoT) are going through a variety of processing (batch and real time) in order to accomplish transitioning captured and cleansed data to information and to knowledge. Data is emerging as the most significant corporate asset to do predictive, prescriptive and personalized analytics. Cloud is the optimized, automated, and virtualized infrastructure for next-generation analytics. That is, with the excellent infrastructure support from Clouds, we can easily expect a lot of distinct improvements in the days ahead so that the ultimate goal of real-time insights can be realized very fluently and flawlessly for producing real-world applications and services.

Automated and Affordable IT—This is definitely a concrete output with the adoption of path-breaking technologies. A number of manual activities for system and software configuration, operation, administration, and maintenance are being automated through a host of templates-based, patterns-centric, and policy-based tools.

In short, the arrival and accentuation of the Cloud idea and ideals have brought in a flurry of praiseworthy improvisations in the IT field, which in turn guarantees business efficacy. That is why there is a rush of Cloud technologies and tools by individuals, innovators, and institutions.

1.10   The Cognitive IT

With billions of connected devices and trillions of digitized objects, the data getting generated due to their on-demand and purposeful interactions are massive in volumes. The data speed, structure, schema, size, and scope are varying, and this changing phenomenon presents a huge challenge for data scientists, IT teams, and business executives. The data mining domain is being empowered with additional technologies and tools in order to collect and crunch big, fast, streaming, and IoT data to extricate useful information and actionable insights in time. Thus, the connected world expects enhanced cognition in order to make sense out of data heaps. The cognition capability of IT systems, networks, and storage appliances is therefore explicitly welcome toward the realization of smarter environments such as smarter hotels, homes, and hospitals. There is an arsenal of pioneering technologies and tools (machine and deep learning algorithms, real-time data analytics, natural language processing, image, audio and video processing, cognitive computing, context-awareness, and edge analytics) emerging in the IT industry to smoothen the route toward the projected cognitive IT.

1.11   The Hyper converged IT

Hyper converged infrastructure (HCI) is a data center architecture that embraces Cloud ergonomics and economics. Based on software, hyper converged infrastructure consolidates server compute, storage, network switch, hypervisor, data protection, data efficiency, global management, and other enterprise functionality on commodity ×86 building blocks to simplify IT and increase efficiency, enable seamless scalability, improve agility, and reduce costs. Hyper converged infrastructure is the culmination and conglomeration of several trends that provide specific value to the modern enterprise.

At the highest level, this emerges as a way forward to enable cloud-like affordability and scale without compromising the performance, resiliency, and availability expected in our own data centers. Hyper converged infrastructure provides significant benefits.

- **Data efficiency**—Hyper converged infrastructure reduces storage, bandwidth, and IOPS requirements.
- **Elasticity**—Hyper converged infrastructure makes it easy to scale out/in resources as required by business demands.
- **Workload-centricity**—A focus on the workload as the cornerstone of enterprise IT, with all supporting constructs focused on applications.
- **Data protection**—Ensuring data restoration in the event of loss or corruption is a key IT requirement, made far easier by hyper converged infrastructure.
- **VM mobility**—Hyper converged infrastructure enables greater application/workload mobility.
- **Resiliency**—Hyper converged infrastructure enables higher levels of data availability than possible in legacy systems.
- **Cost efficiency**—Hyper converged infrastructure brings to IT a sustainable step-based economic model that eliminates waste.

Convergence comes in many forms. At its most basic, convergence simply brings together existing individual storage, compute, and network-switching products into pre-tested, pre-validated solutions sold as a single solution. However, this level of convergence only simplifies the purchase and upgrade cycle. It fails to address ongoing operational challenges often introduced with the advent of virtualization. There are still LUNs to create, WAN optimizers to acquire and configure, and third-party backup and replication products to purchase and maintain. Hyper converged infrastructure seamlessly combines compute, storage, networking, and data services in a single solution, a single physical system. The software that enables hyper convergence runs on industry-standard ×86 systems, with the intention of running virtualized or containerized workloads. Distributed architecture let to cluster multiple systems within and between sites, forming a shared resource pool which enables high availability, workload mobility, and efficient scaling of performance and capacity. Typically managed through a single interface, hyper converged infrastructures let you define policy and execute activities at the VM/container level. The results are significant and include lower CAPEX as a result of lower upfront infrastructure costs, lower OPEX through reductions in operational costs and personnel, and faster time-to-value for new business needs. On the technical side, newly emerging IT generalists—IT staff with broad knowledge of infrastructure and business needs—can easily support hyper converged systems. No longer do organizations need to maintain islands of resource engineers to manage each aspect of the data center.

1.12   Conclusion

We have discussed the trends and transitions happening in the IT domain. And IT has become a complete and comprehensive paradigm for industry verticals. Newer capabilities are being rolled out due to the incessant advancements in the IT landscape, and hence, we are hearing about fresh possibilities and opportunities. IT software has the most domineering effect on business sentiments. It is definitely a good news that IT is consistently on the growth path. Its application areas are growing continuously. Its power and grip on various industry domains are growing as never before. Hitherto unknown benefits are being accrued out of the innovations being unearthed in the IT space. New sectors are greatly embracing the IT to be elegantly productive, delightful to their esteemed customers, clients, and consumers, and extremely affordable.

Now, IT is internally empowered to do more with less. There are rationalization, optimization, modernization, compartmentalization (virtualization and containerization), cloudification (consolidation, centralization, federation, orchestration, integration, etc.) techniques and tips in plenty to automate most of the IT infrastructure operations. The new fields such as DevOps, NoOps, AIOps. DataOps, site reliability engineering (SRE), customer reliability engineering (CRE) are bringing forth a number of advancements for sustaining IT for the years ahead. The role of data analytics, artificial intelligence (AI) methods (machine and deep learning algorithms), real-time log, operational, performance, security, correlational and customer analytics, etc., is enabling IT to be right and relevant for institutions, innovators, and individuals.

Chapter 2
Demystifying Software-Defined Cloud Environments

2.1 Introduction

There are several useful links in the portal pointing to a number of resources on the software-defined Cloud environments. The readers are encouraged to visit the portal to get the links to highly beneficial information on SDDCs. This chapter is designed to explain the distinct features and facilities of software-defined Cloud centers. Large-scale Cloud centers are to get immense benefits with the software-defined resources. Besides virtualization, containerization is the popular mechanism for software-enabling IT infrastructures. Precise and enhanced utilization of IT resources are being guaranteed through the smart application of containerization concepts. The accessibility, flexibility, extensibility, portability, and modifiability of various IT infrastructure modules get simplified and streamlined through software enablement. The distributed deployment of servers, storage appliances, and arrays, network and security solutions and their centralized monitoring, measurement, and management are also facilitated through software-defined infrastructures. There are a number of benefits being accrued out of the software enablement, and hence, Cloud infrastructures in order to get deeper and decisive optimization are being software defined. A variety of log and operational data gets accumulated and they are consciously collected, cleansed, and crunched in order to extricate operational insights for administrators and others to take a timely decision and to plunge into action with all the clarity and confidence.

2.2 Reflecting the Cloud Journey

The Cloud journey is rigorously on the right track. The principal objective of the hugely popular Cloud paradigm is to realize highly organized and optimized IT environments for enabling business automation, acceleration, and augmentation. Most of the enterprise IT environments across the globe are bloated, closed, inflexible, static, complex, and expensive. The brewing business and IT challenges are therefore how to make IT elastic, extensible, programmable, dynamic, modular, and cost-effective.

© Springer International Publishing AG, part of Springer Nature 2018
P. Raj and A. Raman, *Software-Defined Cloud Centers*,
Computer Communications and Networks,
https://doi.org/10.1007/978-3-319-78637-7_2

Especially with the worldwide businesses are cutting down their IT budgets gradually year after year, the enterprise IT team has left with no other option other than to embark on a meticulous and measured journey to accomplish more with less through a host of pioneering and promising technological solutions. Organizations are clearly coming to the conclusion that business operations can run without any hitch and hurdle with less IT resources through effective commoditization, consolidation, centralization, compartmentalization (virtualization and containerization), federation, and rationalization of various IT solutions (servers, storage appliances, and networking components). IT operations also go through a variety of technologies-induced innovations and disruptions to bring in the desired rationalization and optimization. The acts of simplification and standardization for achieving IT industrialization are drawing a lot of attention these days. The various IT resources such as memory, disk storage, processing power, and I/O consumption are critically and cognitively monitored, measured, and managed toward their utmost utilization. The pooling and sharing of IT solutions and services are being given the prime importance toward the strategic IT optimization.

Even with all the unprecedented advancements in the Cloud landscape, there are opportunities and possibilities. The concept of software-defined Clouds (SDCs) is, therefore, gaining a lot of accreditation these days. Product vendors, Cloud service providers, system integrators, and other principal stakeholders are looking forward to having SDCs. The right and relevant technologies for the realization and sustenance of software-defined Cloud environments are fast maturing and stabilizing, and hence, the days of SDCs are not too far away. This chapter is specially crafted for expressing and exposing all the appropriate details regarding the elicitation and engineering of various requirements (functional as well as non-functional).

2.3 Elucidating the Cloudification Process

The mesmerizing Cloud paradigm has become the mainstream concept in IT today and its primary and ancillary technologies are flourishing. The cloudification movement has blossomed these days, and most of the IT infrastructures and platforms along with business applications are being remedied to be cloud-ready in order to reap all the originally envisaged benefits of the Cloud idea.

The virtualization technique has put in a firm and fabulous foundation for the runaway success of Cloud computing. Especially, server machines are being logically partitioned to carve out a few highly insulated virtual machines (VMs). Then, there are a number of standards-compliant and industry-strength automation tools for resource provisioning, configuration, orchestration, monitoring, and management, software deployment and delivery. A 360° view of IT infrastructural components through an integrated dashboard is the new normal. Thus, powerful tools play out a very interesting and inspiring role in making Cloud pervasive, persuasive, and penetrative. Most of the manual activities associated with the establishment of IT infrastructures, software installation, IT administration and operation, IT services management and maintenance are being automated through a variety of technologies. The concept of DevOps is very enticing these days in order to ensure the incredible requirements of IT agility, adaptivity, and affordability. Automation through templates, patterns, and tools is becoming a common affair in IT lately and to substantially reduce human errors. The productivity of IT systems is being remarkably increased through various ways and means. The processes are synchronized to be lean yet efficient. Domain-specific languages (DSLs) are being brought into bring the required automation. Platforms are being readied to accelerate IT management, governance, and enhancement. There are standards such as OpenStack and their optimal implementations in order to enforce resource portability, interoperability, accessibility, scalability, live-in migration, etc. That is, the distributed deployment of compute instances and storage appliances under the centralized management is the key differentiator for the prodigious success of Cloud computing.

Technology Choice is critical—There are several competent yet contrasting technologies in the IT space today, and hence, the selection of implementation technologies has to be strategically planned and carefully played out. Not only the technologies but also the methodologies need to be smartly carried out. In other words, the technology embarkation and usage have to be done with all seriousness and sagacity otherwise, even if the technologies chosen might be sound yet projects would not see the originally emphasized success. Further on, the history clearly says that many technologies emerged and disappeared from the scene without contributing anything substantial due to the lack of inherent strengths and sagacity. Very few technologies could survive and contribute copiously for a long time. Primarily, the intrinsic complexity toward technologies' all-around utilization and the lack of revered innovations are being touted as the chief reasons for their abject and abysmal failure and the subsequent banishment into the thin air. Thus, the factors such as the fitment/suitability, adaptability, sustainability, simplicity, and extensibility of technologies ought to be taken into serious consideration while deciding technologies and tools for enterprise-scale, transformational, and mission-critical projects. The Cloud technology is being positioned as the best-in-class technology in the engrossing IT domain with all the necessary wherewithal, power, and potential for handsomely and hurriedly contributing for the business disruption, innovation, and transformation needs. Precisely speaking, the Cloud idea is the aggregation of several proven techniques and tools for realizing the most efficient, elegant and elastic IT infrastructure for the ensuing knowledge era.

2.4   The IT Commoditization and Compartmentalization

The arrival of Cloud concepts has brought in remarkable changes in the IT landscape that in turn lead in realizing big transitions in the delivery of business applications and services and in the solid enhancement of business flexibility, productivity, and sustainability. Formally, Cloud infrastructures are centralized, virtualized, automated, and shared IT infrastructures. The utilization rate of Cloud infrastructures has gone up significantly. Still, there are dependencies curtailing the full usage of expensive IT resources. Employing the decoupling technique among various modules to decimate all kinds of constricting dependencies, more intensive and insightful process automation through orchestration and policy-based configuration, operation, management, delivery, and maintenance, attaching external knowledge bases are widely prescribed to achieve still more IT utilization to cut costs remarkably. Lately, the aroma of commoditization and compartmentalization is picking up. These two are the most important ingredients of cloudification. Let us begin with the commoditization technique.

- **The Commoditization of Compute Machines**—The tried and time-tested abstraction aspect is being recommended for fulfilling the commoditization need. There is a technological maturity as far as physical/bare metal machines getting commoditized through partitioning. The server commoditization has reached a state of semblance and stability. Servers are virtualized, containerized, shared across many clients, publicly discovered and leveraged over any network, delivered as a service, billed for the appropriate usage, automatically provisioned, composed toward large-scale clusters, monitored, measured, and managed through tools, performance tuned, made policy-aware, automatically scaled up and out based on brewing user, data and processing needs, etc. In short, Cloud servers are being made workloads-aware. However, that is not the case with networking and storage portions.
- **The Commoditization of Networking Solutions**—On the networking front, the propriety and expensive network switches and routers and other networking solutions in any IT data centers and server farms are consciously commoditized through a kind of separation. That is, the control plane gets abstracted out, and hence, the routers and switches have only the data forwarding plane. That means, there is less intelligence into these systems; thereby, the goal of commoditization of network elements is technologically enabled. The controlling intelligence embedded inside various networking solutions is adroitly segregated and is being separately developed and presented as a software controller. This transition makes routers and switches dumb as they lose out their costly intelligence. Also, this strategically sound segregation comes handy in interchanging one with another one from a different manufacturer. The vendor lock-in problem simply vanishes with the application of the widely dissected and deliberated abstraction concept. Now with the controlling stake is in pure software form, incorporating any kind of patching in addition to configuration and policy changes in the controlling module can be done quickly in a risk-free and rapid manner. With such a neat and nice abstrac-

tion procedure, routers and switches are becoming commoditized entities. There is fresh business and technical advantages as the inflexible networking in present-day IT environments is steadily inching toward to gain the venerable and wholesome benefits of the commoditized networking.

- **The Commoditization of Storage Appliances**—Similar to the commoditization of networking components, all kinds of storage solutions are being commoditized. There are a number of important advantages with such transitions. In the subsequent sections, readers can find more intuitive and informative details on this crucial trait. Currently, commoditization is being realized through the proven abstraction technique.

Thus, commoditization plays a very vital role in shaping up the Cloud idea. For enhanced utilization of IT resources in an affordable fashion and for realizing software-defined Cloud environments, the commoditization techniques are being given more thrusts these days.

The compartmentalization is being realized through the virtualization and containerization technologies. There are several comprehensive books on Docker-enabled containerization in the market, and hence, we skip the details of containerization, which is incidentally being touted as the next best thing in the Cloud era.

As indicated above, virtualization is one of the prime compartmentalization techniques. As widely accepted and articulated, virtualization has been in the forefront in realizing highly optimized, programmable, managed, and autonomic Cloud environments. Virtualization leads to the accumulation of virtualized and software-defined IT resources, which are discoverable, network-accessible, critically assessable, interoperable, composable, elastic, easily manageable, individually maintainable, centrally monitored, and expertly leveraged. The IT capabilities are being given as a service, and hence, we often come across the word "IT as a Service." There is a movement toward the enigma of granting every single IT resource as a service. With the continued availability of path-breaking technologies, resource provisioning is getting automated and this will result in a new concept of "resource as a service (RaaS)."

Bringing in the much-discoursed modularity in order to enable programmable IT infrastructures, extracting, and centralizing all the embedded intelligence via robust and resilient software, distributed deployment, centralized management, and federation are being touted as the viable and venerable course of actions for attaining the originally envisaged success. That is, creating a dynamic pool of virtualized resources, allocating them on demand to accomplish their fullest utilization, charging them for the exact usage, putting unutilized resources back to the pool, monitoring, measuring, and managing resource performance, etc., are the hallmarks of next-generation IT infrastructures. Precisely speaking, IT infrastructures are being software-defined to bring in much-needed accessibility, consumability, malleability, elasticity, and extensibility.

On-demand IT has been the perpetual goal. All kinds of IT resources need to have the inherent capability of pre-emptively knowing of users' as well as applications' IT resource requirements and accordingly fulfil them without any instruction, interpretation, and involvement of human resources. IT resources need to be scaled up and down based on the changing needs so that the cost can be under control. That is, perfect provisioning of resources is the mandate. Overprovisioning raises up the pricing, whereas underprovisioning is a cause for performance degradation worries. The Cloud paradigm transparently leverages a number of software solutions and specialized tools in order to provide scalability of applications through resource elasticity. The expected dynamism in resource provisioning and de-provisioning has to become a core and concrete capability of Clouds.

That is, providing right-sized IT resources (compute, storage, and networking) for all kinds of business software solutions is the need of the hour. Users increasingly expect their service providers' infrastructures to deliver these resources elastically in response to their changing needs. There is no Cloud services infrastructure available today capable of simultaneously delivering scalability, flexibility, and high operational efficiency. The methodical virtualization of every component of a Cloud center ultimately leads to software-defined environments.

2.5 Switching to Software-Defined Data Centers (SDDCs)

An increasing number of enterprises are realizing the benefits of utilizing Cloud infrastructures, platforms, and applications to support employee productivity, collaboration, and business innovation. Definitely, the Cloud embarkation journey brings forth business, technical, and use cases. The key advantages include reduced operational costs, higher accessibility, and lower maintenance. These technological advancements have paved the way for innovators to come up with a wide range of Cloud products to meet changing business needs.

As articulated above, the key transformation from the traditional data environment is none other than the software-defined data center (SDDC) concept. This new offering has laid a stimulating and sustainable foundation for a number of innovations in the hugely popular Cloud paradigm. A data center is a facility that keeps all of a company's data centrally housed. Think of a data center as the hub for IT operations and equipment. Some data centers are specific to a single company while others house data for multiple companies. Those who operate data centers specialize in keeping data secure and servers running. The purpose is to ensure business continuity. A software-defined data center is an advanced data center. It is a completely virtualized and cloud-enabled data center. SDDCs deliver a programmatic approach to the functions of a traditional data center via a virtualized environment. These functions include:

- Computing
- Networking
- Security
- Server availability
- Storage

SDDCs use automation to keep business-critical functions operational around the clock, reducing the need for IT manpower and hardware. They deliver on each feature via a software platform accessible by the organization. Virtualized I/O is a term used to describe input/output functions in a virtual environment. It is a key principle of how SDDCs operate. In a traditional network, servers have certain hardware requirements that enable to physically connect them to one another to share data and other functions. But in an SDDC, each virtual machine must be imprinted with a part of I/O and bandwidth belonging to its host server. With the advent of converged I/O, network technology has the power to support SDDC and ITaaS initiatives. This transition has enabled certain things as explained below.

Business agility—Implementing an SDDC offers a number of benefits that increase business agility with a focus on three key areas: balance, flexibility, and adaptability. SDDCs increase business productivity by consolidating duplicate functions. This means that IT resources are freed up to spend their time solving other problems, resulting in greater agility. In addition, SDDCs help businesses increase their ROI so they have more funds to spend on adding newer business capabilities.

Reduced cost—In general, it costs less to operate an SDDC compared with housing data in conventional data centers. Traditional data centers, due to the nature of the business, have to charge more to cover the cost of round-the-clock employees, security, and operational needs like building leases and hardware. Organizations that house their data in-house require additional IT manpower, expensive equipment, time, and maintenance. Those that have not put much thought into data storage may suffer the possible costs of a potential data breach. An expensive hardware malfunction is yet another possibility that could cause loss of data. SDDCs just charge a recurring monthly cost. This is usually an affordable rate, making an SDDC accessible to all types of businesses, even those who may not have a large technology budget.

Increased scalability—By design, SDDCs can easily expand along with business. Increasing storage space or adding functions is usually as easy as contacting the data facility to get a revised monthly service quote. This offers a significant advantage compared to organizations who have to scale by making more room for additional servers, purchasing hardware and software, not to mention bringing in manpower to make the transition. The appeal of traditional data centers has always been that they ease the burden off an organization's shoulders, leaving their in-house IT team to focus on strategy as they scale. But SDDCs take this benefit a step further, offering potentially unlimited scalability.

In summary, SDDCs are not yet commonplace in today's digital economy, but technology trends suggest that they will be. Until then, as more businesses virtualize automated IT functions, demand for both products like SDDCs and DevOps professionals who can code them will continue to increase. Indeed, SDDCs offer an innovative way to store data suitable for enterprise organizations interested in successfully using DevOps to advance digital transformation.

Overall, organizations face pressure for continual innovation in the digital enterprise that drives the need to deliver IT services faster and support agile application development and deployment. More specifically, to gain a competitive advantage, enterprises must:

- Power digital innovation with fast, automated provisioning of multi-tier applications
- Drive down costs by managing complex, heterogeneous environments at scale
- Reduce risk of automated Cloud compliance and governance

These business outcomes can be achieved by implementing a Cloud management strategy that can support business agility while managing risk across complex environments.

2.6   The Emergence of Software-Defined Infrastructures (SDI)

We have discussed the commoditization tenet above. Now, the buzzword of software-defined everything (SDE) is all over the place as a fulfilling mechanism for next-generation Cloud environments. As widely accepted, software is penetrating into every tangible thing in order to bring in decisive and deterministic automation. Decision-enabling, activating, controlling, routing, switching, management, governance, and other associated policies and rules are being coded in software form in order to bring in the desired flexibilities in product installation, administration, configuration, customization, etc. In short, the behavior of any IT products (compute, storage, and networking) is being defined through software. Traditionally, all the right and relevant intelligence are embedded into IT systems. Now, those insights are being detached from those systems and run in a separate appliance or in virtual machines or in bare metal servers. This detached controlling machine could work with multiple IT systems. It is easy and quick to bring in modifications to the policies in software controller rather on the firmware, which is embedded inside IT systems. Precisely speaking, deeper automation and software-based configuration, controlling and operation of hardware resources are the principal enablers behind the long-standing vision of software-defined infrastructure (SDI).

A software-defined infrastructure is supposed to be aware and adaptive to the business needs and sentiments. Such infrastructures are automatically governed and managed according to the business changes. That is, the complex IT infrastructure management is automatically accomplished in consonance with the business direction and destination. Business goals are being literally programmed in and spelt in a software definition. The business policies, compliance and configuration requirements, and other critical requirements are etched in a software form. It is a combination of reusable and rapidly deployable patterns of expertise, recommended configurations, etc. in order to run businesses on the right path. There are orchestration templates and tools, Cloud management platforms such as OpenStack, automated software deployment solutions, configuration management and workflow scheduling solutions in order to accelerate and automate resource provisioning, monitoring, management, and delivery needs. These solutions are able to absorb the above-mentioned software definitions and could deliver on them perfectly and precisely. The SDI automatically orchestrates all its resources to meet the varying workload requirements in near real time. Infrastructures are being stuffed with real-time analytics through additional platforms such as operational, log, performance, and security analytics. As enunciated above, the SDI is a nimble, supple, highly optimized and organized, and workload-aware. The agility gained out of SDI is bound to propagate and penetrate further to bring the much-needed business agility. The gap between the business expectations and the IT supplies gets closed down with the arrival of software-defined infrastructures. SDI comprises not only the virtualized servers but also virtualized storages and networks. There are a few other names for SDI. VMware calls it software-defined data centers (SDDCs), while others call it software-defined environments (SDEs), software-defined Clouds (SDCs), cloud-enabled data centers (CeDCs). We can settle for the name "software-defined Clouds (SDCs)."

2.7   The Major Building Blocks of Software-Defined Clouds (SDCs)

Software-defined infrastructures are the key ingredients of SDCs. That is, an SDC encompasses software-defined compute, storage, and networking components. The substantially matured server virtualization leads to the realization of software-defined compute machines. Highly intelligent hypervisors (alternatively recognized as virtual machine monitors (VMMs) act as the perfect software solution to take care of the creation, provisioning, de-provisioning, live-in migration, decommissioning of computing machines (virtual machines and bare metal servers), etc. Most of the servers across leading Cloud centers are virtualized and it is clear that the server virtualization is reaching a state of stability. In a sense, the SDC is simply the logical extension of server virtualization. The server virtualization dramatically maximizes the deployment of computing power. Similarly, the SDC does the same for all of the resources needed to host an application, including storage, networking, and security.

In the past, provisioning a server machine to host an application took weeks of time. Today, a VM can be provisioned in a few minutes. Even containers can be provisioned in a few seconds. That is the power of virtualization and containerization. This sort of speed and scale being made possible through virtualization platforms is being extended to other IT resources. That is, the whole Cloud center is getting fully virtualized in order to tend toward the days of software-defined Clouds.

In SDCs, all IT resources are virtualized so they can be automatically configured and provisioned and made ready to install applications without any human intervention, involvement, and interpretation. Applications can be operational in minutes; thereby, the time to value has come down sharply. The IT cost gets reduced significantly. There are a number of noteworthy advancements in the field of server virtualization in the form of a host of automated tools, design and deployment patterns, easy-to-use templates, etc. The Cloud paradigm became a famous and fantastic approach for data center transformation and optimization because of the unprecedented success of server virtualization. This riveting success has since then penetrated into other important ingredients of data centers. IT resources are virtualized thereby are extremely elastic, remotely programmable, easily consumable, predictable, measurable, and manageable. With the comprehensive yet compact virtualization sweeping each and every component of data centers, the goals of distributed deployment of various resources but centrally monitored, measured, and managed is nearing the reality. Server virtualization has greatly improved data center operations, providing significant gains in performance, efficiency, and cost-effectiveness by enabling IT departments to consolidate and pool computing resources. Considering the strategic impacts of 100% virtualization, we would like to focus on network and storage virtualization methods in the sections to follow.

Network Virtualization—Server virtualization has played a pivotal and paramount role in Cloud computing. Through server virtualization, the goals of on-demand and faster provisioning besides the flexible management of computing resources are readily and rewardingly fulfilled. Strictly speaking, server virtualization also includes the virtualization of network interfaces from the operating system (OS) point of view. However, it does not involve any virtualization of the networking solutions such as switches and routers. The crux of the network virtualization is to derive multiple isolated virtual networks from sharing the same physical network. This paradigm shift blesses virtual networks with truly differentiated capabilities to coexist on the same infrastructure and to bring forth several benefits toward data center automation and transformation. Further on, VMs across geographically distributed Cloud centers can be connected to work together to achieve bigger and better things for businesses. These virtual networks can be crafted and deployed on demand and dynamically allocated for meeting differently expressed networking demands of different business applications. The functionalities of virtual networks are decisively varying. That is, virtual networks come handy in fulfilling not only the basic connectivity requirement but also are capable of getting tweaked to get heightened performance for specific workloads. Figure 2.1 vividly illustrates the difference between server and network virtualization.

2.8 Network Functions Virtualization (NFV)

There are several network functions such as load balancing, firewalling, routing, switching in any IT environment. The idea is to bring forth the established virtualization capabilities into the networking arena so that we can have virtualized load balancing, firewalling, etc. The fast-emerging domain of network functions virtual-

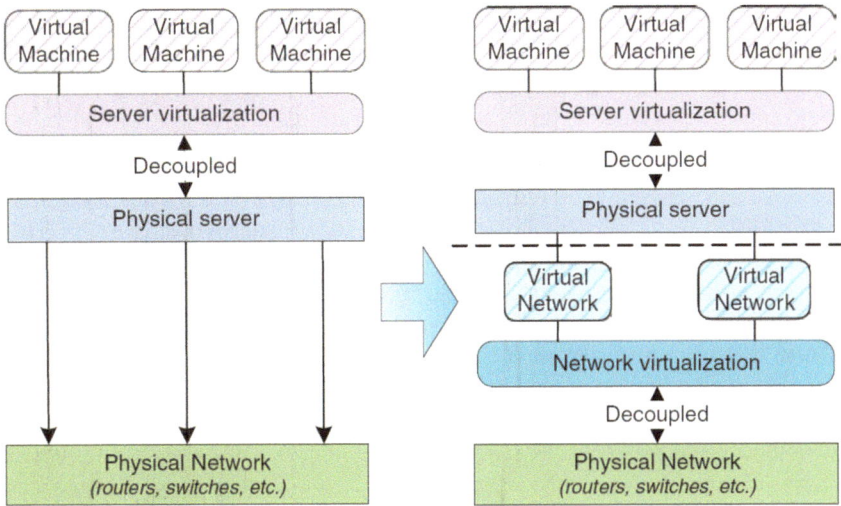

Fig. 2.1 Differences between server and network virtualization

ization aims to transform the way that network operators and communication service providers architect and operate communication networks and their network services.

Network Functions Virtualization (NFV) is getting a lot of attention these days and network service providers have teamed up well to convince their product vendors to move away from special-purpose equipment and appliances toward software-only solutions. These software solutions run on commodity servers, storages, and network elements such as switches, routers, application delivery controllers (ADCs). By embracing the NFV technology, communication and Cloud service providers could bring down their capital as well as operational costs significantly. The power consumption goes down, the heat dissipation too goes down sharply, and the cost of employing expert resources for administering and operating special equipment is bound to come down significantly, and time-to-market for conceiving and concretizing newer and premium services. Due to its software-driven approach, NFV also allows service providers to achieve a much higher degree of operational automation and to simplify operational processes such as capacity planning, job scheduling, workload consolidation, VM placement.

In an NFV environment, the prominent operational processes such as service deployment, on-demand allocation of network resources such as bandwidth, failure detection, on-time recovery, and software upgrades can be easily programmed and executed in an automated fashion. This software-induced automation brings down the process time to minutes rather than weeks and months. There is no need for the operational team to personally and physically visit remote locations to install, con ure, diagnose, and repair network solutions. Instead, all kinds of network components can be remotely monitored, measured, and managed.

In short, it is all about consolidating diverse network equipment types (firewall, switching, routing, ADC, EPC, etc.) onto industry-standard ×86 servers using virtualization. The immediate and strategic benefits include the operational agility, which could empower business agility, autonomy, and affordability.

Software-Defined Network (SDN)—The brewing technology trends indicate that networks and network management are bound to change once for all. Today's data centers (DCs) extensively use physical switches and appliances that have not yet been virtualized and are statically and slowly provisioned. Further on, the current environment mandate for significant and certified expertise in operating each vendor's equipment. The networking solutions also lack an API ecosystem toward facilitating remote discovery and activation. In short, the current situation clearly points out the absence of programmable networks. It is quite difficult to bring in the expected automation (resource provisioning, scaling, etc.) on the currently running inflexible, monolithic and closed network and connectivity solutions. The result is the underutilization of expensive network equipment. Also, the cost of employing highly educated and experienced network administrators is definitely on the higher side. Thus besides bringing in a bevy of pragmatic yet frugal innovations in the networking arena, the expressed mandate is for substantially reducing the capital as well as the operational expenses being incurred by the traditional network architecture is clearly playing in the minds of technical professionals and business executives.

As the virtualization principle has been contributing immensely to server consolidation and optimization, the idea of network virtualization has picked up in the recent past. The virtualization aspect on the networking side takes a different route compared to the matured server virtualization. The extraction and centralization of network intelligence embedded inside all kinds of network appliances such as routers, switches into a centralized controller aesthetically bring in a number of strategic advantages for data centers. The policy setting, configuration, and maneuvring activities are being activated through software libraries that are modular, service-oriented and centralized in a controller module, and hence, the new terminology "Software-Defined Network" (SDN) have blossomed and hugely popular. That is, instead of managing network assets separately using separate interfaces, they are controlled collectively through a comprehensive, easy-to-use, and fine-grained interface. The application programming interface (API) approach has the intrinsic capability of putting a stimulating and sustainable foundation for all kinds of IT resources and assets to be easily discoverable, accessible, usable, and composable. Simplistically speaking, the aspect of hardware infrastructure programming is seeing the reality and thereby the remote manipulations and machinations of various IT resources are gaining momentum.

The control plane manages switch and routing tables while the forwarding plane actually performs the Layer 2 and 3 filtering, forwarding, and routing. In short, SDN decouples the system that makes decisions about where traffic is sent (the control plane) from the underlying system that forwards traffic to the selected destination (the data plane). This well-intended segregation leads to a variety of innovations and inventions. Therefore, standards-compliant SDN controllers provide a widely adopted API ecosystem, which can be used to centrally control multiple devices in different layers. Such an abstracted and centralized approach offers many strategically significant improvements over traditional networking approaches. For instance, it becomes possible to completely decouple the network's control plane and its data plane. The control plane runs in a cluster setup and can configure all kinds of data plane switches and routers to support business expectations as demanded. That means data flow is regulated at the network level in an efficient manner. Data can be sent where it is needed or blocked if it is deemed a security threat.

A detached and deft software implementation of the configuration and controlling aspects of network elements also means that the existing policies can be refurbished, whereas newer policies can be created and inserted on demand to enable all the associated network devices to behave in a situation-aware manner. As we all know, policy establishment and enforcement are the proven mechanisms to bring in the required versatility and vitality in network operations. If a particular application's flow unexpectedly needs more bandwidth, SDN controller proactively recognizes the brewing requirement in real time and accordingly reroute the data flow in the correct network path. Precisely speaking, the physical constraints are getting decimated through the Software-Defined Network. If a security appliance needs to be inserted into two tiers, it is easily accomplished without altering anything at the infrastructure level. Another interesting factor is the most recent phenomenon of "bring your own device (BYOD)." All kinds of employees' own devices can be automatically configured, accordingly authorized and made ready to access the enterprise's network anywhere anytime.

The Key Motivations for SDN—In the IT world, there are several trends mandating the immediate recognition and sagacious adoption of SDN. cloud-enabled data centers (CeDCs) are being established in different cool locations across the globe to provide scores of orchestrated Cloud services to worldwide businesses and individuals over the Internet on a subscription basis. Application and database servers besides integration middleware solutions are increasingly distributed, whereas the governance and the management of distributed resources are being accomplished in a centralized manner to avail the much-needed single point of view (SPoV). Due to the hugeness of data centers, the data traffic therefore internally as well as externally is exploding these days. Flexible traffic management and ensuring "bandwidth on demand" are the principal requirements.

The consumerization of IT is another gripping trend. Enterprise users and executives are being increasingly assisted by a bevy of gadgets and gizmos such as smartphones, laptops, tablets, wearables in their daily chores. As enunciated elsewhere, the "bring your own device (BYOD)" movement requires enterprise networks to inherently support policy-based adjustment, amenability, and amelioration to support users' devices dynamically. Big data analytics (BDA) has a telling effect on IT networks, especially on data storage and transmission. The proprietary nature of network solutions from worldwide product vendors also plays a sickening role in traditional networks, and hence, there is a clarion call for bringing in necessary advancements in the network architecture. Programmable networks are therefore the viable and venerable answer to bring in the desired flexibility and optimization in highly complicated and cumbersome corporate networks. The structural limitations of conventional networks are being overcome with network programming. The growing complexity of traditional networks leads to stasis. That is, adding or releasing devices and incorporating network-related policies are really turning out to be a tough affair at the current setup.

As per the leading market watchers, researchers, and analysts, SDN marks the largest business opportunity in the networking industry since its inception. Recent reports estimate the business impact tied to SDN could be as high as $35 billion by 2018, which represents nearly 40% of the overall networking industry. The future of networking will rely more and more on software, which will accelerate the pace of innovation incredibly for networks as it has in the computing and storage domains (explained below). SDN has all within to transform today's static and sick networks into calculative, competent, and cognitive platforms with the intrinsic intelligence to anticipate and allocate resources dynamically. SDN brings up the scale to support enormous data centers and the virtualization needed to support workloads-optimized, converged, orchestrated, and highly automated Cloud environments. With its many identified advantages and astonishing industry momentum, SDN is on the way to becoming the new norm and normal for not only for Cloud but also corporate networks. With the next-generation hybrid and federated Clouds, the role of SDN for fulfilling network function virtualization (NFV) is bound to shoot up.

In short, SDN is an emerging architecture that is agile, adaptive, cheaper, and ideal for network-intensive and dynamic applications. This architecture decouples the network control and forwarding functions (routing) enabling the network control to become directly programmable and the underlying infrastructure to be abstracted for applications and network services, which can treat the network as a logical or virtual entity.

The Need of SDN for the Cloud—Due to a number of enterprise-wide benefits, the adoption rates of Cloud paradigm have been growing. However, the networking aspect of Cloud environments has typically not kept pace with the rest of the architecture. There came a number of enhancements such as network virtualization (NV), network function virtualization (NFV), and Software-Defined Network (SDN). SDN is definitely the comprehensive and futuristic paradigm. With the explosion of computing machines (both virtual machines as well as bare metal servers) in any Cloud centers, the need for SDN is sharply felt across. Networks today are statically provisioned, with devices that are managed at a box-level scale and are under-utilized. SDN enables end-to-end-based network equipment provisioning, reducing the network provisioning time from days to minutes, and distributing flows more evenly across the fabric allowing for better utilization.

On summarizing, SDN is the definite game-changer for next-generation IT environments. SDN considerably eliminates network complexity in the midst of multiple and heterogeneous network elements. All kinds of network solutions are centrally configured and controlled to eliminate all kinds of dependencies-induced constrictions and to realize their full potential. Network capabilities are provisioned on demand at the optimal level to suit application requirements. In synchronization with other infrastructural models appropriately, the on-demand, instant-on, autonomic, and smart computing goals are easily delivered.

2.9   Accentuating Software-Defined Storage (SDS)

We are slowly yet steadily getting into the virtual world with the faster realization of the goals allied with the concept of virtual IT. The ensuing world is leaning toward the vision of anytime anywhere access to information and services. This projected transformation needs a lot of perceivable and paradigm shifts. Traditional data centers were designed to support specific workloads and users. This has resulted in siloed and heterogeneous storage solutions that are difficult to manage, provision newer resources to serve dynamic needs, and finally to scale out. The existing setup acts as a barrier to business innovations and value. Untangling this goes a long way in facilitating instant access to information and services.

Undoubtedly, storage has been a prominent infrastructural module in data centers. There are different storage types and solutions on the market. In the recent past, the unprecedented growth of data generation, collection, processing, and storage clearly indicates the importance of producing and provisioning of better and bigger storage systems and services. Storage management is another important topic not to be sidestepped. We often read about big, fast, and even extreme data. Due to an array of technology-inspired processes and systems, the data size, scope, structure, and speed are on the climb. For example, digitization is an overwhelming worldwide trend and trick gripping every facet of human life; thereby, the digital data is everywhere and continues to grow at a stunning pace. Statisticians say that every day, approximately 15 petabytes of new data is being generated worldwide and the total amount of digital data doubles approximately every two years. The indisputable fact is that machine-generated data is larger compared to man-generated data. The expectation is that correspondingly there have to be copious innovations in order to cost-effectively accommodate and manage big data.

Software-defined storage (SDS) is a relatively new concept and its popularity is surging due to the abundant success attained in software-defined compute and networking areas. As explained above, SDS is a part and parcel of the vision behind the establishment and sustenance of software-defined data centers (SDDCs). With the virtualization concept penetrating and piercing through every tangible resource, the storage industry also gets inundated by that powerful trend. Software-defined storage is a kind of enterprise-class storage that uses a variety of commoditized and, therefore, cheap hardware with all the important storage and management functions being extricated and performed using an intelligent software controller. With such a clean separation, SDS delivers automated, policy-driven, and application-aware storage services through an orchestration of the underlining storage infrastructure. That is, we get a dynamic pool of virtual storage resources to be picked up dynamically and orchestrate them accordingly to be presented as an appropriate storage solution. Unutilised storage resources could be then incorporated into the pool for serving other requests. All kinds of constricting dependencies on storage solutions simply vanish with such storage virtualization. All storage modules are commoditized, and hence, the cost of storage is to go down with higher utilization. In a nutshell, storage virtualization enables storage scalability, replaceability, substitutability, and manageability.

An SDS solution remarkably increases the flexibility by enabling organizations to use non-proprietary standard hardware and, in many cases, leverage existing storage infrastructures as a part of their enterprise storage solution. Additionally, organizations can achieve massive scale with an SDS by adding heterogeneous hardware components as needed to increase capacity and improve performance in the solution. Automated, policy-driven management of SDS solutions helps drive cost and operational efficiencies. As an example, SDS manages important storage functions including information lifecycle management (ILM), disk caching, snapshots, replication, striping, and clustering. In a nutshell, these SDS capabilities enable you to put the right data in the right place, at the right time, with the right performance, and at the right cost automatically.

Unlike traditional storage systems such as SAN and NAS, SDS simplifies scale out with relatively inexpensive standard hardware, while continuing to manage storage as a single enterprise-class storage system. SDS typically refers to software that manages the capture, placement, protection, and retrieval of data. SDS is characterized by a separation of the storage hardware from the software that manages it. SDS is a key enabler modernizing traditional, monolithic, inflexible, costly, and closed data centers toward software-defined data centers that are highly extensible, open, and cost-effective. The promise of SDS is that separating the software from the hardware enables enterprises to make storage hardware purchase, deployment, and operation independent from concerns about over or under-utilization or interoperability of storage resources.

Cloud-based Big Data Storage—Object storage is the recent phenomenon. Object-based storage systems use containers/buckets to store data known as objects in a flat address space instead of the hierarchical, directory-based file systems that are common in the block and file-based storage systems. Non-structured and semi-structured data are encoded as objects and stored in containers. Typical data includes emails, pdf files, still and dynamic images, etc. Containers stores the associated metadata (date of creation, size, camera type, etc.) and the unique Object ID. The Object ID is stored in a database or application and is used to reference objects in one or more containers. The data in an object-based storage system is typically accessed using HTTP using a Web browser or directly through an API like REST (representational state transfer). The flat address space in an object-based storage system enables simplicity and massive scalability. But the data in these systems cannot be modified and every refresh gets stored as a new object. Object-based storage is predominantly used by Cloud services providers (CSPs) to archive and backup their customers' data.

Analysts estimate that more than 2 million terabytes (or 2 exabytes) of data are created every day. The range of applications that IT has to support today spans everything from social computing, big data analytics, mobile, enterprise, and embedded applications, etc. All the data for all those applications have got to be made available to mobile and wearable devices, and hence, data storage acquires an indispensable status. As per the main findings of Cisco's global IP traffic forecast, in 2016, global IP traffic will reach 1.1 zettabytes per year or 91.3 exabytes (one billion gigabytes) per month, and by 2018, global IP traffic will reach 1.6 zettabytes per year or 131.9 exabytes per month. IDC has predicted that Cloud storage capacity will exceed 7 exabytes in 2014, driven by strong demand for agile and capex-friendly deployment models. Furthermore, IDC had estimated that by 2015, big data workloads will be one of the fastest-growing contributors to storage in the Cloud. In conjunction with these trends, meeting service-level agreements (SLAs) for the agreed performance is a top IT concern. As a result, enterprises will increasingly turn to flash-based SDS solutions to accelerate the performance significantly to meet up emerging storage needs.

The Key Characteristics of Software-Defined Storage—SDS is characterized by several key architectural elements and capabilities that differentiate it from the traditional infrastructure.

Commodity Hardware—With the extraction and centralization of all the intelligence embedded in storage and its associated systems in a specially crafted software layer, all kinds of storage solutions are bound to become cheap, dumb, off-the-shelf, and hence commoditized hardware elements. Not only the physical storage appliances but also all the interconnecting and intermediate fabric is to become commoditized. Such segregation goes a long way in centrally automating, activating, and adapting the full storage landscape.

Scale-Out Architecture—Any SDS setup ought to have the capability of ensuring fluid, flexible, and elastic configuration of storage resources through software. SDS facilitates the realization of storage as a dynamic pool of heterogeneous resources; thereby, the much-needed scale-out requirement can be easily met. The traditional architecture hinders the dynamic addition and release of storage resources due to the extreme dependency. For the software-defined Cloud environments, storage scalability is essential to have a dynamic, highly optimized, and virtual environment.

Resource Pooling—The available storage resources are pooled into a unified logical entity that can be managed centrally. The control plane provides the fine-grained visibility and the control to all available resources in the system.

Abstraction—Physical storage resources are increasingly virtualized and presented to the control plane, which can then configure and deliver them as tiered storage services.

Automation—The storage layer brings in extensive automation that enables it to deliver one-click and policy-based provisioning of storage resources. Administrators and users request storage resources in terms of application need (capacity, performance, and reliability) rather than storage configurations such as RAID levels or physical location of drives. The system automatically configures and delivers storage as needed on the fly. It also monitors and reconfigures storage as required to continue to meet SLAs.

Programmability—In addition to the inbuilt automation, the storage system offers fine-grained visibility and control of underlying resources via rich APIs that allows administrators and third-party applications to integrate the control plane across storage, network and compute layers to deliver workflow automation. The real power of SDS lies in the ability to integrate it with other layers of the infrastructure to build end-to-end application-focused automation.

The maturity of SDS is to quicken the process of setting up and sustaining software-defined environments for the tactic as well as the strategic benefits of Cloud service providers as well as the consumers at large.

2.10 The Key Benefits of Software-Defined Clouds (SDCs)

The new technologies have brought in highly discernible changes in how data centers are being operated to deliver both cloud-enabled and cloud-native applications as network services to worldwide subscribers. Here are a few important implications (business and technical) of SDCs.

The consolidation and centralization of commoditized, easy to use and maintain, and off-the-shelf server, storage, and network hardware solutions obviate the need for having highly specialized and expensive server, storage and networking components in IT environments. This cloud-inspired transition brings down the capital as well as operational costs sharply. The most important aspect is the introduction and incorporation of a variety of policy-aware automated tools in order to quickly provision, deploy, deliver, and manage IT systems. There are other mechanisms such as templates, patterns, and domain-specific languages for automated IT setup and sustenance. Hardware components and application workloads are being provided with well-intended APIs in order to enable remote monitoring, measurement, and management of each of them. The APIs facilitate the system interoperability. The direct fallout here is that we can arrive at highly agile, adaptive, and affordable IT environments. The utilization of hardware resources and applications goes up significantly through sharing and automation. Multiple tenants and users can avail the IT facility comfortably for a cheaper price. The Cloud technologies and their smart leverage ultimately ensure the system elasticity, availability, and security along with application scalability.

Faster Time to Value—The notion of IT as a cost center is slowly disappearing and businesses across the globe have understood the strategic contributions of IT in ensuring the mandated business transformation. IT is being positioned as the most competitive differentiator for worldwide enterprises to be smartly steered in the right direction. However, there is an insistence for more with less as the IT budget is being consistently pruned every year. Thus enterprises started to embrace all kinds of proven and potential innovations and inventions in the IT space. That is, establishing data centers locally or acquiring the right and relevant IT capabilities from multiple Cloud service providers (CSPs) are heavily simplified and accelerated. Further on, resource provisioning, application deployment, and service delivery are automated to a greater extent, and hence, it is easier and faster to realize the business value. In short, the IT agility being accrued through the Cloud idea translates into business agility.

Affordable IT—By expertly pooling and assigning resources, the SDCs greatly maximize the utilization of the physical infrastructures. With enhanced utilization through automation and sharing, the Cloud center brings down the IT costs remarkably while enhancing the business productivity. The operational costs come down due to tools-supported IT automation, augmentation, and acceleration.

Eliminating Vendor Lock-in—Today's data center features an amazing array of custom hardware for storage and networking requirements such as routers, switches, firewall appliances, VPN concentrators, application delivery controllers (ADCs), storage controllers, intrusion detection and prevention components. With the storage and network virtualization, the above functions are performed by software running on commodity ×86 servers. Instead of being locked into the vendor's hardware, IT managers can buy commodity servers in quantity and use them for running the network and storage controlling software. With this transition, the perpetual vendor lock-in issue gets simply solved and surmounted. The modifying source code is quite easy and fast, policies can be established and enforced, software-based activation and acceleration of IT network, and storage solutions are found to be simple, supple, and smart, etc.

Less Human Intervention and Interpretation—SDCs are commoditized and compartmentalized through abstraction, virtualization, and containerization mechanisms. As accentuated above, there are infrastructure management platforms, integration, and orchestration engines, integrated brokerage services, configuration, deployment and delivery systems, service integration and management solutions, etc., in order to bring in deeper and decisive automation. That is, hitherto manually performed tasks are getting automated through toolsets. This enablement sharply lessens the workloads of the system, storage, and server administrators. All kinds of routine, redundant, and repetitive tasks are getting automated on a priority basis. The IT experts, therefore, can focus on their technical expertise to come up with a series of innovations and inventions that subsequently facilitate heightened business resiliency and robustness.

Hosting a range of Applications—All kinds of operational, transactional, and analytical workloads can be run on SDCs, which is emerging as the comprehensive yet compact and cognitive IT infrastructure to ensure business operations at the top speed, scale, and sagacity. Business continuity, backup and archival, data and disaster recovery, high availability, and fault tolerance are the other critical requirements that can be easily fulfilled by SDCs. As we expectantly move into the era of big data, real-time analytics, mobility, cognitive computing, social networking, Web-scale systems, the Internet of Things (IoT), artificial intelligence, deep learning, etc., the SDCs are bound to play a very stellar and sparkling role in the days ahead.

Distributed Deployment and Centralized Management—IT resources and business applications are being extremely distributed these days by giving considerations for cost, location, performance, risk, etc. However, a 360° view through a single pane of glass is required in order to have a firm and fine grip on each of the assets and applications. The centralized monitoring, measurement, and management is the most sought-after feature for any SDC. The highly synchronized and unified management of various data center resources is getting fulfilled through SDC capabilities.

Streamlined Resource Provisioning and Software Deployment—There are orchestration tools for systematic and swift provisioning of servers, storages, and network components. As each resource is blessed with RESTful or other APIs, the resource provisioning and management become simpler. Policies are the other important ingredient in SDCs in order to have intelligent operations. As we all know, there are several configuration management tools and in the recent past, with the culture of DevOps spreads widens overwhelmingly, there are automated software deployment solutions. Primarily orchestration platforms are for infrastructure, middleware, and database installation, whereas software deployment tools take care of application installation.

Containerized Platforms and Workloads—With the unprecedented acceptance of Docker-enabled containerization and with the growing Docker ecosystem, there is a wave of containerization across the data centers and their operations. Packaged, home-grown, customized, and off-the-shelf business applications are being containerized, IT platforms, database systems, and middleware are getting containerized through the open-source Docker platform and IT infrastructures are increasingly presented as a dynamic pool of containers. Thus, SDCs are the most appropriate one for containerized workloads and infrastructures.

Adaptive Networks—As inscribed above, SDC comprises network virtualization that in turn guarantees network function virtualization (NFC) and Software-Defined Network (SDN). Network bandwidth resource can be provisioned and provided on demand as per the application requirement. Managing networking solutions such as switches and routers remains a challenging assignment for data center operators. In an SDC, all network hardware in the data center is responsive to a centralized controlling authority, which automates network provisioning based on defined policies and rules. A dynamic pool of network resources comes handy in fulfilling any varying network requirements.

Software-Defined Security—Cloud security has been a challenge for Cloud center professionals. Hosting mission-critical applications and storing customer, confidential, and corporate information on Cloud environments are still a risky affair. Software-defined security is emerging as the viable and venerable proposition for ensuring unbreakable and impenetrable security for IT assets, business workloads, and data sources. Policy-based management, the crux of software-defined security, is able to ensure the much-required compliance with security policies and principles. SDC is innately stuffed with software-defined security capabilities.

Green Computing—SDCs enhance resource utilization through workload consolidation and optimization, VM placement, workflow scheduling, dynamic capacity planning, and management. Energy-awareness is being insisted as the most vital parameter for SDCs. When the electricity consumption goes down, the heat dissipation too goes down remarkably; thereby, the goal of green and lean computing gets fulfilled. This results in environmental sustainability through the reduced release of harmful greenhouse gasses.

In summary, applications that once ran on static, monolithic and dedicated servers are today hosted in software-defined, policy-aware, consolidated, virtualized, automated and shared IT environments that can be scaled and shaped to meet brewing demands dynamically. Resource allocation requests that took days and weeks to fulfil now can be accomplished in hours or even in minutes. Virtualization and containerization have empowered data center operations, enabling enterprises to deploy commoditized and compartmentalized servers, storages and network solutions that can be readily pooled and allocated to fast-shifting application demand.

2.11 Conclusion

The aspect of IT optimization is continuously getting rapt and apt attention from technology leaders and luminaries across the globe. A number of generic, as well as specific improvisations, are being brought into make IT aware and adaptive. The Cloud paradigm is being touted as the game-changer in empowering and elevating IT to the desired heights. There have been notable achievements in making IT being the core and cost-effective enabler of both personal as well as professional activities. There are definite improvements in business automation, acceleration, and augmentation. Still, there are opportunities and possibilities waiting for IT to move up further.

The pioneering virtualization technology is being taken to every kind of infrastructures such as networking and storage to complete the IT ecosystem. The abstraction and decoupling techniques are lavishly utilized here in order to bring in the necessary malleability, extensibility, and serviceability. That is, all the configuration and operational functionalities hitherto embedded inside hardware components are now neatly identified, extracted and centralized and implemented as a separate software controller. That is, the embedded intelligence is being developed now as a self-contained entity so that hardware components could be commoditized. Thus, the software-defined compute, networking, and storage disciplines have become the hot topic for discussion and dissertation. The journey of data centers (DCs) to software-defined environments (SDEs) is being pursued with vigor and rigor. In this chapter, we have primarily focused on the industry mechanism for capturing and collecting requirements details from clients.

Chapter 3
Software-Defined Storage (SDS) for Storage Virtualization

3.1 Introduction

During the early stages of its evolution, Storage Area Network (SAN) was typically designed as a client server system with the server connected to a group of storage devices by means of some interconnection media which was called bus. In some situations, the client systems were communicating directly to the storage devices. These types of storage architectures in which the client/server systems communicated directly with the storage devices (without any communication network) were referred to as Direct-Attached Storage (DAS). The high-level architectural overview of a DAS system is summarized in Fig. 3.1.

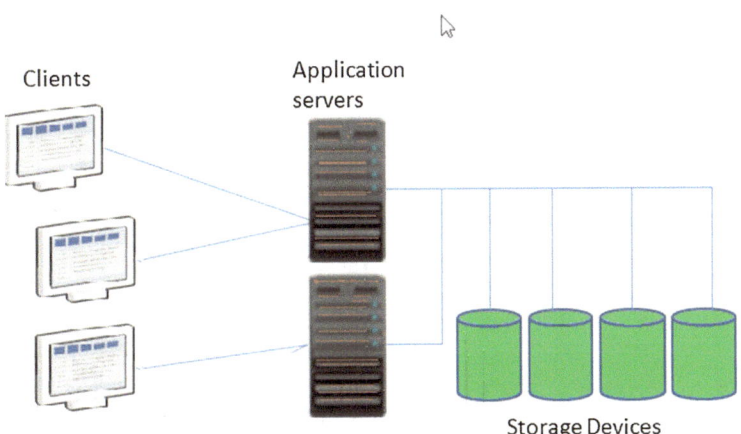

Fig. 3.1 Architecture of DAS

© Springer International Publishing AG, part of Springer Nature 2018
P. Raj and A. Raman, *Software-Defined Cloud Centers*,
Computer Communications and Networks,
https://doi.org/10.1007/978-3-319-78637-7_3

There are three main tiers in the architecture given above, and they are:

Tier 1 : Client Systems which access the applications

- They are connected to the application servers typically using some kind of switch or connector

Tier 2 : Application servers where applications are hosted

- The application servers have (Input /Output) I/O controllers to control input/output operations to the attached storage devices. The I/O controllers are designed to work according to the specific interfaces which are used for connecting to the storage devices. If the attached storage devices support different types of interfaces, there will be an I/O controller for each type of interface.

Tier 3 : Storage Devices

- They are used for storing data which is generated by the application which runs in the application server.

Popular I/O Interfaces Supported by Storage Devices in DAS Architecture

Small Computer System Interface (SCSI)
It is one of the most popular electronic interfaces which were developed by American National Standards Institute (ANSI). Parallel SCSI (also called as SCSI) is one of the most popular forms of storage interface. SCSI connectors/interfaces are mainly used to connect disk drives and tape drives directly to the servers or client devices. SCSI connectors can be also be used to establish connection to other peripheral devices like printers and scanners. The source (servers/client devices) communicates with the attached storage devices using the SCSI command set. The most recent version of SCSI which is called SCSI ultra 320 provides data transfer speeds of 320 MB/s. There is also another variant of SCSI which performs serial transmission and is called **Serial Attached SCSI (SAS)**. It offers enhanced performance and scalability features when compared to its parallel counterpart. SAS at present supports data transfer rates of up to 6 Gab/s.

Integrated Device Electronics/Advanced Technology Attachment (IDE/ATA)
The term IDE/ATA actually represents dual-naming conventions. The IDE component in IDE/ATA denotes the specification of the controllers which are connected to the computer's motherboard for communicating with the attached devices. The ATA component specifies the interface which is used for connecting storage devices, such as CD-ROMs, disk drives, and tape drives, to

the motherboard. The most recent version of IDE/ATA is called Ultra-DMA (UDMA), and it supports data transfer rates of up to 133 MB/s. There is also a serial version of the IDE/ATA specification which is called Serial ATA (SATA). SATA offers enhanced data transfer speeds when compared to its parallel variant, and it can offer data transfer speeds of up to 6 Gb/s.

Activity time !!!!!

Open your computer and make a list of all the other I/O interfaces which are used for communication with storage devices in DAS architecture. Make a comparative study and identify the best I/O interface option. Consider parameters like data transfer speeds, different types of peripheral devices supported, and maximum number of devices supported.

Tape Drives Versus Disk Drives—Which is a Better Option?
Disk drives are a more popular choice as storage media when compared to tape drives because of the following limitations of the tape drives:
- Data is stored linearly on the tape. Search and retrieval operations of data are performed using sequential operations which will take several seconds to complete. This imposes limitations on the usage of tapes by real-time and other performance-intensive application.
- In a multi-user environment, it is not possible for multiple applications to simultaneously access data stored on tape.
- In a tape drive, the read/write head touches the surface of the tape which leads to quick wear and tear of the tape surface.
- The space requirements and the overhead for managing tape media are significant when compared to disk drives.

However, even with all these limitations, tape is still a preferred low-cost option to store backup data and other types of data which are not accessed frequently. Disk drives allow random access operations on data which is stored in them, and they also support access by multiple users/applications simultaneously. Disk drives also have more storage capacity when compared to tape drives.

Tier three comprises of the storage devices. The connections to these storage devices are controlled by means of an I/O controller which is attached to the application server.

3.1.1 Shortcomings of DAS

(1) Static Configuration: If the configuration of the bus needs to changed dynamically to add new storage devices in order to resolve I/O bottlenecks, that option is not supported by DAS architecture.

(2) Expensive: Maintenance of DAS systems is quite expensive. DAS architecture does not allow sharing of storage devices among servers according to the variation in workloads of the servers. This in turn implies that each server needs to have its own spare storage capacity to be used in times of peak load. This would increase the cost drastically.

(3) Limited scalability/supported data transmission distance: The scalability of the DAS architecture is limited by number of ports which are available in each storage device and also the data transmission distance supported by the bus and cables which are used to connect servers to the storage devices.

RAID (Redundant Array of Independent Disks) for Disk Drives

RAID is a mechanism which is used to combine a set of disk drives and use them as a single storage device. The underlying objective of RAID is to improve the performance and the fault tolerance of the disk drives. These objectives are achieved using two techniques:

- Striping: the task of splitting the data to be written across multiple disk drives in order to improve the performance of disk drives by balancing the load across them equally.
- Mirroring: the task of storing copies of data in multiple disks in order to ensure that even if one disk fails, data in the other disk will serve as backup copy.

3.1.2 Getting Started with Storage Area Networks (SAN)

There are several shortcomings in DAS architecture, and this has led to the emergence of a separate category of networks to connect servers to the storage devices. This category of networks is referred to as Storage Area Networks. The high-level generic architecture of a SAN is depicted in Fig. 3.2.

In this architecture, as discussed above, the application servers access the storage devices through a dedicated network. This dedicated network for accessing storage devices is called Storage Area Networks. Having a dedicated network for handling storage device traffic facilitates centralized storage and management. It also adds a lot of scalability to the architecture. The two main transmission protocols which are used by majority of the SANs are: Fiber Channel (FC) protocol or Transmission

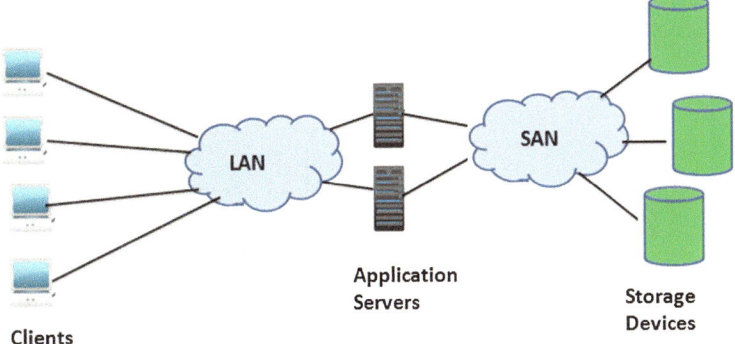

Fig. 3.2 Architecture of storage area networks

Control Protocol/Internet Protocol (TCP/IP). SANs are classified into FC SAN and IP SAN based on the protocol used by them. There are mainly three ways in which data is accessed from the storage devices, and they are: block-level access, file-level access, and object-level access. Among these, object-based access mechanisms are prominently used by high-performance big data applications.

3.1.3 Block-Level Access

Block-level access mechanism is the typical data access mechanisms used in a SAN. In block-level access mechanism, data access is done in terms of blocks or chunks. The blocks are of fixed size, and it is typically 512 bytes in most of the scenarios. Block-level access of data is done by specifying linear block addresses which correspond to the location where the data is stored in the disk.

3.1.4 File-Level Access

In file-level access mechanism, data access is done in terms of files which are retrieved by specifying their name and path. This method is most commonly used for accessing files from file servers. File servers provide a shared storage infrastructure which can be accessed using an IP network. These file servers are referred to as Network-Attached Storage (NAS). More details of NAS will be covered in the latter half of this chapter.

Fig. 3.3 Metadata present in object-based storage

Picture properties   More

Type: JPEG Image
Dimensions: 3264 x 2448 pixels
Size: 3.42 MB
Modified: 11/3/2012 6:30:38 PM
Location: C:\Documents and Setting
Description:

Camera properties   More

Camera Model: iPhone 4S
Date Taken: 10/28/2012 8:43:13 AM

3.1.5 Object-Level Access

In object-level access mechanisms, data is accessed in terms of variable-sized chunks called objects. Each object is a container which holds data and its associated attributes. Object-based access mechanism is the preferred option for accessing unstructured data because of the following reasons:

• Immense scalability
• A flat address space instead of a hierarchical one which offers good performance
• Capability to store rich metadata associated with each object.

One of the main features offered by object-based storage is the capability to provide rich metadata for each object which is stored in it. This metadata facilitates efficient data manipulation and management especially of unstructured data. Figure 3.3 shows a sample of the amount of metadata which can be attached to an object in an object-based storage system.

Data in object-based storage devices is manipulated using commands which include an object in its entirety. For example, some examples of commands used in object-based storage devices are create, delete, put, and so on. Each object is uniquely identified with the help of an identifier which is called Object ID. Object ID is generated with the help of a 128-bit random number generator, and this helps to ensure that object ID is unique. Other details about the objects like location and size are stored in the form of metadata.

Data that is stored in object-based storage devices can be accessed using Web service APIs such as Representational State Transfer (REST) and Simple Object Access Protocol (SOAP). Some types of object-based storage devices also offer support for protocols like Hypertext Transfer Protocol (HTTP) and XML. Object-based storage devices incur very less overhead to perform concurrent read/writes, file locks, and permissions. This provides significant performance improvement and massive scaling capabilities to object-based storage devices. In addition to that, the amount of rich metadata associated with each object offers support to perform analytical operations very efficiently and hence object-based storage devices are ideal candidates for storing data which is generated/used by high-performance big data applications. In the next section of this chapter, we will examine the storage infrastructure requirements for storing big data.

3.1.6 Storage Infrastructure Requirements for Storing Big Data

Big data comprises of huge volumes of constantly changing data which come in from a variety of sources and will be a mix of structured and unstructured data. The key objective of using big data is to derive actionable insights by performing analytical operations. Because of the peculiar nature of big data, the storage infrastructure which is used to store big data should have some unique features which will make them suitable for handling big data. The unique features are:

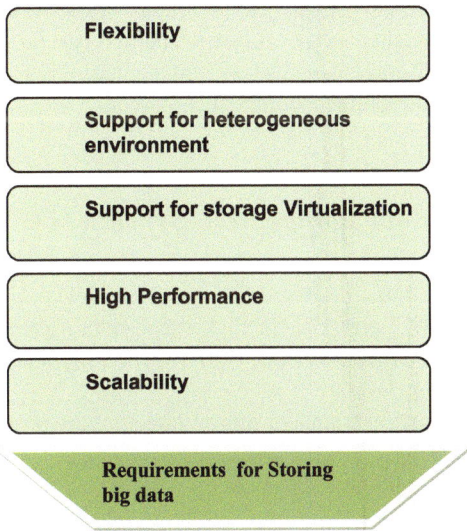

Flexibility: They should have the capability to store diverse types and formats of data. This is mainly to accommodate 3V's of big data, namely volume, velocity, and variety.

Support for heterogeneous environment: They should have application servers which have the capability to access files from LAN or SAN. This will help them to access data from a variety of sources without any additional configuration changes.

Support for storage Virtualization: Storage virtualization is a technique which helps to manage storage resources efficiently. It provides the capability to aggregate heterogeneous types of storage devices and manage them as a single unit. This will be very helpful to allocate storage resources according to the constantly changing storage requirements of big data applications.

High performance: One of the key requirements of big data applications is that many of them require real-time or near real-time responses for their operation. In order to support this requirement, the storage infrastructures should have high-speed data processing capabilities.

Scalability: They should be able to scale quickly as per the requirements of big data applications.

All these storage infrastructure requirements are the main motivation for the evolution of software-defined storage technologies

In the next section, we will analyze the various types of software-defined storage technologies and we will also map their suitability for big data applications.

3.2   Chapter Organization

The organization of the chapter is as follows. The first part provides a general explanation of the various Storage Area Networking technologies, and the second part of the chapter, the software-defined storage technologies.

3.2.1   Fiber Channel Storage Area Network (FC SAN)

FC SAN is one of the most preferred Storage Area Networking technology which uses Fiber Channel (FC) protocol for high-speed data transmission. Storage Area Networking in simple terms refers to FC SAN. The high-level architecture of a FC SAN is depicted in Fig. 3.4.

Note: Note that several variants of this architecture are possible.

The main components of an FC SAN are:

- Clients
- Storage devices/storage arrays which support FC protocol
- Fabric which facilitates transmission
- Switches/routers

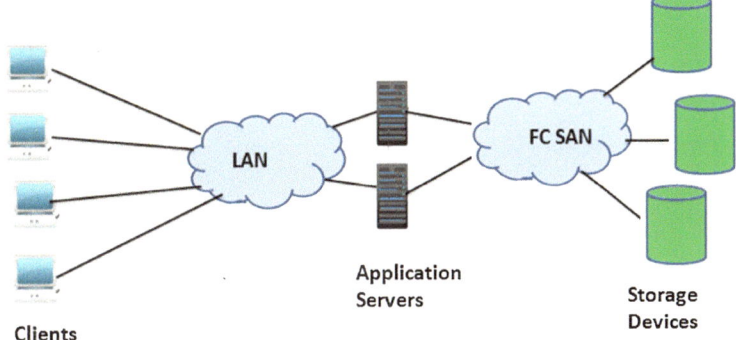

Fig. 3.4 Architecture of FC SAN

- Host bus adapter which connects the application servers or hosts systems to storage devices.

FC SAN uses block-level access mechanisms to access data from the storage devices. They offer excellent performance by providing very high data transmission speeds. Most recent versions of FC SAN offer data transfer speeds of up to 16 Gb/s. FC SAN architecture is highly scalable. The key concern with FC SAN is the fact that cost to setup infrastructure is very high as FC SAN requires its custom set of cables, connectors, and switches.

The high infrastructure cost involved in setting up the FC network and its inability to support file-level access are the two major factors which have blocked their adoption by big data applications. Nowadays, the cost of 10 Gb Ethernet and other IP-based technologies are far less when compared to FC technology.

3.2.2   Internet Protocol Storage Area Network (IP SAN)

An IP SAN network is also referred to as iSCSI (SCSI over IP). In this network, storage devices are accessed over a TCP/IP-based network using SCSI commands. Ethernet is the physical media which used for data transmission. Ethernet is a cost-effective option which makes IP SAN more popular when compared to FC SAN. Data in an IP SAN is also accessed by using block-level access mechanisms. The high-level overview architecture of IP SAN is depicted in Fig. 3.5.

iSCSI is definitely a preferred technology choice for big data storage because of the following reasons:

- It uses 1/10 Gb Ethernet transport, which significantly reduces the network complexity.
- It has less cost when compared to FC SAN.

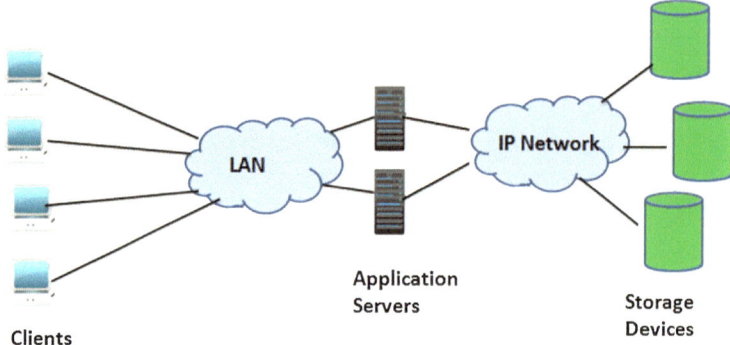

Fig. 3.5 Architecture of IP SAN

- It offers more flexibility as it provides option to leverage the existing IP infrastructure.
- It offers excellent performance as there are several iSCSI-supported storage arrays
  which are capable of providing millions of iSCSI IOPS to handle the huge performance requirements of big data applications.

But the main disadvantages of choosing iSCSI for big data are its inability to support
file-level access.

3.2.3 Fiber Channel Over Ethernet (FCoE)

The FCoE technology allows encapsulation and transmission of Fiber Channel
frames over the conventional Ethernet network without using the Ethernet default
forwarding scheme. These features of FCoE allow transmission of SAN traffic and
Ethernet traffic using a common 10 Gb network infrastructure. This allows organizations to perform consolidation of their LAN and SAN over the same network
infrastructure. FCoE also allows organizations to cut down their infrastructure cost
by reducing the number of cables, Network Interface Cards (NICs) and switches.
The main component of FCoE infrastructure is the FCoE switch which does the
separation of LAN and SAN traffic.

   FCoE is not a preferred technology for big data applications because of the following reasons:

- For FCoE to work properly, it is essential to ensure that storage traffic is fully
  separated from the LAN traffic. This is not a possibility in case of big data storage
  applications because of the unpredicted and huge amounts of data that needs to be
  stored and retrieved frequently.
- There should be some strong error detection and recovery mechanism in order to
  ensure that no storage packets are dropped during transmission. This is mainly due

to the fact that Fiber Channel protocol is slow in recovering from packet errors. This is also another consideration which has practical implementation difficulties.

3.2.4 Network-Attached Storage (NAS)

NAS is a shareable storage device/server which performs the dedicated function of storing files which can be accessed by all types of clients and servers which are connected to the network. In short, NAS is a dedicated shareable file server. NAS is accessed over an IP network, and it is a preferred file sharing option as it has minimum storage overhead. NAS helps to offload the task of file sharing from the expensive application servers which can be then be used for performing other critical operations. The common protocols used for file sharing in NAS are Network File System (NFS) and Common Internet File System (CIFS). One major disadvantage of NAS is that as sharing of files and other related data operations happen through the same network, it often creates a bottleneck for the performance of NAS (Fig. 3.6).

Nowadays, a variant of NAS called **Scale-out NAS** is emerging as a popular storage option for big data application. Scale-out NAS provides an extremely scalable architecture in which the disk space can be expanded as per the requirement, by adding new disk drives from other storage disk arrays or other storage devices. This scalability feature of Scale-out NAS makes it a preferred file storage option for big data applications. Scale-out NAS is also called clustered NAS. Another feature of Scale-out NAS is that even if additional storage resources are added, they can all be managed as a single resource which offers a great deal of flexibility for the organizations.

To summarize, following features of Scale-out NAS make it a preferred big data storage option for many organizations:

- Scalability: It is possible to add additional storage non-disruptively as per the requirements. This offers lot of cost benefits for the organizations and also helps in storage consolidation.
- Improved flexibility: It is compatible and can be accessed by clients and servers which are running on both UNIX and Windows platforms.

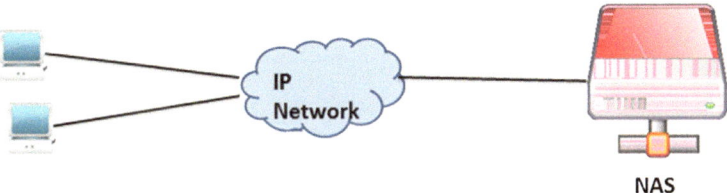

Fig. 3.6 Architecture of NAS

- High performance: Use of 10 Gb Ethernet media for data transfer offers high data transfer rates and improved performance.

Some of the prominent Scale-out NAS storage providers in the market are EMC Isilon, IBM Scale-out Network-Attached Storage (SONAS), and Net App NAS.

3.3 Popular File Systems Used For High-Performance Storage Application

In this section, we will discuss some of the popular file systems which are used by high-performance storage and big data analytical applications. Some of the prominent file systems are:

- Google File System (GFS)
- Hadoop Distributed File System (HDFS)
- PANASAS File System.

3.3.1 Google File System (GFS)

Some of the key characteristics of GFS which makes it a preferred choice for high-performance big data applications are the following:

- Capacity to store large number of files which are of huge size. The smallest file size which can be stored in GFS is assumed to be 1 GB. This file system is optimized to store and process huge number of big files which is typically the characteristic of data which is generated and used by high-performance big data analytical applications.
- GFS is made up of large number of commodity server components which are deployed in a clustered mode and are highly scalable. At present, some of the current deployments have over 1000 storage nodes, with over 300 TB of disk space. These deployments are very robust and highly scalable and are heavily accessed by hundreds of clients on a continuous basis. In addition to this, GFS has a fault-tolerant architecture.
- GFS has in-memory architecture which is best suited and used by majority of high-performance big data analytical applications.

The architecture of GFS is depicted in the diagram which is given below:

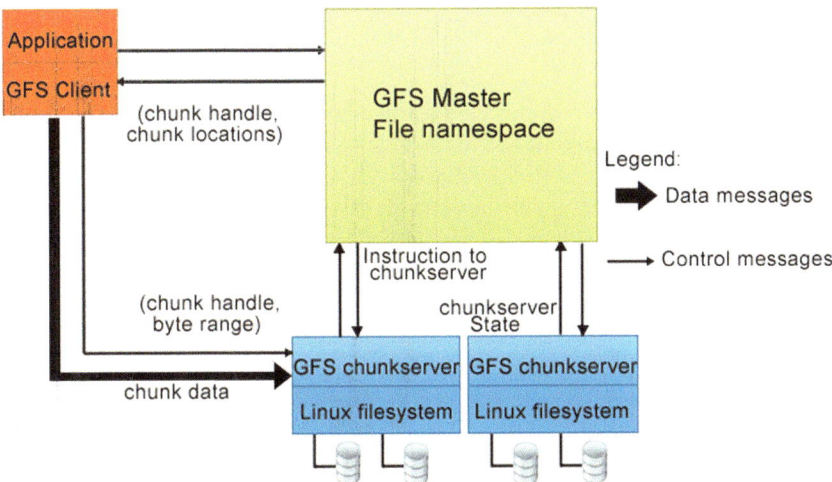

The key components of the architecture are the following:

- GFS master
- GFS chunkserver
- GFS clients which access the data from the file system.

GFS architecture has a master–slave configuration with a single GFS master server and many chunkservers which in turn can be accessed by multiple clients as depicted in the diagram. Each chunk server typically has Linux operating system with a user-level server process running on it. It is also possible to run chunkserver and GFS client run on the same server if the machine has the necessary configuration to support both the components.

Files are stored in GFS in the form of fixed size chunks. Each chunk is identified using a unique 64-bit identifier which is also known as a chunk handle. This chunk handle is assigned to each chunk by the GFS master at the time of its creation. The chunks are stored in local disks of the chunkservers in the form of Linux files. Each Linux file or chunk will have a chunk handle and byte range assigned to it. Each chunk at the time of storage is replicated and stored in multiple chunkservers which provides enhanced reliability to the data stored in the GFS. The default number of replicas which are created for each file is 3. However, there are also provisions to define different replication levels for different types of files as per the requirements.

GFS master stores the metadata information of file system. The metadata parameters which are stored by GFS master are the following:

- Namespace
- Access control information
- Mapping of files to chunks
- Current location of chunks.

GFS master also performs the following chunk management aspects:

- Garbage collection of orphaned chunks
- Migration of chunks between chunkservers
- Chunk lease management.

GFS is always deployed in a clustered configuration. Hence, it is necessary to periodically monitor the health of the various chunkservers. This task is done by GFS master by exchanging heart beat messages with the chunkservers.

GFS clients from each application use the GFS file system API to communicate with the GFS master and chunkservers. GFS clients interact with GFS master only for metadata-related operations. All other types of file operations are performed by the GFS clients by interacting with chunkservers. Caching is not supported by the GFS clients and chunkservers. This is mainly to avoid the performance bottlenecks which are caused due to caching of huge files.

When a GFS client wants to access a file, the client will place a request to the master server. The master server will search and retrieve the file name associated with the location of that particular chunk. The chunk is later retrieved by the client system by going to the chunk location in the respective chunk server. The security and access permissions are maintained by the master server. When a client places a request to a master server, the master server guides the client to the primary copy of the chunk and it will also ensure that all other replicas of this chunk are not updated during this time period. After the modification of the primary chunk is complete, it is passed on to other replicas. The role of the master server can cause a bottleneck in this entire architecture, and the failure can also cause failure of the entire file system.

3.3.2 Hadoop Distributed File System (HDFS)

Apache™ Hadoop® is an open-source software platform which enables distributed processing of huge data sets across server clusters. It has massive scalability and can scale up from a single server to thousands of servers. Apache Hadoop has two main components, and they are:

- Map Reduce—It is a framework that has the capability to understand and distribute work to various nodes that are a part of the Hadoop cluster.
- Hadoop Distributed File System (HDFS)—It is a file system that is spread across all the nodes that form a part of the Hadoop cluster and is used for data storage. It connects the file systems on many local nodes and converts them into one big file system.

Why Hadoop for High-performance big data analytics?

Following are the characteristics of HDFS which makes it suitable for high-performance big data analytics:

- **Massive Scalability**—New nodes can be added non-disruptively; i.e., new nodes can be added without changing the existing data format and without altering the existing data loading mechanisms and applications.
- **Cost-effectiveness**—Hadoop provides big data processing capabilities to commodity servers. This in turn drastically reduces the cost per terabyte of storage for organizations. In short, Hadoop is a cost-effective storage option for all types of organizations
- **Flexibility**—Hadoop does not have any schema structure. This helps Hadoop to store and process all types of data whether it is structured or unstructured, from diverse types of data sources. This feature of Hadoop allows joining and aggregation of data from many sources which in turn facilitate deeper data analyses and better outcomes.
- **Fault tolerance**—When a node in the cluster fails, the system redirects work to another location of the data and continues processing without any drop in performance.

3.3.3 Architecture of HDFS

HDFS has a massively scalable and fault-tolerant architecture. The main components of the architecture are NameNode and DataNode. These nodes work in a master–slave configuration. There is typically one NameNode per cluster, and it acts as the master and performs the following actions:

- Manages file system namespace
- Manages security and regulates access of files by the clients.

Usually, there is a DataNode for every node present in the Hadoop cluster. These nodes keep track of the storage attached to the nodes. HDFs have a file system namespace, and data is stored and retrieved in terms of files. These files may be stored internally as a collection of blocks. These blocks may be split across several DataNodes. All file system namespace-related operations are handled by the NameNodes. They also keep track of the mapping of blocks to DataNodes. The DataNodes are responsible for performing read and write operations based on the client requests.

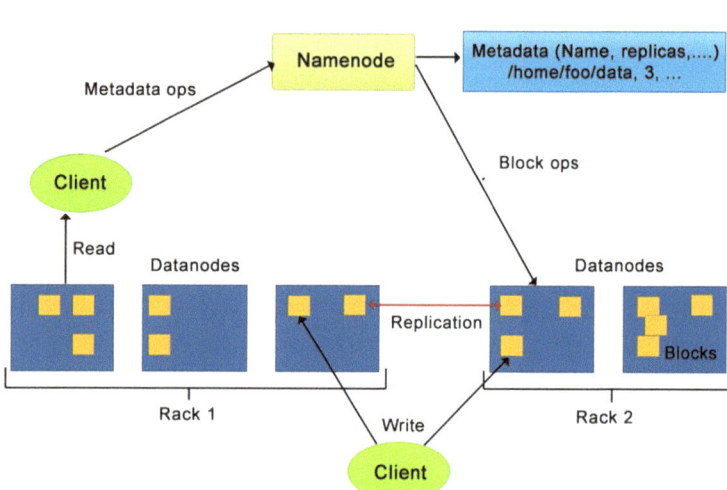

HDFS Architecture

Architecture of HDFS

The main reason for the massive scalability of HDFS is the fact that the namespace and data are stored separately. Usually, metadata operations are very fast, whereas data access and transfer operations will take a long time to complete. If both data and metadata operations are done through the same server, it will create a bottleneck on the server. In the HDFS architecture, metadata operations are handled by the NameNode and data transfer operations are distributed among the data servers utilizing the throughput of the whole cluster.

3.3.4   Panasas

Panasas is high-performance storage system which is available as a file system that can be accessed using a POSIX interface. Hence, it is prominently referred to as Panasas file system and in this chapter also it will be referred to as panasas file systems.

Panasas is a high-performance distributed file system which is used by big data analytical applications. Panasas has a clustered design which provides scalable performance to multiple clients which are accessing the file system simultaneously. The features of Panasas file system which makes it suitable for high-performance big data analytics are the following:

- Per-file client driven RAID
- Object-based storage
- Parallel RAID rebuild

- Fault tolerance
- Cache consistency
- Massive scalability
- Distributed metadata management.

3.3.4.1 Overview of PANASAS File System

PANASAS file system is a high-performance file system which provides file ser-vices to some of the largest server clusters in the world which perform very data-intensive and real-time operations like scientific calculations, space research, seismic data processing, semiconductor manufacturing, and computational fluid dynamics. In all these clusters, there are thousands of clients which access data simultaneously, thereby creating a huge load of I/O operations on the file system. The Panasas system is designed to scale and deliver optimum performance in huge I/O load, and it also offers massive storage capacities which are in the range of petabytes or even more.

The panasas file system is built using object storage technology and uses object-based storage devices for data storage. An object in panasas file system contains both data and attributes packaged into a single container. It is very much similar to the concept of inode which is used in UNIX file system.

The key components of panasas storage cluster are: storage nodes and manager nodes. The default ratio of manager nodes to storage node is 1:10 though it is config-urable as per requirements. The storage nodes have object stores which are accessed by the file system clients to perform I/O operations. These object stores are imple-mented on object-based storage devices. The manager nodes manage various aspects of the storage cluster. The functions of manager node are explained in detail later.

Each file is striped over two or more objects to provide redundancy and high bandwidth access. The file system semantics are implemented by metadata managers that mediate access to objects from clients of the file system. The clients access the object storage using the iSCSI/OSD protocol for read and write operations. The I/O operations proceed directly and in parallel to the storage nodes, bypassing the metadata managers. The clients interact with the out-of-band metadata managers via RPC to obtain access capabilities and location information for the objects that store files.

Object attributes are used to store file-level attributes, and directories are imple-mented with objects that store name to object ID mappings. Thus, the file system metadata is kept in the object store itself, rather than being kept in a separate database or some other form of storage on the metadata nodes

Activity 😊

Open your desktop/laptop, and list down some live examples of panasas file system implementation. Focus more on examples in scientific/research

domain. Do a deep dive on the features of panasas which is making it suitable
for such implementations. Make a list in the space which is provided below:

1 ....
2 ....
3 ....

The main components of the Panasas file system are depicted in the diagram which
is given below.

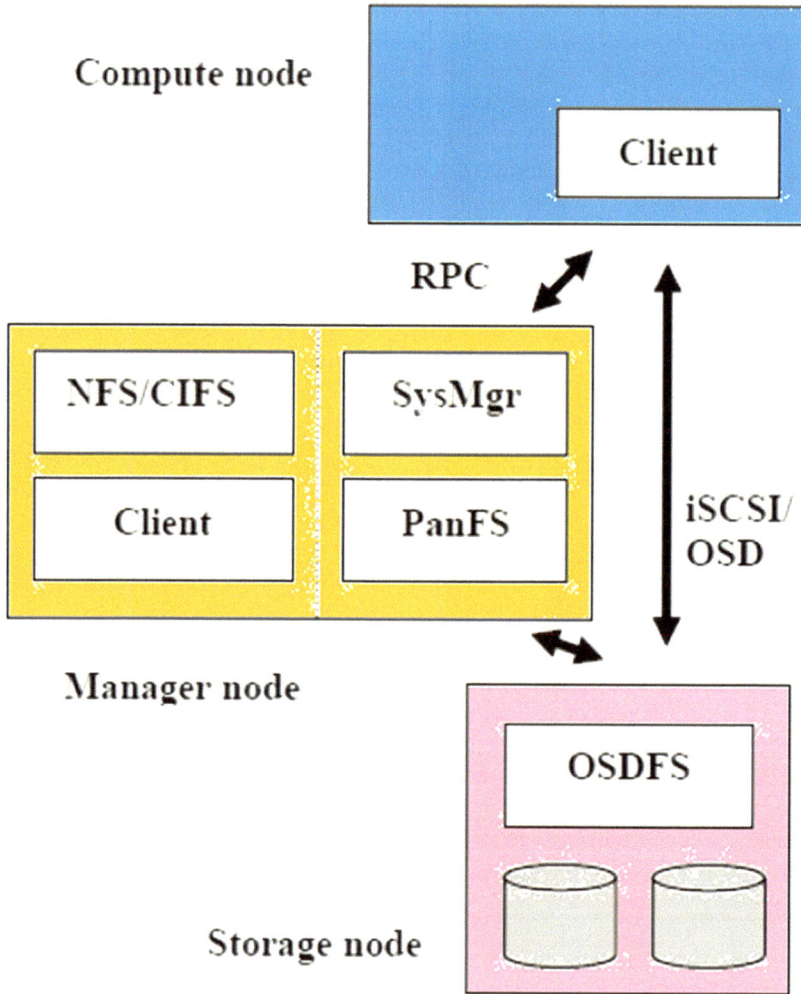

The role of different components of Panasas system is summarized in the table which is given below:

Panasas component	Description
Client	The panasas client is available in the form of a installable kernel module. The client runs inside a Linux kernel. The client uses the standard VFS interface for its implementation. The host systems which have the panasas client use a posix interface to connect to storage systems
Storage node	Each storage cluster node runs on a Free BSD-based Linux platform. Each storage node has additional functions to perform the following services: • Hardware monitoring • Configuration management • Overall control The storage node uses an object-based storage file system which is called object-based storage file system (OSDFS). OSDFS is accessed as an iSCSI target, and it uses OSD command set for its operations. OSDFS mainly performs file management functions. Some of the additional functions performed by OSDFS are: • Efficient disk arm utilization • Media management • Object-based storage device (OSD) interface management
SysMgr (Cluster Manager)	It maintains the global configuration and controls other services and nodes which are a part of the Panasas storage cluster. It has an application which provides both CLI and GUI. The key functions which are performed by the Cluster Manager are the following: • Membership management of storage clusters • Configuration management • Fault detection • Management of system operations like system restart, updates
Panasas metadata manager (PanFS)	It manages striping of data across object-based storage devices. PanFS runs on every cluster manager node as a user-level application. It performs the following distributed file system functions: • Secure multi-user access • Maintain consistency of file- and object-level metadata • Recovery from client, storage node, and metadata server crashes
NFS/CIFS services	They are used to provide PANASAS file system access to clients which are unable to use the Linux file system installable client. CIFS is a user-level service which is based on Samba. NFS service makes use of tuned version of the standard FreeBSD and runs as a kernel-level process

Now it is Activity Time Again 😊

Match the items on column A correctly to the options which are listed under column B

Column A	Column B
(1) Cluster manager	(a) Manages striping of data
(2) PanFS	(b) Maintains global configuration
(3) Storage node	(c) Hardware monitoring

Storage Management in panasas

Client systems which access Panasas have a single mount point through which they can access the entire system. Client systems can learn about the location of metadata service instances in cluster manager with the help of the/etc./fstab file. It is possible for a storage administrator to add new storage to the storage pool of panasas non-disruptively. In addition to this, panasas also has automatic storage discovery capabilities embedded in it.

In order to understand storage management in Panasas, it is necessary for you to understand two basic storage terms in the context of panasas: BladeSet which is a physical storage pool and Volume which is a logical quota tree. BladeSet refers to collection of storageblade modules which form part of the RAID fault domain. A BladeSet also marks the physical boundary for the volumes which are present in it. It is possible to expand the BladeSet any time either by storageblade modules or by combining multiple Bladesets together.

Volume refers to directory hierarchy and has a quota assigned to the particular BladeSet to which it belongs. Value of quota assigned to a volume can be changed any time. However, capacity is not allocated to a Volume until it is used. This leads to competition between multiple volumes for space within their Bladeset which in turn will grow in size as per the demand. Volumes appear as directories in the file system namespace below the single mount point for the entire panasas file system. It is not necessary to update mount points to panasas file system when new volumes are added, deleted, or updated. Each volume is tracked and managed by a single metadata manager. The file system error recovery check is done independently on each volume, and errors on one volume do not disrupt the functioning of other volumes.

3.4 Introduction to Cloud Storage

Cloud computing has brought about a revolutionary change in the techniques used to store information and run applications. Instead of running programs and storing data on an individual desktop/laptop, everything is hosted in the "Cloud." When you talk about accessing everything from Cloud, there should be some storage mechanism also which will help you to store and retrieve data from the Cloud as when required. This in turn leads to the concept of Cloud storage.

Cloud storage does not refer to any specific storage device/technology, but instead refers to a large collection of storage devices and servers which are used for storing data within a Cloud computing environment. Cloud storage users are not using a particular storage device; instead, they are using the Cloud storage system using some kind of access service. The following parameters of Cloud storage make it a preferred option for high-performance big data applications:

- Resource pooling: Storage resources are maintained as a pool, and they are allocated instantaneously as per the demand.
- Capacity on demand: From the storage pool, organizations can leverage storage resources as per the requirements of big data applications. There is no limit on the scalability as Cloud infrastructure is highly elastic and scalable.
- Cost-effective: The ability to pay for the resources according to the usage provides significant economies of scale for organizations.

Note: The Cloud storage architecture given below is not very specific to public or private Cloud. It depicts the generic Cloud storage architecture in any type of Cloud. However, storage in private Cloud is any day a preferred option because of the enhanced security it provides to the organization.

3.4.1 Architecture Model of a Cloud Storage System

The layered architecture of a Cloud storage system is depicted in Fig. 3.7.

Storage Layer

Storage layer is the bottommost layer in the architecture of Cloud storage which is given above. It contains different types of storage devices. Some example of storage devices in this layer could be:

- Fiber Channel storage devices
- IP storage devices such as NAS and iSCSI
- DAS storage devices such as SCSI
- Object-based storage devices.

These storage devices may be present in geographically dispersed regions and connected to each other by means of some networking technology like Internet or

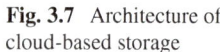

Fig. 3.7 Architecture of cloud-based storage

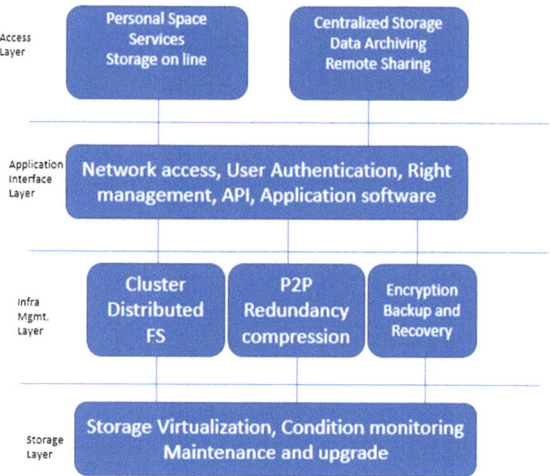

Wide Area network (WAN). This layer has a unified storage management system which is capable of managing all these heterogeneous types of devices in a single storage pool and provisioning them as per requirements in the form of a service like storage as a service or infrastructure as a service. The key underlying concept used in this layer is storage virtualization. This technology provides capabilities to manage heterogeneous storage devices with different performance levels as a single entity. Hence, the unified storage management activity which is performed in this layer can also be called as virtual storage management.

Infrastructure Management Layer

Infrastructure management layer is the layer which is present above the storage layer, and as the name implies, this layer provides the necessary infrastructure which is required for unified management of underlying storage devices in the storage layer. This infrastructure is very critical as it provides various vital functions like security, space management, backup, and storage consolidation using various techniques like clusters and grids. The following are the key services which are provided by this layer:

- Backup: It takes multiple copies in order to ensure that data stored in Cloud in not lost in any situation.
- Disaster Recovery: It takes steps to recover data in the event of any kind of data loss.
- Encryption: It provides enhanced security for the data by converting them into a format which cannot be interpreted by an attacker or malicious user.
- Compression: It reduces the space consumed by the data by removing blank spaces which are present in the data.
- Cluster: It aggregates multiple storage devices/servers to provide more storage capacity.

Application Interface Layer

Application interface layer is used to provide various interfaces/APIs to support the Cloud storage use cases which are provided/used by the organization. Some common examples of Cloud storage use cases are data archive applications, backup applications, and so on. Different Cloud storage service providers develop their own custom application interfaces as per the services offered by them.

Access Layer

Any authorized user who is registered to access the Cloud services from the specific Cloud service provider can login to the Cloud storage system via a standard public application interface to use the required Cloud storage service. Different Cloud storage service providers use different types of access mechanisms. The access layer will have catalogue which provides the pricing and other usage details and will also have the service-level agreement details which are given by the specific service provider.

One of the important concepts which need to be mentioned in this regard is the concept of Cloud drive. Cloud drive acts as a gateway to access Cloud storage which is provided by many vendors. The architecture of Cloud drive is given in the figure which is given below.

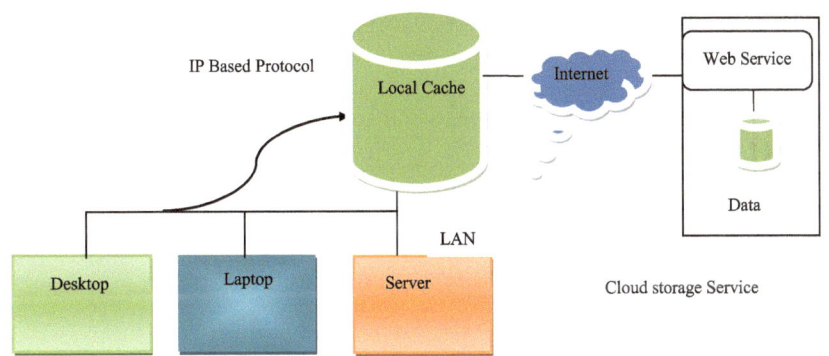

Cloud Drive supports access to storage services offered by many leading Cloud storage service providers including Microsoft Azure, Amazon S3 Amazon EC2, EMC Atmos. Cloud drive masks the complexity of the underlying storage devices and allows the end user to access Cloud storage like a local storage. Computers are connected to the LAN access data which is stored on Cloud Drive using some IP-based protocol. The Cloud Drive service communicates using Internet connection with the Cloud storage service provider. Whenever data generated increases, Cloud drive service starts moving data to the storage infrastructure of Cloud storage service provider. If the data that is request by the user is available in the local cache of the Cloud drive, it will provide a significant performance improvement.

One of the most important requirements of any Cloud storage system is that it should allow sharing of data between various heterogeneous commercial applications. In order to ensure smooth sharing of data among these applications, it is important to implement multi-level locking mechanisms for data. Another important aspect to be kept in mind is that cache consistency should be ensured in order to maintain consistent copies of the same data.

Apart from all these, the most important feature in the storage layer of Cloud storage architecture is storage virtualization. Storage virtualization is the technology which is at the core of the Cloud storage architecture. The concept of storage virtualization is explained in the next section.

3.5   Storage Virtualization

Storage virtualization is a mechanism to ensure that different heterogeneous types of storage devices are stored and managed as a single unit. This in turn will enable unified storage management, easier deployment, and integrated monitoring of entire storage infrastructure. Storage virtualization mainly involves splitting the available storage into virtual volumes. Virtual volumes can be created by combining different types of storage devices. These virtual volumes are then presented to the operating system as storage devices after abstracting the details of the storage devices which are present in that volume. Virtual volumes can be expanded, created, and deleted as per the storage requirements without any downtime. There are various techniques used in the creation of virtual volumes. Some of the most commonly used techniques in Cloud storage are storage tiering and thin provisioning. Some of the key benefits offered by storage virtualization are the following:

- It provides unified storage management capabilities.
- It facilitates aggregation of heterogeneous storage devices.
- It allows storage resources to be allocated and freed as per the changing storage requirements.
- It provides scalability to the storage infrastructure.

3.5.1   Thin Provisioning

One of the major challenges faced by the present-day organizations is that most of the storage capacities allocated to various applications remain unused and this turns out to be an expensive affair for the organizations. Majority of such situations arise due to over provisioning of storage needs. In some cases, this situation also arises due to upfront investment on storage capacity though it may be change later on. Let us consider a scenario to understand this situation better. It is estimated that the archival requirements of an ABC organization need approximately 50 TB of storage over a 2-year period with an average usage of 12.5 TB once in every 6 months. In most of the situations, the organization will purchase 50 TB of storage upfront and then plan to use it over the 2-year period. Imagine the cost invested by the organization upfront

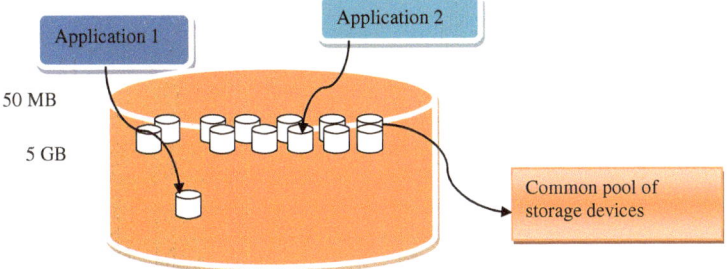

Fig. 3.8 Virtual provisioning

though more than 50 percent of the storage will be used only in the next year? Apart from the initial capital expenditure, the following are the other hidden costs involved in unused storage capacity management:

- Energy wastage: The unused storage consumes power and generates heat which will add on to the power consumption requirements. This will also violate the "go green" policy which is adopted by most of the organizations.
- Floor space: The unused storage devices will consume unnecessary floor space which could have been allocated otherwise to other useful infrastructure components.

It is also possible that the predicted storage needs of the archival application considered in the above example may drastically reduce due to various unanticipated factors. In such a situation, what happens to the amount invested in procuring the storage capacity? Situations like this are quite common across organizations. In order to tackle all such situations, virtual provisioning or thin provisioning comes as a life saver.

Virtual Provisioning refers to the provisioning of storage as per the actual need. In this technique, logical storage is allocated to applications based on the anticipated requirements. Actual storage allocated is much lesser than the logical storage and is based on the current need of the applications. Whenever the storage need of the application increases, the storage is allocated to the applications from a common pool of storage. In this manner, thin provisioning provides efficient utilization of storage and reduces the waste due to unused physical storage. The concept of thin provisioning is depicted in Fig. 3.8. In the example given below, application 1's anticipated storage requirement is 1 GB; however, it is allocated only 50 MB of storage as per the current requirements of the application. More storage will be given to the application as and when it needs it (The total available storage capacity is 5 GB).

Activity for you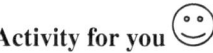
Based on the concept of virtual provisioning, how can the ABC organization described in the above example optimize their archival storage costs?.

Interesting Fact About Virtual Provisioning

One example of virtual provisioning technique which is used in Cloud storage is the concept of **ephemeral storage**. In ephemeral storage, storage allocated to a virtual machine instance exists only till the time of existence of the virtual machine instance. When the virtual machine instance is deleted, the storage gets destroyed along with it. In contrast to this concept, **persistent storage** is a form of storage which continues to exist even if the virtual machine instance with which it is associated currently is not being used or deleted. This allows persistent storage to be reused across virtual machine instances.

3.5.2 Storage Tiering

Let us consider the example of the ABC organization which was used to describe virtual provisioning concept. Imagine that the organization has purchased a mix of storage devices which offer varying performance, cost, etc. Applications like archival require only low-cost, low-performance storage devices. However, there will be other real-time applications which will require quick access to data which in turn is dependent on the number of input/output operations supported by the storage device. It would have been so helpful for the organization if there was a way to allocate storage as per the performance requirements of the various applications. In short, organizations require techniques that enable them to store the right data in the right type of storage device so that they can be made available at the correct point in time to the various applications. Storage tiering is a technique which provides this capability. It is a mechanism to establish a hierarchy/tier of storage devices and then store data in them based on performance and availability requirements of the application which uses the data stored in them. Each storage tier will have different levels of protection, performance, data access frequency, cost, and other considerations.

For example, high-performance FC drives may be configured as tier 1 storage for real-time applications and low-cost SATA drives may be configured as tier 2 storage to keep less frequently accessed data like archival data. Moving the active data (frequently used data) to Flash or FC improves application performance, while moving inactive data (less frequently used) to SATA can free up storage capacity in high-performance drives and reduce the cost of storage. This movement of data happens based on predefined policies. The policy may be based on parameters such as file type, frequency of access, performance, etc., and can be configured by the storage administrators. An example of storage tiering is depicted in the diagram which is given below:

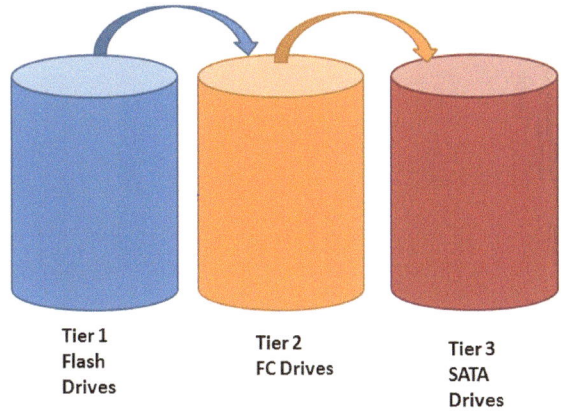

Tier 1
Flash
Drives

Tier 2
FC Drives

Tier 3
SATA
Drives

3.5.3   Storage Optimization Techniques Used in Cloud Storage

In this section, we will examine the various storage optimization techniques which are used in Cloud storage. The two commonly used techniques are deduplication and compression.

- Deduplication: It is a technique to ensure that duplication of data is not present in the storage system or in other words ensure that no duplicate copies of data are stored in the system. This technique will drastically reduce the storage requirements. Deduplication works with the help of a hashing method. This hashing method is used to generate a unique hash value for each file based on the contents of the file. Each time a new file reaches the storage system, and the deduplication software generates a hash value for the file and compares it with the existing set of hash values. If there is a matching hash value, it indicates that the same file is already stored in the system and will not be stored again. If there is a minimal change between the new version of the file and the file which is present in the system, the delta or difference is updated to the file stored in the system instead of storing the entire file. The process of deduplication is depicted in the diagram which is given below:

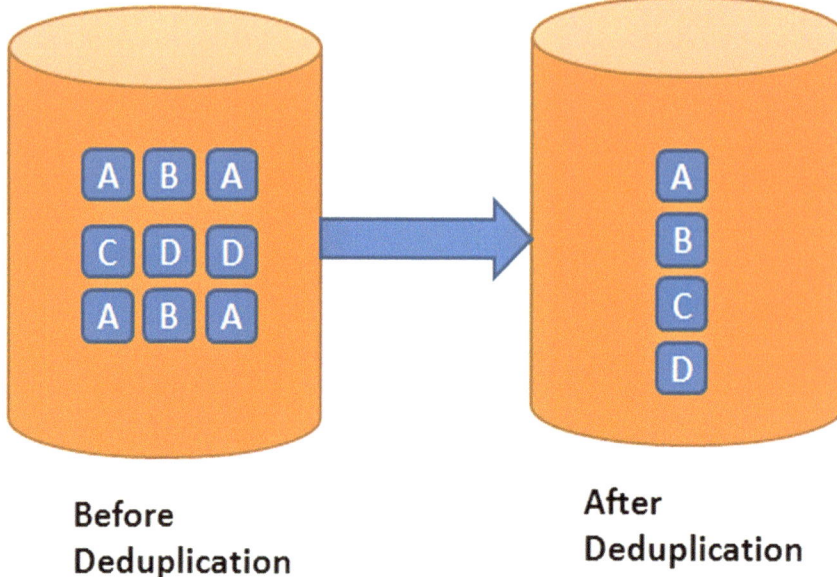

Before
Deduplication

After
Deduplication

Deduplication can be performed at two levels: file level and block level. File-level deduplication is done on the files, and it ensures that only a single copy of each file exists in the system. In block-level deduplication, the deduplication file is split into blocks and the software ensures that only a single copy of the file is stored in each block. Identical files or blocks are detected by comparing the generated hash value with a preexisting list of hash values for files or blocks.

- Compression: Compression reduces the amount of data by removing the blank spaces which are present in the data. A major drawback of compression technique is that it consumes computing cycles. This in turn may cause performance concerns to users of storage services as transmission of data to the Cloud is a continuous process.

3.5.4   Advantages of Cloud Storage

Storage technologies like Storage Area Networks (SAN) and Network-Attached Storage (NAS) provide benefits like high performance, high availability, and accessibility using industry standard interfaces. However, these storage systems have many drawbacks:

- They are very costly.
- They have limited life.
- They require backup and recovery systems to ensure that data is fully protected.
- These technologies operate only under specific environmental conditions.

- They require storage personnel to manage them.
- They consume considerable amount of power for their functioning and cooling.

Cloud data storage providers provide cheap and unlimited data storage which can be used as per the requirements. Cloud storage can be accessed via the Internet or Wide Area Network (WAN). Economies of scale enable providers to supply data storage cheaper than the equivalent electronic data storage devices/technologies [1]. Cloud storage is much cheaper when compared to other conventional storage systems, and they do not require any maintenance cost. They also have inbuilt backup and recovery systems to ensure data protection, and they do not consume any additional energy for power and cooling as they run on the Cloud infrastructure which is hosted remotely most of the times.

Thought for the brain 😊

John doe has a question in his mind and he approaches his professor to get an answer. The question is as follows:

Is object-based storage the preferred storage choice of Cloud storage service providers? If so, what are the reasons?

The answer given by the professor is as follows:

Yes it is the preferred choice of most of the Cloud storage service providers because of the following reasons:

- They provide unlimited and highly scalable storage with multi-tenancy features.
- They have a Scale-out architecture which can be accessed using Web interfaces like HTTP and REST.
- They have single-flat namespace, location-independent addressing, and auto-configuring features.

3.6 Summary/Conclusion

In the first half of the chapter, we discussed the basic storage area networking technologies and their evolution. The advantages and disadvantages of each of these technologies were discussed in detail.

In the second half of the chapter, the variants of key storage technologies which are used to storage huge amounts of data were discussed. Some important file systems like HDFS and GFS were discussed in this regard. The concept of Cloud storage was discussed in detail, and the storage optimization techniques which are used in Cloud storage was also discussed in this chapter.

Reference

1. Advantages of cloud data storage (2013, March 09) Retrieved from Borthakur D (2007) Architecture of HDFS. Retrieved from http://hadoop.apache.org/docs/r0.18.0/hdfs_design.pdf

Chapter 4
Software-Defined Network (SDN) for Network Virtualization

4.1 Introduction

The core elements of any data center are:

- Compute
- Network
- Storage

All these elements in traditional data centers are used to operate in silos. The components which were used for maintaining and monitoring these elements were also maintained separately. With the passage of time, changes in technology contributed to the evolution of low-cost compute, network, and storage elements which in turn forced the data centers to revisit their policies and devise techniques to maintain and manage these data center elements more closely.

In traditional data centers, each compute system was used to run dedicated application like email. The other elements like the storage attached to this compute system and the network used for transferring data to this compute system were also handled as discrete components with little or no interaction. This siloed working of data center components posed lot of changes for organizations which were operating at the enterprise level and handling huge volume of data and transactions. One such challenge was that the IT departments of those organizations had to procure all data center elements and store them in bulk for the anticipated usage in the future. Many of these components which were procured in bulk had to wait for months together to see their optimal utilization. In some instances, it was also becoming a dead investment for the organizations if these resources were not used at all. Another issue which was caused due to the siloed nature of these data center components is the huge amount of power, space, and cooling requirements of these data center elements.

© Springer International Publishing AG, part of Springer Nature 2018   65
P. Raj and A. Raman, *Software-Defined Cloud Centers*,
Computer Communications and Networks,
https://doi.org/10.1007/978-3-319-78637-7_4

All these burning issues which existed in the traditional data centers forced organizations to look at ways to optimize usage of the data center core elements. At around this time, VMware came up with the concept of virtualization. Using virtualization, it was possible for a single host operating system to run multiple client operating systems using a supervisory program called hypervisor. The hypervisor was also responsible for allocation of all the hardware resources of the host among the various client operating systems and applications which run on each of them as per their operational requirements. The introduction of the virtualization concept opened a whole new era for the organizations to revisit ways at which their data centers were being operated. Some of the interesting concepts which came into existence with the evolution of virtualization and the associated terminologies are summarized below:

Serial No.	Terminology	Explanation
1.	Virtual machine (VM)	A physical machine which runs an operating system and other applications. In the presence of a hypervisor, multiple virtual machines can operate concurrently on a single host system
2.	Virtual network or network virtualization	A software which provides capabilities to present multiple logical network services on top of a single physical network
3.	Virtual storage and storage virtualization	A software which provides capability to create logical groups of storage resources and make them appear as a particular group to the end user/application

From the table, let us focus only on the network virtualization component. All other types of virtualization are discussed in detail in another chapter. Network virtualization is closely tied to two other concepts which are the following:

- Software-Defined Network (SDN)
- Network function virtualization (NFV)

We will cover these concepts in this chapter. The chapter is organized as follows:

Evoluton of networking	Traditional networking
	Software Defined Networking (SDN)
	Network Functions Virtualization (NFV)
	Network Virtualization

4.2   Network Infrastructure Limitations of Present-Day Networks

In this section, we will analyze some of the limitations of the present-day networks in terms of their capabilities:

(1) Static Nature of Networks—The present-day network infrastructure has a bunch of protocols which are used to interconnect systems over long distances reliably and with good performance and security. However, most of these protocols are designed for specific requirements and hence they tend to isolate the network into silos which in turn increases the complexity of handling them and altering them when there is a need. For example, in order to add any specific networking device, it is required to alter multiple network components like access control lists, switches, routers, firewalls, and in some cases portals also. Due to the complexity of altering each of these components, networks of today are more or less static in nature as IT personnel defer not to create service disruption in an attempt to alter these huge number of network components. But is this the present-day requirement? In the present-day infrastructure, server virtualization is a common trend in an attempt to optimize the use of server resources. With server virtualization, each server in a data center may have the necessity to communicate with hundreds and thousands of servers which may be colocated or in geographically dispersed data centers. This is in contrast to the existing architectures which typically support interactions between one server to multiple clients or one server to limited number of other servers. But with virtualization becoming very prominent, each server has to communicate with hundreds of servers which may be running several other applications on their virtual machines. To add on to this complexity, virtual machines have several techniques like live VM migration to increase fault tolerance and disaster recovery. All these aspects which are related to virtual machines pose tough challenges for many design aspects of conventional networks like addressing schemes, namespaces, and routing.

In addition to virtualization, another aspect which poses a tough challenge for the existing network infrastructure is the concept of converged network or use of the same IP network for handling different types of IP data like voice, data, and video streams. Though most of the networks have the capability to adjust the quality of service parameters for each type of data differently, most of the provisioning tasks to handle each of this type of data need to be done manually. Owing to the static nature of the network design, the networks lack the capability to change their parameters like QoS, bandwidth as per the changing demands of applications and users.

(2) Rigid Network Policies—It is a very cumbersome task to implement new network policies in the existing network infrastructure because of its rigid and siloed nature. In order to change a specific network policy, it may be necessary to change hundreds of different network devices which are a part of the network. In an attempt to alter each of the network components as per a new policy, the network administrators may induce several attacking surfaces for hackers and other malicious elements.

(3) Inability to Scale—Today's infrastructures are designed with massively parallel algorithms to speed up the pace at which data is processed. These parallel algorithms involve huge number of data exchanges between the various servers which are involved in processing/computation. This kind of scenario demands hyper-scale high-performance networks with limited or no manual intervention. The rigid and static nature of present-day networks leaves no options to cater to these types of requirements of organizations.

Another prominent trend which is evolving nowadays is the concept of multi-tenancy due to the proliferation of cloud-based model of service delivery. This model requires servicing diverse groups of users with different applications which may have different performance needs. These aspects are very difficult to implement in the traditional network infrastructure.

(4) Vendor Dependence—Present-day organizations demand a lot of new features in the network infrastructure which will help them to scale as per the changing needs of the business environment. But in many situations, it may not be possible to implement those features as they may not be supported by the network infrastructure equipment vendors. This makes things very difficult for present-day organizations and necessitates decoupling of components from the underlying hardware as this will go a long way in eliminating vendor dependence.

Activity time ☺

Now that you have learnt the limitations of the traditional network infrastructure, what could be the techniques that can be used to overcome these limitations and make the network infrastructure big data ready?

Hint: Use each challenge discussed above and convert them into a possibility. Summarize your observations in the space which is given below:

1..
2..
3..

4.3 Approaches for the Design of Network Infrastructures Software-Defined Data Centers

The following are the approaches which we are going to use to describe the network infrastructure which is required for software-defined data centers:

Network virtualization	Software Defined Networking
Two tier leaf spine architecture	Network Functions virtualization

Network Virtualization
Network virtualization decouples the network functions from the underlying hardware that delivers them. This is done by creating virtual instances which can be plugged onto any off-the-shelf platforms and used immediately.

Software-Defined Network (SDN)
SDN offers a centralized point for the orchestration and control of the underlying network traffic. This is done with the help of specialized components called SDN controllers which function as the brain of the network.

Two-Tier Leaf/Spine Architecture
This is a fat tree architecture with two types of switches: one to connect the servers and the other one to connect the switches. This provides more scalability when compared to traditional three-tier architecture.

Network Functions Virtualization (NFV)
It refers to the virtualization of network services. This refers to set of techniques which accelerates the provisioning of network services without much of dependencies on the underlying hardware components. This is something which is still evolving.

Each of these techniques will be discussed in detail in this chapter.

4.3.1 Network Virtualization

Network virtualization refers to the creation of multiple logical network partitions over a single network infrastructure. This segments the network into multiple logical networks. A network which is logically segmented using the network virtualization technique is called a virtualized network or a virtual network. A virtual network appears as a physical network to the nodes connected to it. Two nodes connected to a virtual network can communicate among themselves without routing of frames, even if they are in different physical networks. Network traffic must be routed when two nodes in different virtual networks are communicating, even if they are connected to the same physical network. Network management traffic including "network broad-cast" within a virtual network does not propagate to any other nodes that belong to a different virtual network. This enables functional grouping of nodes with a common set of requirements in a virtual network, regardless of the geographic location of the nodes. The logical network partitions are created using many networking techniques like virtual local area network (VLAN), VXLAN, virtual storage area network (VSAN) which will be described later in this chapter. The diagram given below gives a high-level overview about the concept of network virtualization (Fig. 4.1).

Network virtualization is performed by the hypervisor and physical switch operating system (OS). These softwares allow an administrator to create virtual networks on physical and virtual machine networks.

A physical switch runs an operating system which performs network traffic switching. The operating system must have network virtualization functionality to create virtual networks on the switch. Hypervisor has built-in networking and network virtualization functionalities. These functionalities can be leveraged to create a virtual switch and configure virtual networks on it. These functionalities are also provided by third-party software, which may be installed onto the hypervisor. Then, the third-party software module replaces the native networking functionality of the hypervisor.

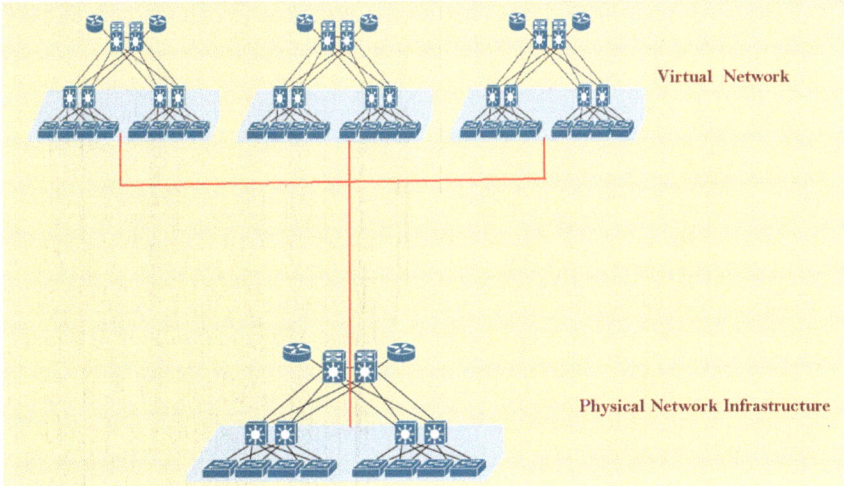

Fig. 4.1 Networking infrastructure

The following are the key benefits of network virtualization:

- **Secure Guest and Partner Access**—Many organizations allow customers and other business partners to access their some of their resources using the Internet. A virtualized network helps to provide separate access to these parties. This in turn will help to protect the confidential information and other confidential assets of the organizations.
- **Role-Based Access Control Implementation**—Information access policies define who can access what data and resources. Using network virtualization techniques, it is possible to create separate user groups or business divisions. This in turn helps to ensure that individuals of only specific user group/business division will have access to certain sensitive information pertaining to them.
- **Device Isolation**—Certain devices/device components may need to be isolated from others for security or performance reasons. For example, banks can isolate ATMs on a dedicated virtual network to protect transactions and customer privacy.
- **Secured Services Delivery**—Many organizations may need to offer services to multiple customers by ensuring fully privacy and security of data for each customer. This can be achieved by routing each customer data through a virtual network which is dedicated to them.
- **Improves Utilization and Reduces Capital Expenditure**—Network virtualization allows multiple virtual networks to share the same physical network. This improves utilization of network resources. Network virtualization also cuts down the capital expenditure (CAPEX) in procuring network equipments for different node groups.

Some of the important use cases of network virtualization are the following:

- Mergers and Acquisitions—Organizations nowadays focus a lot on acquisition for business benefits, new product skills/domain addition, and so on. In such situations, it becomes necessary to merge the infrastructure of the organizations in a seamless manner. Network virtualization becomes very important in this scenario to combine the various networking components of the organizations to ensure a smooth and synchronized functioning.
- Globalization of Enterprises—Present-day organizations have branches distributed across the world. But they tend to work more or less using the concept of borderless enterprises. Network virtualization proves very handy to handle such situations by creating multiple virtualized domains according to the business divisions, guest and partner access, IT maintenance and administration, geographic regions, and so on. One important aspect which needs to be mentioned in this regard is that the creation of virtualized domains does not act as a barrier for sharing of resources, tools, and staff members from time to time as per the changing business requirements. Network virtualization also helps to optimize the use of networks and provides improved performance.
- Retail Sector—Retail is a fast-growing sector across the world with new retail giants with worldwide presence emerging every now and then in the market. Most of the retail groups have the tendency to outsource many maintenance aspects to a third-party agency/partner. In such situation, virtualized networks help to isolate the traffic of each third-party agency/partner from the retail store traffic. This ensures optimal usage of network resources and also provides improved performance.
- Regulatory Compliance—Healthcare organizations in the USA are required to ensure the privacy of patient data as per the Health Insurance Portability and Accountability Act (HIPAA). Network virtualization is very helpful in these situations as it helps to create separate networks for different categories of people as per their access control permissions.
- Government Sector—There are many departments in a government sector. Many times it becomes necessary to ensure that these departments use separate networks for security and privacy reasons. IT departments of governments can segment department services, applications, databases, and directories by using network virtualization techniques. This in turn facilitates resource consolidation and cost benefits.

Now that we have seen enough use cases of network virtualization; in the next section, we will discuss some of the key components of a virtual network.

4.4   Components of a Virtual Network

Virtual machines run on top of a complete system on which some kind of virtualization software has been implemented. But these virtual machines (VMs) need a virtual network which has all the characteristics and components of a physical

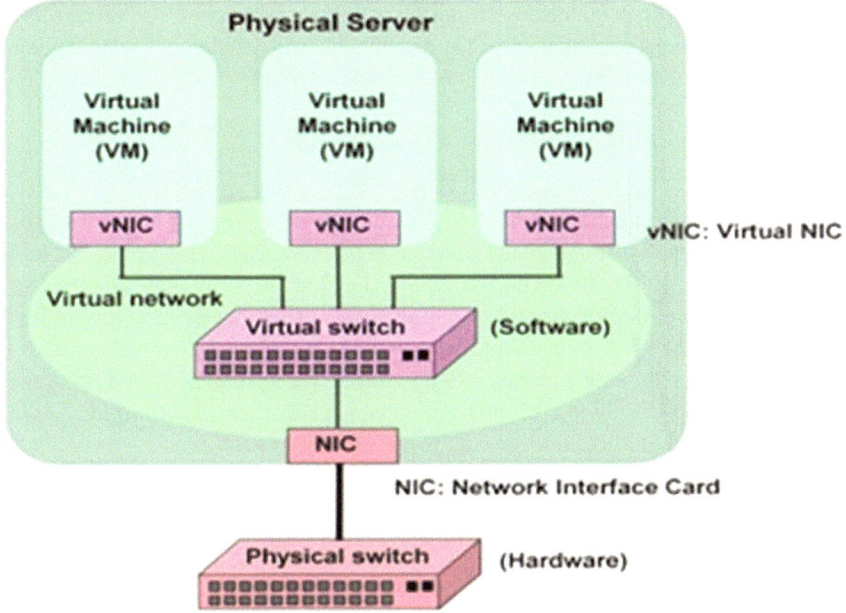

Fig. 4.2 Virtual switch

network. They also need to be connected to a virtual switch in the server. A virtual switch is a logical layer 2 (OSI model) switch that resides inside a physical server within the hypervisor. Virtual switches are created and configured using hypervisor. The high-level diagram of a virtual switch is shown in Fig. 4.2.

Virtual switches provide traffic management by routing packets to the virtual machines which are hosted within a hypervisor. Routing of packets requires a Media Access Control (MAC) address to specify the destination VM to which a packet needs to be routed. These MAC addresses of the virtual machines are stored and maintained in a MAC address table. Apart from MAC addresses, this table also maintains the details of the virtual switch ports to which packets need to be forwarded.

Virtual switches also facilitate communication among VMs within a physical server and direct VM traffic to physical network. Switching of VM traffic to physical network allows VMs to communicate with their clients or VMs hosted on another physical server. A virtual switch may be connected to multiple physical Network Interface Cards (NICs). This helps in traffic management by distributing outbound traffic to multiple physical NICs. It also provides fault tolerance capabilities by allowing virtual switches to route traffic to an alternate NIC in case of failure of a specific NIC. For handling different types of traffic, different types of virtual ports are configured on a virtual switch. The different types of virtual switch ports are given below:

- Uplink ports: They connect a virtual switch to the physical NICs present in the server on which the virtual switch is present. Virtual switches can transfer data to a physical network only when it has multiple or at least one NIC attached to its uplink port.
- VM ports: They connect VNICs to a virtual switch.
- Hypervisor kernel port: They connect hypervisor kernel to a virtual switch.

Port grouping is a mechanism used to group the ports according to specific criteria like security, type of traffic. This can be done in many ways. One of the commonly used methods is policy-based port grouping. This involves creation and application of a policy to a group of virtual switch ports as per specific requirements. This is typically done by the administrator and provides a lot of flexibility and time savings by facilitating creation of a common configuration for a group of switch ports at one time rather than the individual configuration which is very time consuming. A virtual switch may have multiple port groups as per the requirement.

Another important component of a virtual network is a Virtual Network Interface Card (VNIC).

A virtual machine may be connected to multiple Virtual Network Interface Cards. The working of a VNIC is very similar to that of a physical NIC. The main difference between NIC and VNIC is that NIC is used to connect physical machines to a physical switch whereas VNIC is used to connect virtual machines to a virtual switch.

The guest operating of the virtual machine sends data to the VNIC using a device driver software. VNIC performs routing of data to the virtual switches in the form of frames. Each VNIC has a unique MAC address and IP address and follows Ethernet protocol for transmission of frames. These MAC addresses are generated by the hypervisor, and they are assigned to each VNIC during virtual machine creation. Some of the mechanisms to implement network virtualization are discussed in the next section.

4.5 Techniques to Implement Network Virtualization

4.5.1 Virtual LAN (VLAN)

A VLAN is a logical network created on a LAN or across multiple LANs consisting of virtual and/or physical switches. VLAN technology can divide a large LAN into smaller virtual LANs or combine separate LANs into one or more virtual LANs. A VLAN enables communication among a group of nodes based on functional requirements of an organization, independent of nodes location in the network. All nodes in a VLAN may be connected to a single LAN or distributed across multiple LANs.

A virtual LAN is implemented by grouping switch ports in such a way that all the workstations connected to those specific switch ports receive the data that is sent to those switch ports. This creates a logical grouping or partition among the workstations in a LAN based on specific business requirements like projects, domain,

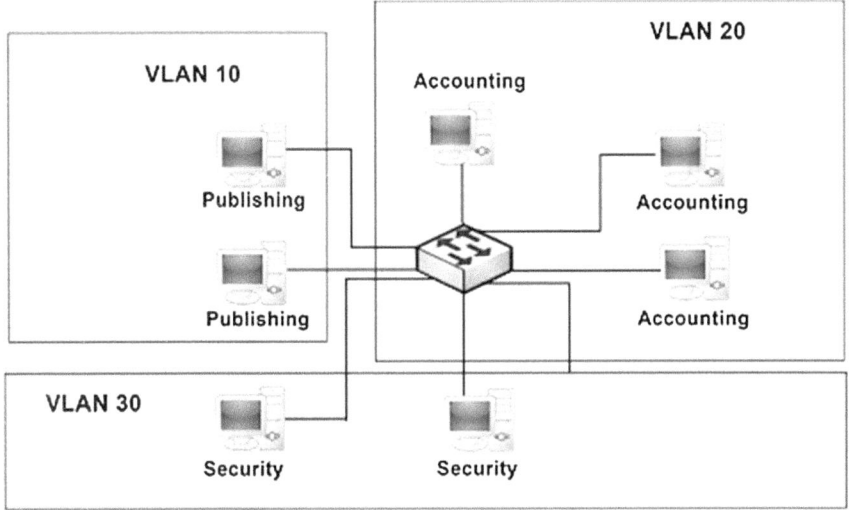

Fig. 4.3 VLAN architecture

business unit. This in short ensures that the entire network is segmented into multiple virtual networks. As this grouping mechanism mainly uses switch ports as a basis for grouping, these types of VLANs are also called port-based VLANs. A high-level implementation of port-based VLAN technique is shown in the diagram given below. In the diagram given below, VLANs are created based on various departments in an organization (Fig. 4.3).

In port based VLANs, VLAN with the switch ports are just assigned a VLAN ID. Workstations which are connected to a particular switch port will automatically receive the membership of that specific VLAN. One simple scenario pertaining to the example given above is summarized in the table given below:

Port number	VLAN ID
1	10
2	10
3	20
4	30

The benefits of VLAN are as follows:

- Broadcast traffic within a specific VLAN is restricted from propagating to another VLAN. For example, a node receives all broadcast frames within its associated VLAN but not from other VLANs. This imposes a restriction on the traffic which enters a specific VLAN. This restriction on VLAN traffic frees bandwidth for user traffic, which thereby improves performance.

- VLANs facilitate easy, flexible, and less expensive way to manage networks. VLANs are created using software. Therefore, they can be configured easily and quickly compared to building separate physical LANs for various communication groups. If it is required to regroup nodes, an administrator simply changes VLAN configurations without moving nodes and doing recabling.
- VLANs also provide enhanced security by isolating sensitive data of one VLAN from any other VLANs. It is also possible to impose restrictions at the OSI layer 3 routing device to prevent inter-VLAN routing.
- Since a physical LAN switch can be shared by multiple VLANs, the utilization of the switch increases. It reduces capital expenditure (CAPEX) in procuring network equipments for different node groups.
- Facilitates the easy formation of virtual workgroups as VLANs provide the flexibility to the workstations to change from one VLAN to another by easily changing the switch configuration. This allows the formation of virtual workgroups and also facilitates sharing of organization resources like printers, servers.

4.5.2   VLAN Tagging

Many times it becomes necessary to distribute a single VLAN across multiple switches. Though there exist many ways to do this, the most popular method is VLAN tagging. Let us try to understand the necessity of VLAN tagging by using the VLAN example given above. In the example, assume that VLAN 20 is distributed across multiple switches. When a switch receives a broadcast packet for VLAN 20, it is necessary to make sure that the switch knows that the packet needs to be broadcasted to some other switch of which VLAN 20 is a member.

This is done by means of a frame tagging technique which is called VLAN tagging. The only limitation of this technique is the fact that it requires a change to the fundamental format of an Ethernet header. VLAN tagging involves insertion of four additional bytes to the header of an Ethernet packet. The Ethernet header structure after addition of four additional bytes is shown in Fig. 4.4.

The main fields of the header are TPID and TCI.

TPID: This is the tag protocol identifier. The main purpose of TPID is to represent the fact that there is tag header which is present and contains the following fields:

User priority: This is a 3-bit field and conveys the priority information which needs to be included in the frame. There are eight priority levels which are allowed: Zero denotes the lowest priority level, and seven denotes the highest priority level.

CFI: This is a 1-bit field which is always set to zero for Ethernet switches. This field is mainly used to indicate priority between Ethernet and token ring networks. If this field has a value of 1, then it indicates the fact that the frame should not be bridged to a port which is untagged.

VID: This field corresponds to the virtual LAN identifier, and this field plays a key role for the distribution of VLAN across multiple switches.

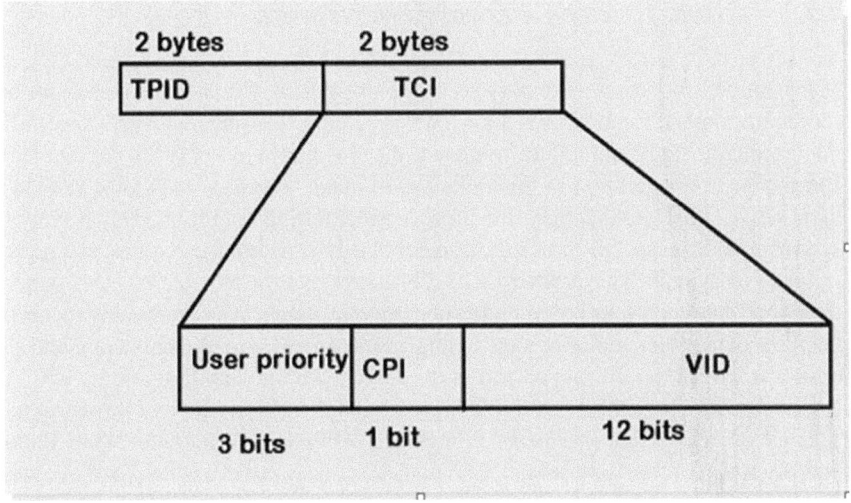

Fig. 4.4 VLAN tagging

Now let us try to understand how this tagging mechanism helps to solve the problem which we described in the previous section. To understand it better, let us consider a broadcast packet which arrives at a specific switch port. This packet is associated with VLAN 20; i.e., its VLAN ID is 20. Let us assume that port 10 of this switch is connected to port 15 of another switch which also is a part of VLAN 20. Now what needs to be done to configure VLAN tagging is to ensure that ports 10 and 15 should be configured as tagged member ports of VLAN 20. This is typically done by the network administrator. Once this is done, it makes switch 1 aware of the fact that once it receives a broadcast, it needs to send it out through port 10 as a broadcast packet with VLAN ID = 20 in the tag. It makes switch 2 aware of the fact that it should receive the tagged packet and associate it with VLAN 20. Switch 2 will also send out the packet to all the member ports of VLAN 20. This makes it very easy for switch 2 to understand what needs to be done with the packets belonging to VLAN 20. So in short, this concept can be summarized as follows:

- If a port is tagged to be a member of a particular VLAN, then all packets which are sent to that port by the VLAN should have a VLAN tag inserted into it.
- If a port receives a tagged packet with a specific VLAN ID, then the packet needs to be associated with that VLAN.

Virtual LAN has its limitations, and the main limitation is its scalability. Scalability becomes a bigger concern if the network under consideration is used in Cloud infrastructure. These scalability concerns can be addressed using another technique called virtual extensible local area network (VXLAN). This technique is used extensively in data centers where massive scalability is a key requirement. More details are explained in the next section.

4.5.3   Virtual Extensible Local Area Network

Many times it becomes necessary to move or migrate virtual machines from one server to another for purposes like load balancing, disaster recovery, and traffic management. Many techniques to ensure the live migration of VMs are available. But the key consideration in this regard is to make sure that VMs must remain in their native subnet so that they remain accessible during migration. This becomes a serious concern especially when the number of subnets, virtual machines, and servers is huge in the count. This is where VXLAN comes into the picture. VXLAN helps to overcome the limitations posed by IP subnetting by using layer 2 tunneling feature. It helps the data center administrators to implement a good layer 3 architecture and also ensure that VMs can be moved across the servers without any limitations. VXLAN uses techniques to combine multiple layer 3 subnetworks to a layer 3 infrastructure. This allows the virtual machines on multiple networks to communicate as though they are a part of the same subnet. The high-level working of a VXLAN is shown in Fig. 4.5.

VXLAN traffic is managed transparently by most of the networking devices. For VXLAN, IP-encapsulated traffic is routed like normal IP traffic. The encapsulation or decapsulation is done by the VXLAN gateways which are also called Virtual Tunnel End Points (VTEPs). These VTEPs play a major role in VXLAN. VTEPs can be implemented in one of the following ways:

- Virtual bridges in the hypervisor
- VXLAN-aware virtual machine applications
- VXLAN-enabled switch hardware.

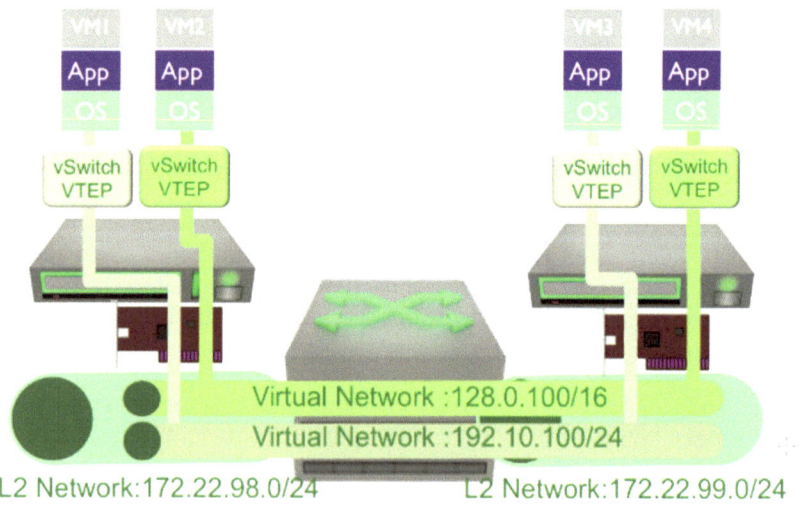

Fig. 4.5 Virtual extensible local area network

Each VXLAN network segment has a 24-bit identifier which is unique. This identifier is also called VXLAN Network Identifier or VNI. The 24-bit address space allows massively scalable virtual networks. However in most of the cases, the number of useable virtual network addresses is limited by multi-cast and by the limitations of the network hardware. Virtual machines in a logical layer 2 domain use the same subnet and are mapped using a common VNI. This common mapping allows the virtual machines to communicate with one another. It should be noted that the IP addressing rules which are followed in the physical layer 2 are applicable to virtual networks as well.

VXLANs maintain the uniqueness of the virtual machines by combining the virtual machine's MAC address and the VNI. This sometimes leads to the duplication of MAC addresses within a data center. The only restriction in this scenario is that duplication of MAC addresses cannot happen within a same VNI. Virtual machines which belong to a particular subnet do not require any special configuration to support VXLAN traffic. This is mainly due to the presence of VTEP which is typically a part of hypervisor itself. The configuration on the VTEPs should include layer 2 or IP subnet to VNI network mapping and VNI to IP multi-cast group mapping. The first mapping allows building of forwarding tables to facilitate VNI/MAC traffic flow. The second mapping helps VTEPs to perform broadcast or multi-cast functions across the network.

Next, we will try to understand virtual networking in Storage Area Networks. This is referred to as virtual storage area network and is described below.

4.5.4 Virtual Storage Area Network (VSAN)

Virtual SAN is a logical grouping of servers or storage devices, created on a Storage Area Network, in order to facilitate communication among a group of nodes with a common set of requirements regardless of their physical location. VSAN conceptually functions in the same way as that of a VLAN.

Each VSAN acts as an independent fabric and is being managed independently. Each VSAN has its own set of fabric services, configuration, and set of unique Fiber Channel addresses. Configurations on a specific VSAN do not affect any other VSAN. Similar to VLAN tagging, VSAN has its tagging mechanism. The purpose of VSAN tagging is similar to VLAN tagging in LAN.

4.5.5 Traffic Management in a Virtual Network

Network traffic must be managed in order to optimize performance and availability of networked resources. Many techniques exist to monitor and control the network traffic in a physical network. Some of them could be applied to manage the virtual network traffic. Load balancing is a key objective of managing network traffic. It is a technique to distribute workload across multiple physical or virtual machines and parallel network links to prevent overutilization or underutilization of these resources and optimize performance. It is provided by dedicated software or hardware.

It is possible for the network administrators to apply a policy for distribution of network traffic across VMs and network links. Network traffic management techniques can also be used to set a policy to ensure failover of network traffic across network links. In the event of a network failure, the traffic from the failed link will failover to another available link, based on pre-defined policy. Network administrators have the flexibility to change a policy as per the requirement.

When multiple VM traffics share bandwidth, network traffic management techniques ensure guaranteed service levels of traffic generated by each VM. Traffic management techniques allow an administrator to set priority for allocating bandwidth for different types of network traffic such as VM, VM migration, IP storage, and management. In this section, we will understand some techniques which are used for traffic management.

4.5.6 Link Aggregation

Link aggregation is a technique used to aggregate multiple network connections into a single connection in order to provide an increased throughput which in turn provides significant performance improvement. Some variants of the link aggregation techniques which may be applied to virtual networks are:

- VLAN trunking: VLAN trunking is a technique which allows traffic from multiple VLANs to traverse through a single link or network connection. This technology allows for a single connection between any two networked devices such as routers, switches, VMs, and storage systems with multiple VLAN traffic traversing the same path. The single connection through which multiple VLAN traffic can traverse is called a trunk link. VLAN trunking enables a single port on a networked device to be used for sending or receiving multiple VLAN traffic over a trunk link. The port, capable of transferring traffic pertaining to multiple VLANs, is called a trunk port. To enable trunking, it is necessary to ensure that the sending and receiving networked devices should have at least one port configured as trunk port. A trunk port on a networked device is included to all the VLANs defined on the networked device and transfers traffic for all those VLANs. The mechanism used to achieve VLAN trunking is called VLAN tagging which was described earlier.
- NIC teaming: NIC teaming is a technique that logically groups (to create a NIC team) physical NICs connected to a virtual switch to form a team. This is done to balance the network traffic and to ensure failover in the event of a NIC failure or a network link outage. NICs within a team can be configured as active and standby. Active NICs are used to send frames, whereas standby NICs remain idle. Load balancing allows distribution of all outbound network traffic across active physical

NICs, giving higher throughput than a single NIC could provide. A standby NIC will not be used for forwarding traffic until a failure occurs on one of the active NICs. In the event of NIC or link failure, traffic from the failed link will failover to another physical NIC. The load balancing and failover across NIC team members are governed by policies which are configured on the virtual switch.

4.5.7 Traffic Shaping

Traffic shaping controls network bandwidth to prevent impact on business-critical application traffic by restricting the non-critical traffic flow. It also helps to guarantee the required quality of service. Traffic shaping can be enabled and configured on the virtual switch level. Traffic shaping uses three parameters to throttle and shape network traffic flow: average bandwidth, peak bandwidth, and burst size.

Average bandwidth is configured to set the allowed data transfer rate (bits per second) across a virtual switch over time. Since this is an averaged value over time, the workload at a virtual switch port can go beyond average bandwidth for a small time interval. The value provided for the peak bandwidth determines the maximum data transfer rate (bits per second) allowed across a virtual switch without queuing or dropping frames. The value of peak bandwidth is always higher than the average bandwidth.

When the traffic rate at a virtual switch exceeds the average bandwidth, it is called burst. Burst is an intermittent event and typically exists in a small time interval. The burst size defines the maximum amount of data (bytes) allowed to transfer in a burst, provided it does not exceed the peak bandwidth. The burst size is a calculation of bandwidth multiplied by the time interval during which the burst exists. Therefore, the higher the available bandwidth, the less time the burst can stay for a particular burst size. If a burst exceeds the configured burst size, the remaining frames will be queued for later transmission. If the queue is full, the frames will be dropped.

In the next section, we will discuss Software-Defined Networks (SDN).

4.5.8 Software-Defined Network (SDN)

The advent of virtualization allowed any number of operating systems and applications to be run on a single compute system in the form of virtual machines or VMs. This also necessitated the need for the assignment of IP addresses to access each of these VMs from both internal and external networks. When a router delivers a packet of data, it does so using a combination of Ethernet and IP. A concept called VM mobility poses serious challenges to the delivery of packets. VM mobility refers to the relocation of VMs for power saving, cooling, compacting resources, etc. In this case, due to relocation, there is a change in the physical address also. This demands a change in the layer 3 routing to ensure that packets which were destined for the original location should now be altered to reflect the new location address. This posed a challenge to the network operators. This was one of the motivations for the evolution of Software-Defined Network.

Most of the switchers, routers, etc., which are available in the market come with specialized management interfaces which can be used to access and manage the network devices. Though these management interfaces provide the capability to access network device's capabilities, yet they mask some low-level details of the details which are required for performing certain operations like configuration of static routes. This is also another reason for the evolution of Software-Defined Network.

In a generic scenario, any network device comes with a data plane which essentially refers to the switch fabric which is used to interconnect the various network ports which are present in the switch. Switches also contain a control plane which functions as brain of the switch. For example, activities like implementing network routing protocols are done on the control plane of the switch. That is, each device in the network has a control plane that implements the protocol. These control planes communicate with each other to perform activities like network path construction. But in scenarios of centralized control plane, there would be only one control plane. Hardware which was used to create data plane was costly, whereas the cost of control plane hardware was less. All these aspects attributed to the development of the concept called Software-Defined Network.

It was also observed by the proponents of SDN that vendors of network devices were very slow in meeting the needs of feature development and innovation. High-end routing and switching equipment was also viewed as being highly overpriced for at least the control plane components of their devices. At around the same time, the cost of raw, elastic computing power started falling rapidly. It was then decided that this cheap processing power could be used to run a logically centralized control plane which could also use inexpensive, commodity-priced switching hardware. Based on this idea, few engineers from Stanford University created a protocol called OpenFlow. This led to the start of an entirely new era in networking called Software-Defined Network or SDN.

OpenFlow was designed in such a way that network devices with data planes only respond to commands which are sent to them from the single control plane of the network which contains the centralized controller. This controller acts as the master brain of the network, performs several functions like maintaining all the paths in the network, and also programs all the network devices which are controlled by it. All these concepts form the foundation of SDN.

Software-Defined Networks (SDN) is an architectural approach that aims to optimize and simplify network operations by closely binding the interaction among the various components of the network like applications, various types of network devices and network services (whether they are real or virtualized). This task is often achieved creating a logically centralized control point in the network. This control point is often called an SDN controller. This SDN controller acts as an intermediary and facilitates communication between the applications and the network elements which want to start communication. The SDN controller also exposes and abstracts network functions and operations via modern, application-friendly, and bidirectional programmatic interfaces.

4.5.9 *Layered Architecture of an SDN*

Software-Defined Network is a paradigm in which network control is decoupled from the underlying network devices and is embedded into a software-based component called SDN controller. This separation of control enables the network services to be abstracted from the underlying components and helps network to be treated like a logical entity. The high-level architecture of SDN is depicted in the diagram which is given below:

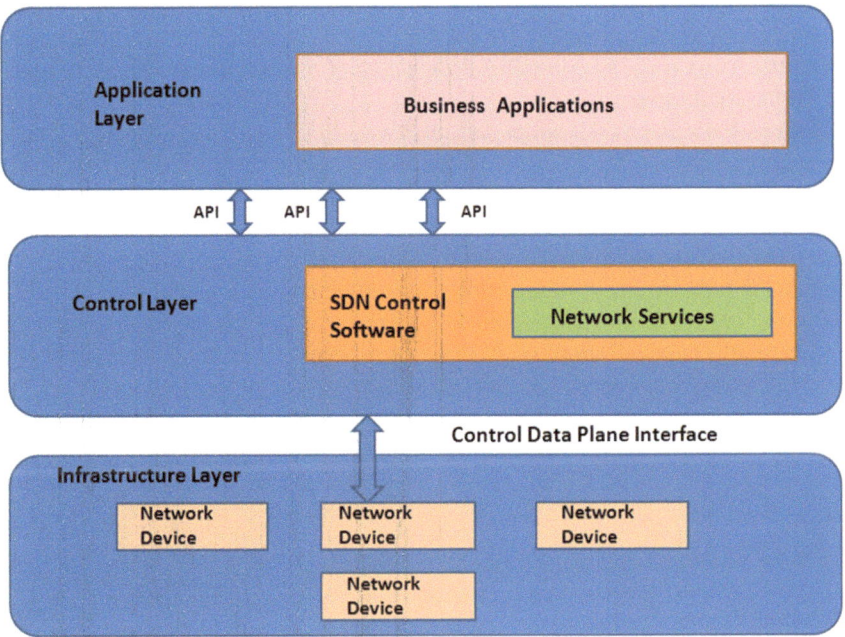

All the business applications which run on the network are a part of the applications layer. All the components of the network are a part of the infrastructure layer. The SDN software component resides in the control layer and interacts both with the applications and with the infrastructure components.

The core of the SDN is the software component which is called the SDN controller. The entire network can be controlled by means of the SDN controller, and the SDN controller appears to all other components of the network as a logical switch. SDN controller can be used to monitor and control the operations of the entire network. This greatly eliminates the hassles of configuring hundreds of network devices. The network administrators can now change network settings dynamically using SDN programs. SDN controller interacts with the business applications using SDN APIs. SDN controller interacts with infrastructure components of the network using some protocols like OpenFlow. OpenFlow is one of the most prominent protocols used in SDN, though there are many other protocols as well as for SDN. SDN helps intelligent orchestration and provisioning of the network quickly using software programs which are written in the control layer. The development of OpenFlow API's in progress for SDN architecture and this will give a great deal of vendor independence for the SDN architecture. As of now, all the vendor devices which use a common SDN protocol for communication can be controlled centrally from an SDN controller.

Benefits of SDN

Centralized Control of Multi-vendor Network Equipments—All network equipments which use a common SDN protocol for communication can be controlled centrally using an SDN controller irrespective of the vendors who have manufactured the equipments.

Reduced Complexity Through Automation—SDN framework provides features to automate and manage several network-related functions which are otherwise time consuming when done manually. This automation will bring down operational cost and also reduce the errors which are introduced due to manual intervention.

Improved Network Reliability and Security—Network policy implementation which used to take months together previously can now be accomplished in a matter of few days. SDN framework eliminates the need to configure each network device individually, and this in turn reduces the possibility of security breaches and other non-compliance aspects which may arise during policy implementation.

Better User Experience—SDN architecture provides flexibility to dynamically change configuration as per the user requirements. For example, if a user requires specific level of QoS for audio data streams, it can be configured to happen dynamically using SDN controller. This offers better user experience.

Some of the prominent use cases for SDN are:

- Campus
- Data center
- Cloud
- Carriers and service providers

OpenFlow

OpenFlow is the one of the first standard communication interfaces which was defined for an SDN architecture [1]. It allows direct access and configuration of network devices such as switches and routers (these components can be both physical and virtual (hypervisor-based)). It is the absence of such open interfaces that have led to the monolithic, closed, and mainframe-like nature of traditional networks.

OpenFlow is so popular in the field of SDN that many a times, SDN and OpenFlow are used interchangeably.

Activity Time

Divide the class into groups of two, each comprising of equal number of members. For each group, assign the task of finding out a protocol other than OpenFlow which is used in SDN architecture/framework.

Two-tier Leaf/Spine Architecture

The traditional network fabric architecture has three tiers as shown in the diagram which is given below:

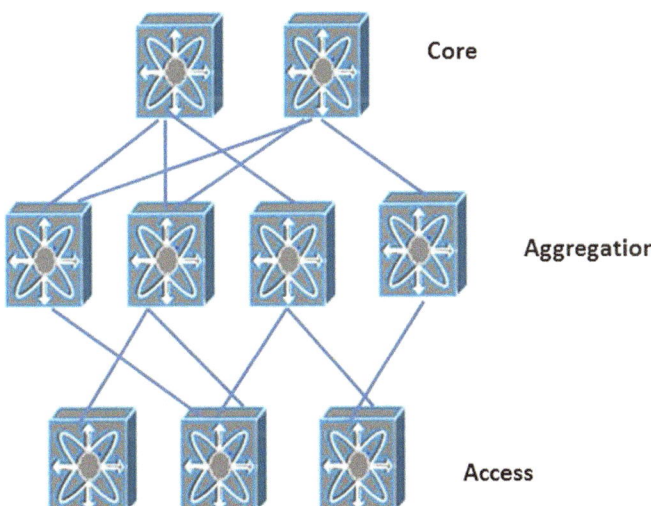

The functions of the three tiers of switches are as follows:

Tier 1 (access switches): The access switches are used to connect servers and other storage devices which are part of the network.

Tier 2 (aggregation switches): The access switches are connected using Ethernet media to aggregation switches. The aggregation switches aggregate and forward traffic from the access switches to the core switches.

Tier 3 (core switches): The core switches or routers forward traffic flows from servers and storage devices to intranet and Internet.

The main limitation of this architecture is that they use layer 2 forwarding techniques as opposed to layer 3 forwarding techniques. In addition to this, it is common to have oversubscription of bandwidth in the access layer and less bandwidth in the aggregation layer. This in turn will lead to latency. All these factors limit the scalability of the architecture as per the present needs. In order to overcome the limitations imposed by this architecture, the two-tier leaf/spine network fabric architecture has been designed. The high-level architecture of two-tier leaf/spine network fabric is depicted in the diagram which is given below:

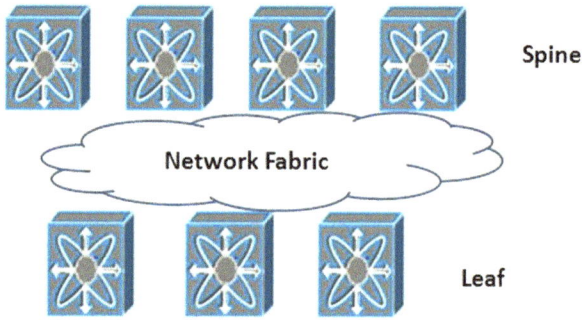

In the two-tier leaf/spine architecture, there are only two tiers of switches: one tier for connecting the servers/storage devices and the other one for connecting the switches. This two-tier architecture creates a non-latency, non-blocking fabric and thus provides a highly scalable architecture which will be suitable to transfer big data.

4.5.10 Network Functions Virtualization (NFV)

NFV is a concept which uses virtualization technologies to provide specific network-related services without the necessity to have custom hardware appliances for each network function. This is the main value proposition offered by NFVs. Some examples of NFVs are virtual firewalls, load balancers, WAN accelerators, and intrusion detection services. NFV can be visualized as a combination of virtualization and SDN, and the relationship is depicted in the diagram which is given below:

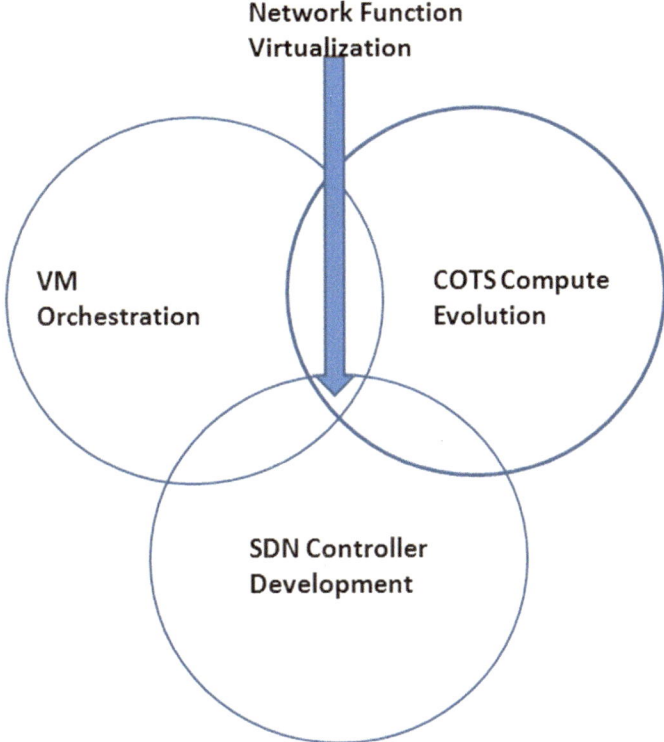

It is not necessary to use SDN to implement NFV, and present-day virtualization techniques are robust enough to build NFVs. However, the orchestration and management capabilities of SDN greatly enhance the capabilities of NFV and hence the use of SDN is being advocated during the development of NFVs. Virtualization of network services does not necessarily mean separate hypervisor-partitioned VMs that contain each service instance; instead, it could also mean: [2]

- Services which are implemented in a machine which has multiple/compartmentalized OS(s)
- Services which are implemented within a single hypervisor
- Services which are implemented as distributed or clustered as composites
- Services which are implemented on bare metal machines
- Services which are implemented in Linux virtual containers

These techniques may use some kind of storage device like NAS to share their state.
  NFVs is still an evolving area; however, following are some of the concerns which should be kept in mind during design of NFVs: [2]

- The use of hypervisor and delivering virtualized services using the same underlying physical hardware can lead to a conflict for physical resources. This may cause a performance drop in the delivery of services which are related to that specific component. NFV orchestration system should monitor such performance degradation very carefully. The NFV orchestration system should also keep track of the hypervisor and the physical resources so that any contention for resources can be carefully sorted out without any drop in performance.

- The virtualized services are hosted on the hypervisor component which could become a single point of failure. This failure will impact all the VMs which are running on that server and will also disrupt the services which are offered by those VMs.
- The virtual switch which is present in the hypervisor can get overloaded in an attempt to serve multiple VNICs of the various VMs which are running on it. The hypervisor should have some mechanism, and to identify and prioritize control traffic in so that application and management, failures can be avoided.
- The hypervisor has the capability to keep the applications unaware of the changes in physical machine state like failure of a NIC port. SDN controller and orchestration cooperation should bridge this awareness gap and perform timely actions.
- In some cases, virtual machines can be migrated from one server to another as a part of a high availability (HA) strategy. This migration can impact a service delivery in several ways. So appropriate steps need to be taken to ensure that no disruption of services happens.

4.6   Summary

In the first part of this chapter, we discussed the various limitations of the present-day networks which in turn led to the evolution of robust networking technologies which use virtualization technology as their foundation. These robust technologies form the foundation of the present-day SDDC.

In the second part of this chapter, we discussed the various approaches which are used in software-defined data centers, and the various approaches are:

- Network virtualization
- Network functions virtualization
- Software-defined storage

The various methods to implement network virtualization and the key components of a virtual network were also discussed. The traffic management techniques used in virtual networks were also discussed in detail. The various aspects of SDN and the architecture of SDN were discussed in this chapter. The chapter finally concludes with the description of NFV and the concerns to be kept in mind while designing service delivery using NFV.

References

1. A white paper on Software Defined Networking—The New Norm for networks by Open Net-working Foundation
2. Nadeau TD, Gray K A book on Authoritative review of network programming technologies. O'Reilly Publishers

Chapter 5
The Hybrid Cloud: The Journey Toward Hybrid IT

5.1 Introduction

Hybrid Cloud ensures fast and frictionless access for Cloud infrastructures, platforms, software, and data along with the much-touted bulletproof governance and IT service management (ITSM) features. However, establishing and sustaining hybrid Cloud facility is beset with a number of challenges including maintaining consistent configuration and developer experiences across geographically distributed Cloud environments. The other prominent issues include workload modernization and migration, IT cost management and monitoring. There are multiple automated solutions for eliminating the known as well as unknown complexities of hybrid Cloud monitoring, measurement, and management. This chapter elucidates the right and relevant things on various capabilities of different hybrid Cloud service providers and the tools they are using for accelerating and augmenting hybrid Cloud processes. The competitive analysis focuses on the following value-adding and decision-enabling parameters.

1. Hybrid Cloud Enablement Capabilities
2. Cloud Migration
3. Cloud Bursting, Connectivity, and Integration Features
4. Cloud Orchestration Capabilities
5. The Realization of Cloud-Enabled and Native Applications
6. Cloud brokerage Services for Multi-Cloud Environments
7. Software Configuration, Deployment, and Management
8. Hybrid Cloud Management Capabilities (through Third-party as well as Home-grown Tools)
9. Application Performance Management (APM)
10. Service Integration and Management
11. Distributed Deployment and Centralized Management (A single pane of glass to manage resources and applications across hybrid Clouds).

Let us see how the various service providers cope up with these identified parameters and this chapter is to give the right and relevant insights such as which provider stands where in the challenging yet promising domain of hybrid Cloud.

© Springer International Publishing AG, part of Springer Nature 2018   91
P. Raj and A. Raman, *Software-Defined Cloud Centers*,
Computer Communications and Networks,
https://doi.org/10.1007/978-3-319-78637-7_5

5.2   Demystifying the Hybrid Cloud Paradigm

Let us start with a brief of the raging hybrid Cloud concept. The Cloud paradigm is definitely recognized as the most disruptive one in the IT space in the recent past. The Cloud idea has brought in a series of well-intended and widely noticed business transformations. It all started with the widespread establishment and sustenance of public Clouds that are typically centralized, consolidated, virtualized, shared, automated, managed, and secured data centers and server farms. This trend clearly indicated and illustrated the overwhelming idea of IT industrialization. The era of commoditization to make IT the fifth social utility has also flourished with the faster maturity and stability of Cloud concepts. That is, public Clouds are made out of a large number of commodity server machines, storage appliances, and networking devices to make IT cost-effective, ubiquitously available and accessible, elastic, and energy-efficient. The volume-based and value-added IT service delivery methods through geographically distributed and standards-compliant Cloud environments have made the Cloud notion commercially viable and enviable. The much-discussed compartmentalization technologies represented by virtualization and containerization are playing a vital role toward the unprecedented success of the Cloud paradigm. The IT agility, adaptability, and affordability succulently imparted by the public Cloud paradigm have led to a bevy of newer business models and the much-anticipated IT operational efficiency.

The astounding success of public Clouds has in turn invigorated worldwide enterprises to explore the process of setting up of enterprise-grade private Clouds. The existing on-premise data centers are being systematically Cloud enabled to establish a seamless integration with publicly available Clouds. On the other hand, the proven and promising Cloud technologies and tools are being applied to establish local Cloud environments from the ground up. There are several crucial requirements for having on-premise private Clouds for certain industry verticals. That is, to ensure an exemplary control, visibility, and security of enterprise IT, private Clouds are being insisted. The business-critical requirements such as high performance, availability, and reliability also have forced worldwide enterprises to have their own Clouds on their premises.

The aspect of convergence has become the new normal in the IT space. Having understood that there are elegant and extra advantages with the combination of private and public Clouds, there is a renewed interest and rush by businesses to embrace the hybrid version and vision of Clouds. There are certain scenarios and benefits with hybrid Clouds. Cloud service providers are equally keen on providing hybrid capabilities to their clients and consumers.

Hybrid Cloud is a combination of on-premises and public Cloud services to bring forth an exemplary value for businesses. The Hybrid IT is the most influential and important moment for worldwide businesses in order to guarantee enhanced value for their customers, consumers, partners, employees, etc. The hybrid environment provides customers with all the flexibility and extensibility to select and consume the most appropriate service offering for specific workloads based on several critical factors such as cost, security, and performance. For example, a customer may choose a public Cloud service to test and develop a new application and then move that workload to a private Cloud or traditional IT environment when the application becomes operational. Enterprises that need to support a variety of workloads can leverage the flexibility of a hybrid Cloud approach to ensure they have the ability to scale up and scale down as needed. The emerging hybrid capability through a bevy of automated tools is a blessing in disguise for worldwide enterprises to meet up the fast-evolving business sentiments.

5.3 The Key Drivers for Hybrid Clouds

Hybrid Cloud is a kind of converged Cloud computing environment which uses a mix of on-premise private Cloud and public Cloud services with seamless interaction and orchestration between the participating platforms. While some of the organizations are looking to put selective IT functions onto a public Cloud, they still prefer keeping the higher-risk or more bespoke functions in a private/on-premise environment. Sometimes, the best infrastructure for an application requires both Cloud and dedicated environments. That is being touted as the prime reason for having hybrid Clouds (as illustrated in Fig. 5.1).

- **Public Cloud** for cost-effective scalability and ideal for heavy or unpredictable traffic
- **Private Cloud** for complete control and security aspects
- **Dedicated servers** for super-fast performance and reliability.

A hybrid Cloud configuration offers the following features:

- **Flexibility**—The availability of both scalable, cost-effective public resource, and secure resource can provide better opportunities for organizations to explore different operational avenues.
- **Cost efficiencies**—Public Clouds are likely to offer significant economies of scale (such as centralized management) and greater cost efficiencies than the private

Fig. 5.1 Formation of hybrid Cloud

Cloud. Hybrid Cloud model, therefore, allows organizations to unlock these savings for as many business functions as possible and still keeping sensitive operations secure.

- **Security**—The private Cloud feature in the hybrid Cloud model not only provides the security where it is required for sensitive operations but can also meet regulatory requirements for data handling and storage where it is applicable.
- **Scalability**—Although private Clouds offer a certain level of scalability based on the configurations (whether they are hosted externally or internally), public Cloud services do offer scalability with fewer boundaries as resources are pulled from the larger Cloud infra. By moving as many non-sensitive functions as possible to the public Cloud infrastructure, this would allow organizations to benefit from public Cloud scalability even as reducing the demands on a private Cloud.

Hybrid Clouds succulently empower enterprises to innovate rapidly while fulfilling the enterprise-grade performance, resiliency, and security requirements. Hybrid Cloud ensures the widely articulated enterprise IT needs by immaculately combining the control and reliability of private Cloud with the scalability, consumability, and cost-efficiency of public Clouds. Leveraging hybrid Cloud environments enables you to run every workload in its optimal place at optimal cost.

Integration of applications, data, and services—A hybrid Cloud creates the transparency needed to see and connect data and applications across infrastructures. For example, a hybrid Cloud approach can foster integration between internal systems of record, often housed on traditional IT or on a private Cloud, and more outward-facing systems of engagement, which are increasingly hosted on a public Cloud.

Composition and management of workloads—An agile and competitive business is increasingly a composable business. In any composable business, all sorts of processes, applications, services, and data become building blocks. These blocks are quickly and easily found, bound and assembled and re-assembled in the Cloud to find new ways to rapidly innovate and engage with customers. Distributed and different Cloud environments combine well to realize composable businesses. A hybrid Cloud enhances developer productivity so applications can be integrated, composed, and delivered.

Portability of data and applications—In a hybrid environment, developers can rapidly connect and compose data and services for the enterprise, the Web, and mobile applications, allowing organizations to act fast. Perhaps you need to make an application available in a new country or move from a development and test environment to production or move from primary capacity to scale-out capacity.

Flexibility with speed—Hybrid Clouds offer the broadest choice of platforms and infrastructures on which to build and deploy a range of applications at the speed required for business needs.

Value-driven with variety—Ubiquitous access to data sources for applications, a growing software market store, and integrated platforms across on-premise and off-premise Clouds.

Reliability with resiliency—Unbreakable and impenetrable data security along with application resiliency is the distinct hallmarks of hybrid Clouds.

Cost optimization—The choice of Cloud environments for efficiently and affordably running application workloads is being facilitated through hybrid Clouds.

Enhanced utilization—By leveraging the already invested and installed IT infrastructures, the IT costs could be kept low. Underutilized and unutilized infrastructural resources can be used to the highest value.

Hybrid Cloud use cases—It is possible to achieve higher levels of control, reliability, availability, elasticity, quality, and performance in hybrid Cloud environments. Customers have acknowledged the following five key use cases for a hybrid Cloud implementation.

Development and testing—Hybrid Cloud provides businesses with the required flexibility to gain the needed capacity for limited time periods without making capital investments for additional IT infrastructures.

Extending existing applications—With a hybrid Cloud, businesses can extend current standard applications to the Cloud to meet the needs of rapid growth or free up onsite resources for more business-critical projects.

Disaster recovery—Every organization fears an outage, or outright loss, of business-critical information. While on-site disaster recovery solutions can be expensive, preventing businesses from adopting the protection plans they need, a hybrid Cloud can offer an affordable disaster recovery solution with flexible commitments, capacity, and cost.

Web and mobile applications—Hybrid Cloud is ideal for cloud-native and mobile applications that are data-intensive and tend to need the elasticity to scale with sudden or unpredictable traffic spikes. With a hybrid Cloud, organizations can keep sensitive data on-site and maintain existing IT policies to meet the application's security and compliance requirements.

Development operations—As developers and operations teams work closely together to increase the rate of delivery and quality of deployed software, a hybrid Cloud allows them to not only blur the lines between the roles, but between Dev/Test and production, and between on-site and off-site placement of workloads.

Capacity expansion—Quickly address resource constraints by bursting workloads into VMware on IBM Cloud.

Data center consolidation—Consolidate legacy infrastructures onto an automated and centrally managed software-defined data center.

The adoption of hybrid Clouds is being driven due to several parameters as articulated above. The mandate toward highly optimized and organization Cloud environments for enabling smarter organizations is the key force for hybrid Clouds. The heightened stability and surging popularity of hybrid Clouds ultimately lead to multi-Cloud environments.

5.4   VMware Cloud Management Platform for Hybrid Clouds

VMware vRealize Suite delivers a comprehensive Cloud management platform that can manage hybrid (multi-Cloud) environments running anything from traditional to container (cloud-native) workloads. To make the shift to a hybrid Cloud computing environment, a few key best practices will help ensure success:

Automate services—Hybrid Clouds are designed to thrive on automation. For example, using a next-generation load-balancing solution allows predictive application auto-scaling. Such systems are analytics-driven and can automatically recognize changing traffic patterns in real-time and spin up additional instances without human intervention. This end-to-end automation across the environment is made possible when a hybrid Cloud traffic management system is in place. IT services teams can build this self-service infrastructure to not only optimize computing resources and provisions on the fly but also to shift workloads as needed. These types of capabilities provide the agility that hybrid Clouds promise with built-in elasticity, responsiveness, and efficiency.

Manage services across Cloud environments—Managing Cloud services with multiple providers or across environments do not need to be challenging; network teams simply need a single and central point of management across all environments, no matter where applications are running. Because public and private Cloud infrastructures operate independently, it is critical to use technology that provides portability of data and applications between Clouds. For example, when it comes to application networking services, software load balancers that combine central management together with per-app delivery services enable a high degree of customization and flexibility. The alternative of deploying an expensive, monolithic hardware load balancer in front of multiple applications creates problems when each application needs to be maintained or updated, causing downtime for others.

Use vendor-agnostic services—Now is the time to take advantage of the healthy competition that is brewing between Cloud providers to avoid getting locked into a single Cloud provider. Because not all Cloud providers deliver consistent services, it behooves companies to remain nimble and test out different services to find the ones that work best. By keeping the marketplace open and utilizing different providers, companies can take advantage of the myriad options to lower costs and increase performance, especially when they build a hybrid Cloud that utilizes the best-of-breed from private and public Clouds.

Hybrid Cloud computing is growing in popularity because it offers companies flexibility, scalability, and agility. To capitalize on this environment, IT teams must spend time creating a strategy that matches their organizational requirements. Putting private and public Clouds together requires automation tools and management capabilities to make a system efficient and cost-effective over the long haul.

5.5   The Hybrid Cloud Challenges

Hybrid Cloud facilitates to run different applications in the best of the environments to reap the required advantages such as the speed, scale, throughput, visibility, control. There are competent solutions and services being offered by different providers in the Cloud space in order to accelerate the hybrid Cloud setup and the sustenance. There is Cloud infrastructure service providers and Cloud managed services providers too in plenty. There are a plethora of open source as well as commercial-grade solutions and toolsets. Service providers have formulated enable frameworks toward risk-free and sustainable hybrid Clouds.

However, there are challenges too. Especially the prickling challenge lies in establishing a high-performing hybrid environment to appropriately and accurately manage and monitor all of its different components. Most of the current infrastructure management and monitoring tools were initially built to manage a single environment only. These point tools are incapable of managing distributed yet connected environments together. These tools lack the much-needed visibility and controllability into different environments; thereby, the activities such as workload migration among the integrated Clouds are not happening smoothly. Further on, the application performance management (APM) across the participating Clouds is also not an easy affair.

Thus, there is an insistence for integrated Cloud management platform (CMP) in order to leverage the fast-evolving hybrid concept to the fullest extent to give utmost flexibility to businesses.

5.6   The Distinct Capabilities of Hybrid Clouds

We are slowly yet steadily heading toward the digital era. The digitization-enablement technologies and tools are bringing a number of rapid and radical changes on how we collaborate, correlate, corroborate, and work. IT professionals are under immense pressure to meticulously capitalize these innovations and help their organization to move with agility and alacrity than today. The mantra of "more with less" has induced a large number of organizations to accurately strategize and implement a private Cloud due to the huge advantages being offered by public Clouds. But with the broad range of Cloud platforms, along with the explosion of new infrastructure and application services, having a private Cloud environment is no longer sufficient and efficient. The clear-cut answer is the realization of hybrid Clouds. The following questions facilitate to understand how hybrid Cloud comes handy in steering businesses in the right direction:

- Are workloads moved from private to public environments?
- Do you develop the Web or mobile application in one Cloud platform but run it in a different Cloud?
- Do your developers want to use multiple public platforms for their projects?

The following are the widely articulated and accepted features of hybrid Cloud service providers.

1. **Cloud bursting**—After all, the promise of running a performant and efficient private data center and leveraging public Cloud providers for the occasional hybrid Cloud bursting is the way forward. On the private side, you can maintain a complete control over privacy, security, and performance for your workloads, and on the public side, you can have "infinite" capacity for those occasional workloads. Imagine a Ruby application that is being used for an online store and the transactional volume is increasing due to a sale, a new promotion or Cyber Monday. The Cloud bursting module will recognize the increased load and recommend the right action to address the issue, effectively answering WHEN it is time to burst.

   It will also give the recommendation of WHERE to clone the instance. So, it is all about deciding WHAT workload to burst and WHERE to burst it including specific placement for computing and storage in a public Cloud environment. That is, the module enables to extend your private Cloud to:

   - Burst load into the Cloud when demand increases and cannot be met with local resources
   - Maintain control on workload performance and resource utilization to decide when to move back when possible
   - Allow application to auto-scale and clone into the Cloud
   - Load balances across private and public Clouds

   The module continuously analyzes the hybrid Cloud resources and IT stack taking into account multi-dimensions of continuously fluctuating tradeoffs. Tradeoffs between QoS versus budget and costs, between workload demand and infrastructure supply, between application performance and infrastructure utilization, between computing, storage and network, etc.

2. **VM migration Support**—As hybrid Clouds increase in popularity, it is important for organizations to be able to move virtual machines (VMs) from an on-premises hypervisor into the public Cloud, and to bring those workloads back to the house if necessary.

3. **Custom image support**—Cloud providers generally allow VMs to be built from predefined images, but these generic OS images do not always meet an organization's needs. As such, a Cloud provider should allow custom virtual machine images to be created and used.

4. **Image library**—Although many organizations try to minimize the number of server operating systems they use, heterogeneous environments are becoming much more common, especially in the Cloud. A good Cloud provider should offer a variety of server OS choices.

5. **Auto-scaling**—Workloads do not typically experience linear demand; instead, demand increases and decreases over time. Ideally, a Cloud provider should allow workloads to automatically scale up or down in response to current demand.

6. **Network connectivity**—Network connectivity is another important consideration when choosing a Cloud provider. There should be a way to connect your on-premises network to your Cloud network, and the provider should offer various connectivity features.

7. **Storage choices**—Storage needs vary depending on workloads. Some workloads can use commodity storage without any issues, while others require high-performance storage. As such, a Cloud provider should offer a variety of storage options.

8. **Regional support**—Sometimes, a business or regulatory requirements mandate hosting resources in a specific geographic region. That being the case, a Cloud provider should ideally give its customers a choice of where VMs will be hosted.

9. **Data backup, archival, and protection**—Cloud environments are turning out to be an excellent mechanism for business continuity and resiliency.

10. **Identity and Access Management (IAM)**—Authentication, authorization, and auditability are the key requirements for ensuring Cloud security and privacy. There are several additional security-ensuring mechanisms for impenetrable and unbreakable security.

11. **Disaster and data recovery**—Whether their applications are running in on-premises private Clouds, hosted private Clouds or public Clouds, enterprises are increasingly seeing the value of using the public Cloud for disaster recovery. One of the major challenges of traditional disaster recovery architectures that span multiple data centers has been the cost of provisioning duplicate infrastructure that is rarely used. By using pay-as-you-go public Cloud as the disaster recovery environment, IT teams can now deliver DR solutions at a much lower cost.

12. **Service integration and management**—IT service management (ITSM) has been an important requirement for different IT service providers, data center operators, and Cloud centers for exemplary service fulfilment. As Clouds emerge as the one-stop IT solution, the aspect of service management and integration garners extreme importance in order to fulfil the agreed SLAs between Cloud service consumers and providers. The various non-functional attributes need to be guaranteed by CSPs to their subscribers through highly competitive ITSM solutions.

13. **Monitoring, measurement, and management**—Hybrid Cloud management platform is a key ingredient for running hybrid Cloud environments successfully and we have extensively written about the role and responsibility of a viable management platform in a hybrid scenario.

14. **Metering and chargeback**—A chargeback model in the Cloud delivers many benefits, including the most obvious:

   - Correlating utilization back to Cloud consumers or corporate departments, so that users can be charged if desired
   - Providing visibility into resource utilization and facilitating capacity planning, forecasting, and budgeting
   - Providing a mechanism for the enterprise IT function to justify and allocate their costs to their stakeholder business units

With the continued evolution of business sentiments and expectations, the capabilities of hybrid Clouds are bound to enlarge consistently through the careful addition of powerful tools, processes, and practices.

5.7 The Cloud Development Solutions

Hybridization is definitely a unique and useful approach for different scenarios. In the Cloud space also, the hybrid capability is all set to penetrate and participate in bringing forth a number of exceptional benefits such as the acceleration of innovations, sharply lessening the time to take fresh products and services to the knowledge-filled market, the means and ways of achieving agile development through continuous integration, deployment and delivery, and guaranteeing the significant enhancement in resource utilization, for worldwide enterprises.

There are a few Cloud development and sustenance solutions in the market.

1. VMware vSphere ESXi is the industry-leading virtualization platform for building Cloud infrastructures. vSphere enables you to run your business-critical applications confidently to meet the most demanding service-level agreements (SLAs) at the lowest TCO. vSphere with operations management combines this leading virtualization platform with the award-winning management capabilities of VMware vCenter Server.

2. OpenStack is the widely leveraged and open-source infrastructure as a service (IaaS) development and management framework. There are other open-source Cloud development environments such as CloudStack,

3. Apache CloudStack is open-source software designed to deploy and manage large networks of virtual machines, as a highly available, highly scalable Infrastructure as a Service (IaaS) Cloud computing platform. CloudStack is used by a number of service providers to offer public Cloud services, and by many companies to provide an on-premises (private) Cloud offering, or as part of a hybrid Cloud solution. CloudStack is a turnkey solution that includes the entire "stack" of features most organizations want with an IaaS Cloud: compute orchestration, Network-as-a-Service, user and account management, a full and open native API, resource accounting, and a first-class User Interface (UI). CloudStack currently supports the most popular hypervisors: VMware, KVM, Citrix XenServer, Xen Cloud Platform (XCP), Oracle VM server, and Microsoft Hyper-V.

4. Microsoft System Center is the other option to develop Cloud environments. Azure Stack is a new hybrid Cloud platform product which enables organizations to deliver Azure services from their own data center in a way which is consistent with Azure. Organizations can create these Azure services from data center resources—enabling developers and IT professionals to quickly provision and scale services using the same self-service experience found in Azure. This all adds up to an environment in which application developers can maximize their productivity using a 'write once, deploy to Azure or Azure Stack' approach

because the Azure APIs are consistent regardless of where the resources are provisioned—Azure Stack is simply an extension of Azure.

5.8 The Hybrid Cloud of Virtual Machines and Containers

Legacy applications need a transition period for moving from VMs to containers. Therefore as an intermediate solution, unified hybrid platforms (https://www.mirantis.com/blog/multi-cloud-application-orchestration-on-mirantis-cloud-platform-using-spinnaker/) are being formed and used. Here, you can split various workloads between containers, VMs, and non-virtualized resources. You can take best-of-breed from all three workloads and tune them for best performance and optimal costs. For example, MCP 1.0 comes with OpenStack, Kubernetes, and OpenContrail, making it possible to create an environment where all those components work together to create a platform for legacy application stacks that are in various stages of transformation.

Let us go through the steps and architecture of this unified platform. First, we needed to provision all hardware nodes in our Cloud center with a basic operation system (OS) and OpenStack provides that capability via the Ironic project, Bare Metal-as-a-Service (BMaaS). These servers then form the foundation nodes for the control plane or support services, as well as compute power for any workloads, as in Fig. 5.2.

For this example, we split our servers into three groups and we deployed Kubernetes cluster on bare metal on one group, standard OpenStack compute nodes on the second group, and left the third group alone to act as non-virtualized servers. OpenContrail SDN enabled us to create a single network layer and connect VMs, containers, and bare metal nodes. OpenContrail has a Neutron plugin for OpenStack, and also a CNI plugin for Kubernetes, which enables us to use same network technology stack for both. Bare metal servers are then connected through Top-of-Rack (ToR) switches via VXLAN and the OVS-DB protocol, as in Fig. 5.3.

In Fig. 5.4, you can see the demo stack, where we have OpenStack and Kubernetes running with two independent OpenContrail control planes, which are federated via BGP. This feature enables you to build independent OpenStack regions and federate their network stack across multiple sites while still maintaining separate failure domains. Any virtual networks can be directly routable by setting a route target, which establishes a direct data path from container to VM. Traffic does not go through any gateway or network node, because vRouter creates an end-to-end MPLSoUDP or VXLAN tunnel. As you can see, we have created a direct path between the Kafka pod (container) and the Spark VM.

Multi-Cloud orchestration with Spinnaker—Now we have a platform that can run any kind of workload, but for developers or operators, what is more important is to how to orchestrate applications. Users do not want to go into OpenStack and manually start a VM, then go to Kubernetes to start a container, and after that plug a

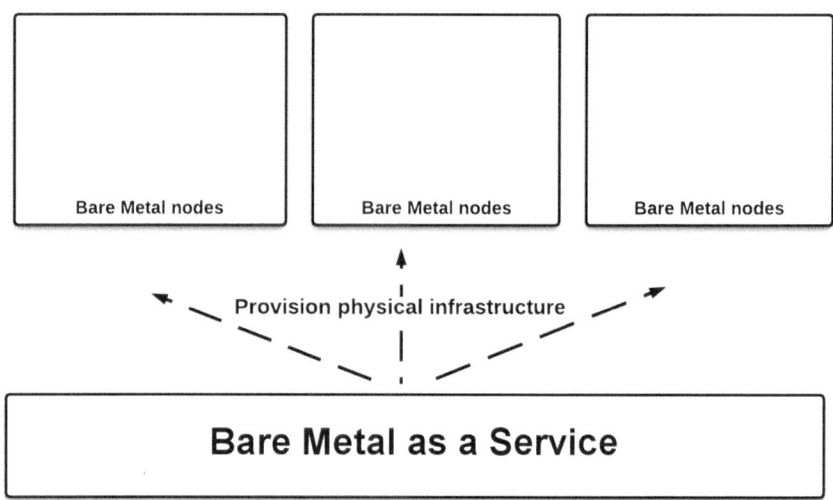

Fig. 5.2 Bare metal (BM) servers are split for hosting different workloads

non-virtualized bare metal node into the network through a ToR switch. That process is complex, error-prone, and time-consuming.

The real value and usability of this platform comes with higher orchestration. Fortunately, we can provide multi-Cloud orchestration using a tool called Spinnaker. Spinnaker is an open-source, multi-Cloud continuous delivery platform for releasing software changes with high velocity and confidence. It was developed primarily by Netflix for AWS, but it is gotten a lot of traction and provides drivers for AWS, OpenStack, Kubernetes, Google Cloud platform, and Microsoft Azure.

Spinnaker's main goal is to bake and rollout immutable images on different providers with different strategies, where you can manage load balancers, security groups and server groups made up of VMs and containers. Figure 5.5 shows that we have enabled two providers: OpenStack and Kubernetes.

Spinnaker has a simple UI, which enables us to build complex pipelines that include stages such as "manual judgement," "run script," "Webhook," or "jenkins job." MCP includes Jenkins as part of DriveTrain, so integration with Spinnaker

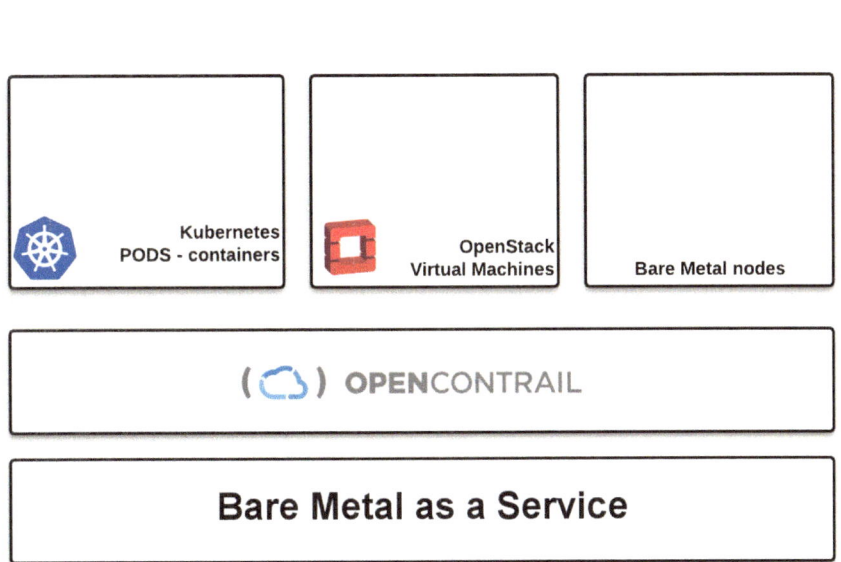

Fig. 5.3 One group of servers is dedicated to Kubernetes, one to OpenStack, and one to bare metal nodes; they are tied together with OpenContrail networking

pipelines is very easy. I can imagine using Spinnaker just for multiple stage Jenkins pipelines for upgrades of hundreds of different OpenStack sites.

Figure 5.6 shows our Big Data infrastructure we want Spinnaker to orchestrate on top of MCP. Basically, we deploy HDFS on couple of bare metal servers, Spark in VMs, and Kafka with zookeeper in containers.

Big Data Twitter analytics—We wanted to use a real example use case and not just show orchestration or ping between VMs and containers, so we picked Big Data because we are working on similar implementations at a couple of customers. To make it manageable for a short demo, we created a simple app, with real-time Twitter streaming API processing, as you can see in Fig. 5.7.

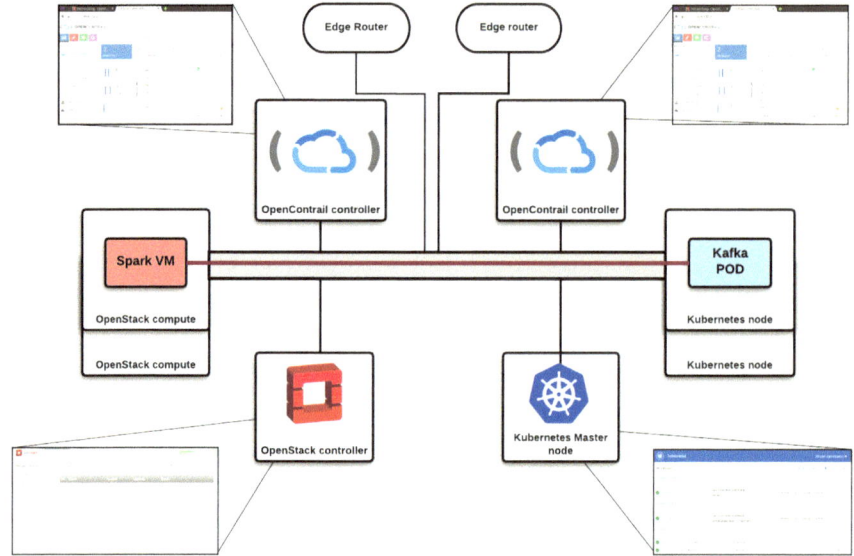

Fig. 5.4   A direct path between VM and container

Fig. 5.5   Spinnaker has two providers enabled: Kubernetes and OpenStack

Our stack consists of following components:

- Tweetpub—Reads tweets from the Twitter Streaming API and puts them into a Kafka topic.
- Apache Kafka—Messaging that transmits data from Twitter into Apache Spark. Alongside Kafka, we run Apache Zookeeper as a requirement.
- Apache Spark—Data processing, running TweeTics job.
- TweeTics—Spark job that parses tweets from Kafka and stores hashtags popularity as text files to HDFS.

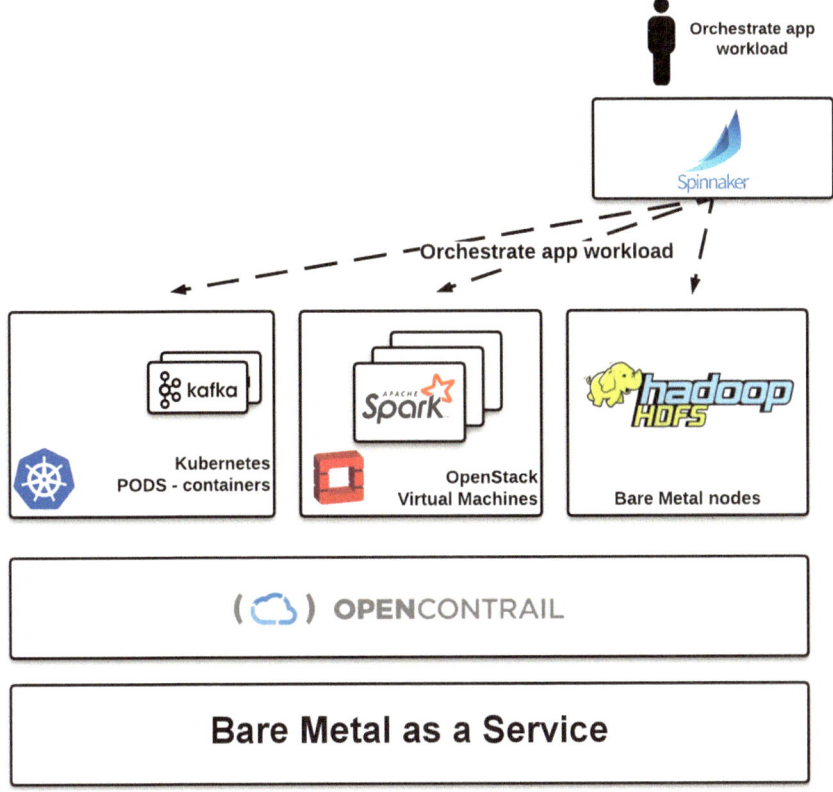

Fig. 5.6 Spinnaker will orchestrate Kafka on our Kubernetes cluster, Apache Spark on our VMs, and Hadoop HDFS on the bare metal nodes

- Apache Hadoop HDFS—Data store for processed data.
- Tweetviz—Reads processed data from HDFS and shows hashtag popularity as a tag Cloud.

We configured Tweetpub to look for tweets that are sent from the Boston, MA area using the location parameters $(-71.4415, 41.9860, -70.4747, 42.9041)$, and tracked the following words:

- openstack
- kubernetes
- k8s
- python
- golang
- sdn
- nfv
- weareopenstack

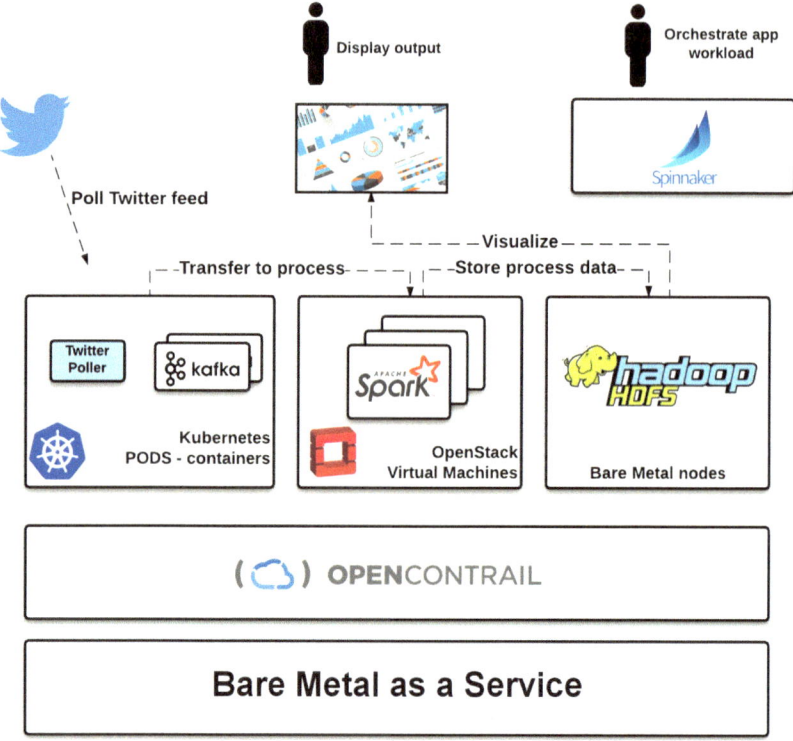

Fig. 5.7 Twitter Poller pulls data into Kafka, which then sends it to Spark for analysis before it gets sent to Hadoop for visualization and storage

- opencontrail
- docker
- hybridCloud
- aws
- azure
- openstacksummit
- mirantis
- coreos
- redhat
- devops
- container
- api
- bigdata
- Cloudcomputing
- iot.

Fig. 5.8 App displays the data in real time, showing the relative popularity of various terms by adjusting their size in the tag Cloud. For example, the two most popular topics were IoT and Big Data

Once everything was running, the job looked at every tweet that contained one of those words and stored a count for the hashtag in real time. Our 3D visualisation page then displayed most popular hashtags. We found that almost every time, IoT, and Big Data are the most common hashtags, regardless of the location or time. OpenStackSummit was number 6, as you can see in Fig. 5.8.

As you can see, once you have a flexible platform such as MCP, it is much easier to tackle various use cases and help customers to onboard their workloads and satisfy their requirements through an open-source platform. We have shown a relatively simple view of this setup.

5.9   Hybrid Cloud Management: The Use Cases and Requirements

Hybrid Cloud management solutions are typically automation and orchestration platforms. They automate manual or scripted tasks and they orchestrate tasks and processes that execute across a number of distributed and disparate Cloud environments. Forrester, one of the leading market analysts, has identified the four most common hybrid Cloud management use cases today.

- Accelerating hybrid Cloud application development and delivery
- Managing and governing the hybrid Cloud infrastructure life cycle
- Migrating Cloud apps and infrastructure among Cloud platforms
- Creating an enterprise Cloud brokering function.

Businesses are involving hybrid Cloud management platforms for solving different requirements. If hybrid Cloud challenges are primarily around the Cloud infrastructure life cycle, then it is logical to focus on features that help package up infrastructure components as per customers' requirements, present them to your Cloud consumers, automate deployment and migration, and monitor consumption and performance. If you are more concerned with accelerating Cloud development, look for prepack-aged application templates, cloud-agnostic and developer-friendly APIs, integrations with application release automation (ARA) tools, and policy-based automation of application lifecycle events like auto-scaling. If cost management is a top concern, prioritize price benchmarking and cost analytics features. The key capabilities are summarized in the reference architecture model.

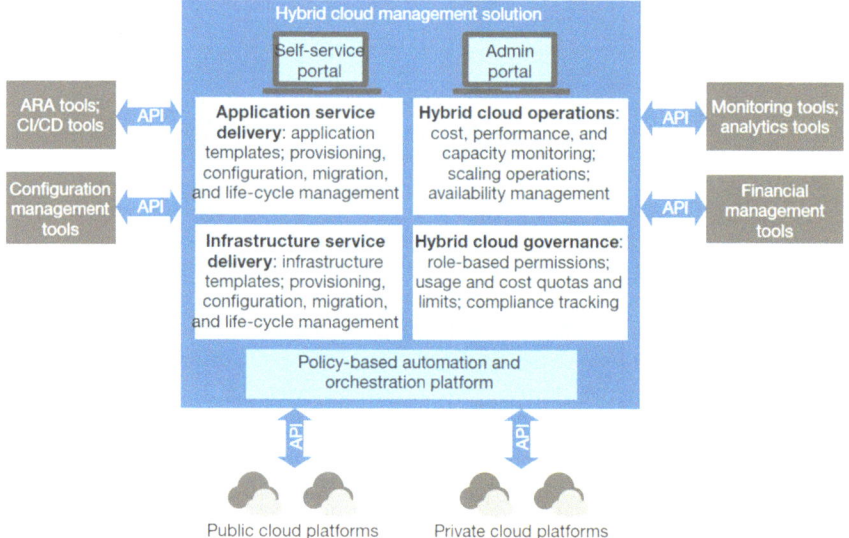

5.10   The Growing Ecosystem of Hybrid Cloud Management Solutions

The hybrid Cloud management landscape is fast enlarging.

- For many incumbent enterprise systems and technology vendors, hybrid Cloud management is just an evolution of existing IT service management (ITSM) suites. These are meticulously extended to manage Cloud infrastructure endpoints using the same automation tools that the vendor sells to manage physical and virtualized infrastructure in the data center.
- Enterprise technology vendors that have built private Cloud solutions often con-sider hybrid Cloud management to be an extension of private Cloud.
- There are smaller software companies that created solutions to manage multiple public Cloud platforms first and they are now refactoring them to manage private Clouds so that they can be categorized as hybrid Cloud management solutions.

There are others who built solutions for Cloud migration or brokerage and are now extending them to have life cycle and governance features to be accommodated in the hybrid Cloud management solutions.

1. Established management solution providers extend existing management suites. Three of the traditional big four enterprise management vendors (BMC Software, HP, and IBM) offer standalone hybrid Cloud management solutions, often integrating with and leveraging other tools from the vendor's existing catalogue. Microsoft and Oracle have added hybrid Cloud management features to System Center and Enterprise Manager, respectively.
2. Enterprise systems vendors add hybrid management to private Cloud platforms. Cisco Systems, Citrix, Computer Sciences Corp (CSC), Dell, HP, IBM, Microsoft, Oracle, and VMware all offer private Cloud suites that may also include hybrid Cloud management capabilities. If private Cloud is critical to your hybrid Cloud strategy, consider whether such an extension of private Cloud meets your needs.
3. Hypervisor and OS vendors target technology managers who own infrastructure. Citrix, Microsoft, Red Hat, and VMware offer virtualization platforms and virtual machine (VM)-focused management tools and focus hybrid Cloud management solutions on the Cloud infrastructure life cycle use case. CloudBolt and Embotics also feature VM-focused management capabilities.
4. Independent software vendors target cloud-focused developers and DevOps. CliQr, CSC, Dell, DivvyCloud, GigaSpaces, RightScale, and Scalr market their solutions primarily at Cloud developers and the DevOps pros who support them. Their solutions are well suited for the Cloud application life cycle use case.
5. Public Cloud platform vendors focus on their own Clouds in hybrid scenarios. Cisco, IBM, Microsoft, Oracle, Red Hat, and VMware offer public Cloud platforms in addition to hybrid Cloud management software. Naturally, these vendors encourage the use of their own platforms for hybrid deployments. Pay attention to how strongly the vendor's own platform is favored when evaluating its hybrid Cloud management capabilities.
6. Cloud migration vendors add more life cycle management features. HotLink and RackWare are Cloud migration tools with added VM-management features that extend to public Cloud platforms. They stress the onboard and disaster recovery use cases for Cloud migration. RISC Networks is a Cloud migration analysis tool. In addition to these vendors, many other hybrid Cloud management vendors in this landscape have migration capabilities.
7. Cloud brokers and brokerage enablers extend beyond cost analytics. AppDirect, Gravitant, Jamcracker, and Ostrato primarily focus on the enterprise Cloud brokerage use case. Each of these vendors, however, offers additional capabilities beyond cost brokering and analytics.

5.11   Conclusion

The Cloud technology has matured and opened up newer possibilities and opportunities in the form of pragmatic hybrid Clouds that in turn comprises elegant private Clouds and elastic public Clouds. Organizations are increasingly leaning toward hybrid Clouds in order to reap the combined benefits of both public and private Clouds. This chapter has explained the unique advantages to be accrued out of hybrid Clouds. Enterprises considering the distinct requirements of their workloads are consciously embracing hybrid Clouds. There are several hybrid Cloud service providers in the market with different capabilities and this chapter has faithfully articulated the various competencies of those hybrid Cloud service providers in order to educate worldwide corporates to take an informed decision.

Chapter 6
Security Management of a Software-Defined Cloud Center

6.1 Introduction

Information and communication technology will be the key foundational component of a software-defined data center. These information and communication technological components will be closely interconnected with one another in order to facilitate efficient coordination among the various data center components. However for this efficient communication and collaboration to happen in real time, it is very critical to ensure the safety and security of the underlying information technology infrastructure.

In this chapter, we will identify the security challenges and the security requirements to be kept in mind for the design of data center infrastructure. In this chapter, we will identify security threats based on the four key platforms and technologies which are used by the data center infrastructure components. They are the following:

- Security concerns in mobile devices and platforms.
- Security concerns in big data platforms.
- Security concerns in Cloud.
- Security concerns in IoT platforms.

We will also examine some of the techniques to be used in order to leverage the underlying technological resources in a smart manner by ensuring that there is no unintentional or malicious access to data which is stored and accessed in the data center components

6.2 Security Requirements of a Software-Defined Data Center (SDDC) Infrastructure

The key security aspects which need to be kept in mind for the security of information technological components which are applicable to a SDDC infrastructure are discussed in this section.

© Springer International Publishing AG, part of Springer Nature 2018   111
P. Raj and A. Raman, *Software-Defined Cloud Centers*,
Computer Communications and Networks,
https://doi.org/10.1007/978-3-319-78637-7_6

- **Confidentiality, Integrity, and Availability (CIA) Triad**— The three fundamental requirements, which need to be kept in mind during the design and development phase of the underlying SDDC infrastructure, are depicted in the diagram which is given below:

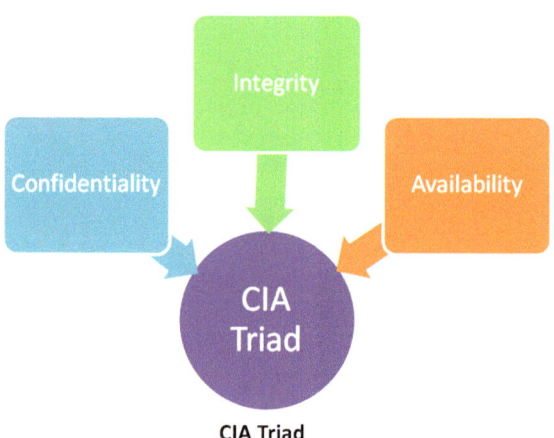

CIA Triad

Confidentiality: It ensures that only authorized users will have access to the underlying information. In other words, it ensures that privacy by preventing unauthorized access to the information which is stored and transmitted using the SDDC infrastructure.

Integrity: It ensures that only authorized users are allowed to modify the underlying information. It ensures that unauthorized users will not be able to alter the information in any manner. Alteration involves write, delete, and update operations.

Availability: It ensures that authorized users have access to the underlying information as and when it is required. This includes ensuring the fact that the SDDC infrastructure has fault tolerance capabilities built into them. Fault tolerance can be built into the SDDC infrastructure by ensuring that backup components are present for each of the SDDC infrastructure components, namely servers, storage, and networks. Server backup can be ensured by clustering the servers in order to provide a high availability environment. It is also important to ensure that the backup server is an identical copy of the primary server and can take over the role of the primary server immediately upon the failure of the primary server. Storage backup can be ensured by using the highly scalable RAID architecture for hard disks in which same data is striped and mirrored across multiple hard disks so that even if one hard disk fails, data will not be lost as it will be stored in the other disks of the array. Fault tolerance in networks can be ensured by providing multiple switches, multiple ports, and multiple cables between the two connecting endpoints in order to ensure that the failure of any network component will not hamper the transfer of data through the network.

These components confidentiality, integrity, and availability are commonly referred to as CIA Triad.

6.3   Authentication, Authorization, and Audit Trial Framework (AAA)

AAA framework is a security requirement which is of paramount importance for the SDDC infrastructure. The various components of the framework are:

Authentication: This process checks to ensure that a user's credentials are valid so that users with invalid credentials will not be allowed to access the underlying information. The simplest way to use authentication is with the help of user names and passwords. But as hacking techniques are evolving day by day, it is very important to ensure that sophisticated authentication techniques are in place. One such authentication mechanism which is used is called multi-factor authentication. Multi-factor authentication is a special authentication technique which uses a combination of parameters to verify a user's credentials. An example of multi-factor authentication mechanism is described below

First factor: A user name and password will be unique for the specific user which may be sometimes unique for the specific session as well.

Second factor: A secret key is generated by a random number generator or a secret key phrase is known only to the user or answer to a secret question which is specific to a particular user.

Third factor: This could be any biometric parameter of the user which could be used as the user's biometric signature. This could include aspects like iris recognition, fingerprint recognition, and so on.

A multi-factor authentication uses a combination of all the parameters mentioned above in order to verify a user's credentials. In some cases, only two factors mentioned above may be used for authentication and in that case, it is called two factor authentication.

Authorization—Authorizationis a process which ensures that a specific user has rights to perform specific operations on a specific object. This is generally by granting different types of permissions to different types of users' based on their role in a city government. For example, a fire station executive will be just able to read the data pertaining to other city departments like water he may not be able to edit it. Edit permissions may be given only to the city supervisors or executives who belong to the water department of the city. The different types of permissions for different users on different objects are mapped and stored in a table which is called access control list (ACL). The different types of permissions which are given for users are classified as the following:

- Read only: The user has permission to only read the object. The user cannot delete or edit the object. These types of permissions are granted to staff who are not required to perform any alteration on the data.
- Read and Write: The user has permission to read and alter the object. These types of permissions are granted to authorities who have the overall authority and discretion to validate the rights and access permissions of other users.

Audit Trial—Audit trial is an activity which is conducted periodically to assess the effectiveness of the security measures which are implemented in the SDDC infrastructure. Audit trial is performed with the help of audit logs which tracks the operations which are performed by different users.

6.4 Defense in Depth

This is a mechanism which should be used to provide high level of security to the SDDC infrastructure. This mechanism ensures that multiple levels or layers of security are present within an SDDC infrastructure to ensure that even if security at one level gets compromised due to some reason, security at other levels should be able to safeguard the underlying SDDC infrastructure. As multiple levels of security are provided in this approach, it is also called a layered approach to security implementation. It gives enhanced security to the SDDC infrastructure by providing multiple layers of security and more time to officials to react to a security breach which has happened in one layer where the other layer security measures will be working to protect it. A high-level architecture of the Defense-in-Depth approach is given below:

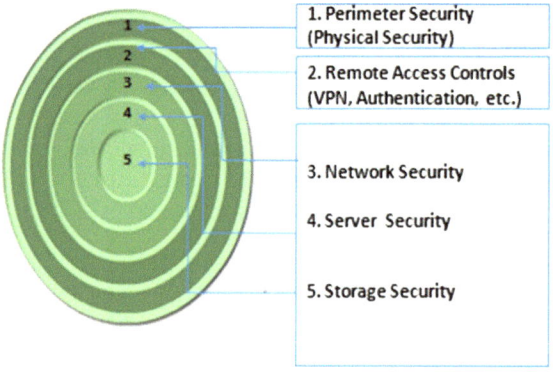

Architecture of Defense –in-Depth

Trusted Computing Base (TCB)—This defines the boundary for the critical information components which form a part of the SDDC infrastructure. Any security breaches which happen within the TCB boundary will affect the entire SDDC infrastructure in an adverse manner. This helps to establish a clear definition between the critical and non-critical components of the SDDC infrastructure. For example, if we take an example of a PC or tablet, operating system and configuration files will be a part of the TCB as any security breaches to the operating system will corrupt the entire PC. It is very important for TCB to be defined for the SDDC infrastructure. It helps to provide multiple additional levels of security for the components which fall under the TCB of the SDDC infrastructure.

Encryption— It is the process of converting data into a format which cannot be interpreted easily and directly by unauthorized users. It is very important to ensure that data which is stored in the SDDC infrastructure and the data which is transmitted via the networks are in encrypted form. This is very helpful to prevent unauthorized deception of data by third-party agents. The process of converting the data back to its original form is called decryption. Several encryption software are available in the market.

Pretty Good Privacy (PGP)
Pretty Good Privacy (PGP) is a strong data encryption and decryption program which is widely used by federal government for protecting all types of government data like mails, files, and entire disk partitions of computers.

Apart from the security requirements which are mentioned above, the additional security requirement of the SDDC infrastructure is resilience. Resilience is the capability of an infrastructure to return back to its original state after it is disturbed due to some factors which are internal or external.

Majority of the SDDC applications will be built and deployed on Cloud platforms. Hence, all security concerns of Cloud platforms will pose security threats for SDDC components as well. In the next section, we will examine some of the security concerns of Cloud platforms.

6.5   Security Concerns of Cloud Platforms

Cloud security architecture has three different layers: software applications layer, platform layer, and infrastructure layer. Each layer has its own set of security concerns. We will discuss some of them in the context of IoT components which would mainly rely on public Cloud for its IT requirements.

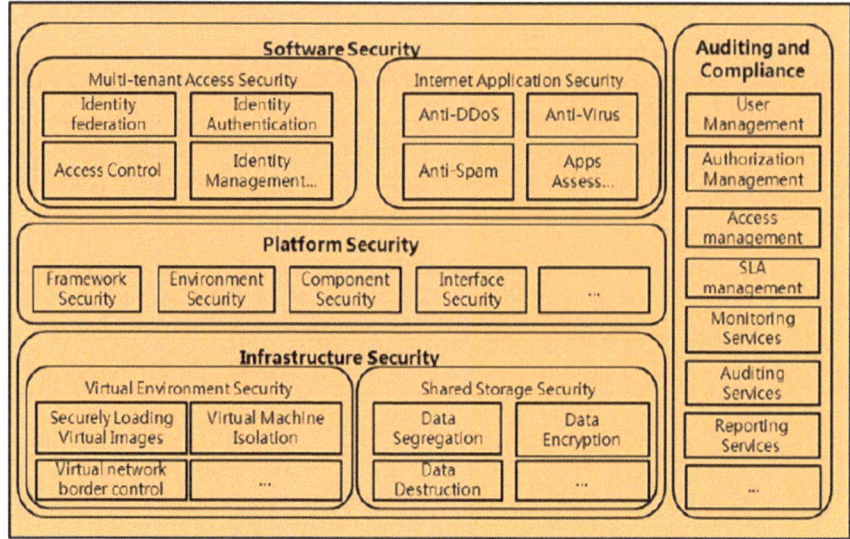

Cloud Security Architecture

One of the main concerns of Cloud is multi tenancy. Multi-tenancy refers to the fact that Cloud infrastructure because of the underlying virtualization platform provides features to service multiple independent clients (tenants) using same set of resources. This consequently increases the risks for data confidentiality and integrity. These risks are especially more severe in case of public Cloud environment. This is because, in Public Cloud, services can be used by competing clients as compared to Private Clouds and also a number of Cloud users are much higher in Public Clouds.

Some of the ways to overcome these concerns which arise due to multi-tenancy are:

- Virtual machine segmentation
- Database segmentation
- Virtual machine introspection.

6.5.1 Virtual Machine Segmentation

Virtualization forms the basis of most of the IaaS offerings. There are many virtualization software available in the market like VMware vSphere, Citrix XenServer, and Microsoft Hyper-V. This software provides the capability to convert a physical machine into multiple virtual machines. These virtual machines serve as databases, Web servers, and file servers. These components which run on virtual platforms are provided to customers as a part of IaaS. The main component of virtualization platform is hypervisor which acts as operating system for the virtual machines and provisions all the resources required for the operation of Virtual machines. The major security concerns in virtualized infrastructure are due to the fact that virtual machines owned by multiple customers reside on the same physical machine. This aspect places the virtual machines in a privileged position with respect to one another. This can introduce several types of security risks like unauthorized connection, monitoring, and malware induction. In order to prevent occurrence of such security concerns, it is very important to ensure that VMs which contain confidential customer data should be segmented and isolated from one another. This process of ensuring that virtual machines are isolated or separated from one another is called virtual machine segmentation.

6.5.2 Database Segmentation

In IaaS, infrastructure resources are offered as a service. In SaaS, apart from software applications, database is also offered as a service. This will introduce a scenario that multiple customers will store their data in the same database as multiple rows which are differentiated based on customer Id which will be assigned to customers. In some situations like application code errors or access control list errors, there is a lot of risk for customer data. For controlling access to database data, there are quite a few tools and technologies available. In order to prevent the occurrence of such situations, there are many tools which are available in the market. These tools work on the basis of a system for authentication and authorization which ensure that only some rows are only modifiable based on certain predefined security policies which ensure that access to data is warranted. Another technique which could be used to reduce security threats in this situation is the encryption of data which is stored in the database. This ensures that even if the security of the data is compromised, it would be difficult to decrypt it.

6.5.3 VM Introspection

Another important technique which could be used to eliminate the risks of multi-tenancy is VM introspection. VM introspection is a service which is provided by the hypervisor. This service examines the internal state of each VM which runs on top of the hypervisor. There are many tools available in the market which leverages the benefits of this service to provide VM segmentation and isolation. VM introspection provides following details of each VM:

- Applications and services which are present
- Configuration details.

With the help of these details of VMs, it is possible to create and implement custom security policies on each VM. An example of a policy could be to ensure that no other

VM should join a specific VM group until it has some matching OS configuration parameters. This ensures that in a multitenant environment, VMs remain segmented and isolated.

6.6 Distributed Denial of Service (DDoS)

In a Cloud system, if a host of messages attack all nodes of the Cloud system and overutilize the server resources, making the resources unavailable for actual requirements, then it is called a DDoS attack. There are multiple versions of DDoS attacks which are available: simple and complex. Example of simple DDoS attack tools is XML-based denial of service (X-Dos) as well as HTTP-based denial of service (H-Dos). Example of complex DDoS attack tools is Agobot, Mstream, and Trinoo. H-DoS is used by attackers who are interested in using less complex Web-based tools for attack. One additional advantage of these simple tools is the ease of implementation of attacks. DX-DoS occurs when XML-based messages are sent to a Web server in such a way that it will use up all their resources. Coercive parsing attack is an X-Dos attack in which web content is parsed using SOAP to transform it into an application. A series of open tags are used by coercive parsing attack to exhaust the CPU resources on the Web server. In case of an H-DoS attack, a series of about 1000 plus threads are started to create HTTP simultaneous random requests to exhaust all the resources. There are several tools available in the market to detect and eliminate DDoS attacks. The Cloud service provider can use these tools at their discretion. One such example is discussed below.

Real-Life Example of DDoS Attack
Bloomberg News reported that hackers used AWS's EC2 Cloud computing unit to launch an attack against Sony's PlayStation Network and Qriocity entertainment networks. The attack reportedly compromised the personal accounts of more than 100 million Sony customers.

6.6.1 Imperva SecureSphere Web Application Firewall to Prevent DDoS Attacks

The Imperva SecureSphere Web Application Firewall is a security appliance which is capable of preventing DDoS attacks in a Cloud infrastructure. In addition to DDoS, this software also has the capability to prevent several types of Web attacks like SQL injection.

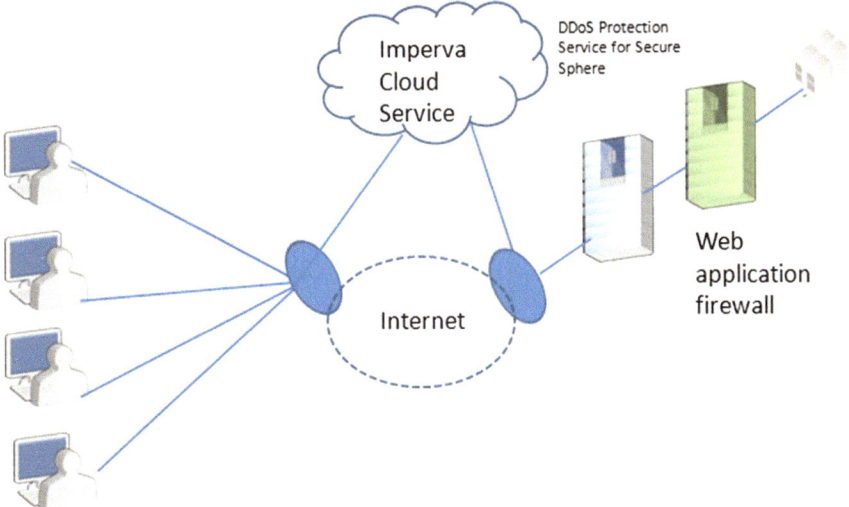

Architecture of Imperva Secure Sphere

The tool uses the following features to prevent DDoS attacks on Cloud infrastructure:

- Threat Radar Reputation: This service keeps track of users who are attacking other Web sites. By using this information, it will filter off any request from those users and prevent them from getting into the Cloud system.
- Up-to-Date Web Attack Signatures: This service helps to monitor and keep track of bot user agents and DDoS attack vectors.
- DDoS Policy Templates: This service helps to detect users who have the pattern of generating and sending HTTP requests with long response times.
- Bot Mitigation Policies: This service has the capability to sends a JavaScript challenge to users' browsers. This JavaScript challenge has the capacity to detect and block bots.
- HTTP Protocol Validation: This service monitors and records buffer overflow attempts and other intrusion techniques.

6.7   Virtual Machine/Hypervisor-Based Security Threats

The virtual machines which forms the basis of Cloud infrastructure is also subjected to various types of vulnerabilities. This poses severe threats to the Cloud infrastructure. Some of them are:

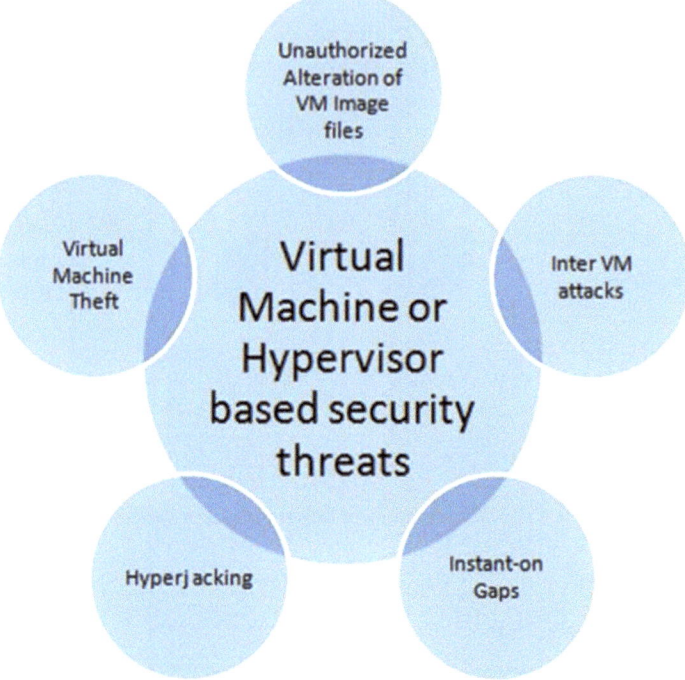

Virtual Machine Based Security Threats

6.7.1 Unauthorized Alteration of Virtual Machine Image Files

Virtual machines are susceptible to security threats when they are running as well as when they are powered off. When a VM is powered off, it is available as a VM image file. This image file is exposed to several security threats like malware infections. Apart from that, if appropriate security measures are not in place, VM image files can be used by hackers to create new unauthorized VMs. It is also possible to patch these VM image files so as to infect the VMs which are created using these image files. VM security can be compromised even during VM migration. At the time of VM migration, the VMs are exposed to several types of network attacks like eavesdropping and unauthorized modification. One technique which could be used to protect the VM image files is to encrypt them when they are powered off or being migrated.

6.7.2 VM Theft

VM theft enables a hacker or attacker to copy or move a VM in an unauthorized manner. This is mainly made possible because of the presence of inadequate controls on VM files. These inadequate controls will allow the unauthorized copy or movement of VM files. VM theft could prove to be very fatal if the VM that is stolen contains confidential data of a customer.

One way to restrict VM theft is to impose required level of copy and move restrictions on VMs. Such restrictions effectively bind a VM to a specific physical machine in such a way that even if there is a forceful copy of the VM, it will not operate on any other physical machine. A VM with required level of copy and move restrictions cannot run on a hypervisor installed on any other physical machine.

Apart from VM theft, another threat which can happen at VM level is known as "VM escape." Normally, virtual machines are encapsulated and isolated from each other and from the underlying parent hypervisor. In normal scenarios, there is no mechanism available for a guest OS and the applications running on it to break out of the virtual machine boundary and directly interact with the hypervisor. The process of breaking out and interacting with the hypervisor is called a VM escape. Since the hypervisor controls the execution of all VMs, due to VM escape, an attacker can gain control over every other VM running on it by bypassing security controls which are placed on those VMs.

6.7.3 Inter-VM Attacks

Multiple VMs run on the same physical machine. So if the security of one VM is compromised, there is a very easy possibility for the security of other VMs running on the same physical machine to be compromised. In one scenario, it is possible for an attacker to compromise one guest VM which can then get passed on to the other VMs which are running on the same physical machine. In order to prevent the occurrence of such scenarios, it is very important to have firewalls and intrusion detection systems which have the capability to detect and prevent malicious activity at the VM level.

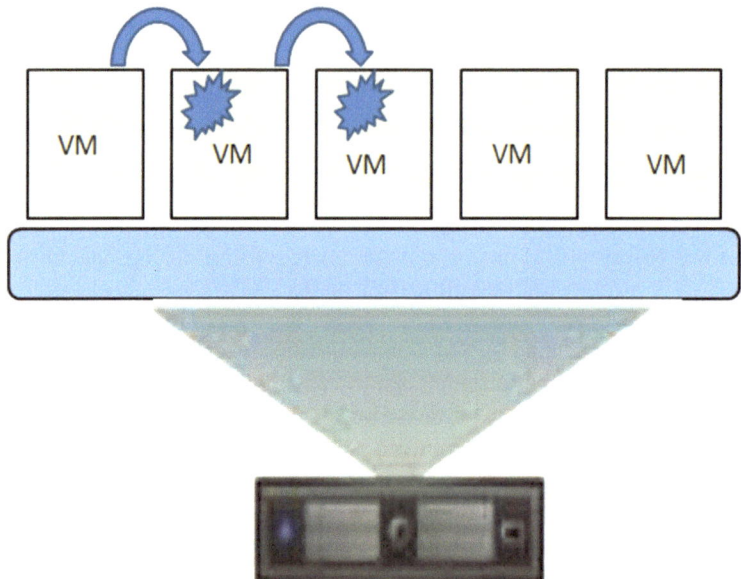

How Inter-VM attacks happen

6.7.4 Instant-on Gaps

Virtual machines have some vulnerabilities which are not present in physical machines. This is mainly due to the techniques which are used to provision, use, and de-provision them. Sometimes these cycles are repeated very frequently. This frequent activation and deactivation of VMs can pose challenges to maintain their security systems constantly updated.

After sometime, these VMs can automatically deviate from their defined security baselines and this in turn can introduce significant levels of security threats. This will give lot of options to attackers to access them. There is also a possibility that new VMs could be cloned and created out of these VMs which have vulnerabilities. If this is done, the security threats will get passed on to the newly created VMs and this will increase the area of the attack surface. It is very important to ensure that VMs possess a security agent which has all the latest security configurations update.

When a VM is not online during an anti-virus update, that VM will have vulnerabilities when it comes online as it would not have got the latest security updates. One solution to this problem could be to have a dedicated security VM in each physical machine to automatically update all VMs running in that physical machine with all latest security updates.

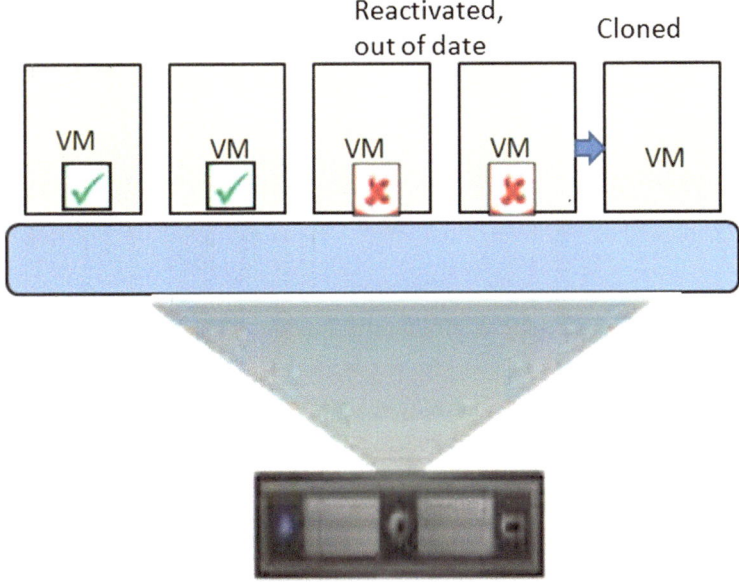

Instant-on Gaps

6.7.5 *Hyperjacking*

Hyperjacking enables an attacker to install a rogue hypervisor that has the capability to take complete control of the underlying physical server. This is a rootkit-level vulnerability. A rootkit is a malicious program which is installed before a hypervisor fully boots on a physical server. In this manner, the rootkit is able to run in the server with privileged access and remains invisible to the system administrators. Once a rootkit is installed, it gives permission to an attacker to mask the ongoing intrusion and maintain privileged access to the physical server by bypassing the normal authentication and authorization mechanisms which are employed by an OS.

Using such a rogue hypervisor, an attacker can run unauthorized applications on a guest OS without the OS realizing the presence of such an application. With hyperjacking, an attacker could control the interaction between the VMs and the underlying physical server. Regular security measures are ineffective against this rogue hypervisor because:

- Guest OS is unaware of the fact that underlying server has been attacked.
- Anti-virus and firewall applications cannot detect the presence of the rogue hypervisor as it is installed directly over the server itself.

Measures against hyperjacking include:

- Hardware assisted secure launching of the hypervisor so that rootkit-level malicious programs cannot launch. This would involve designing and using a TCB for the hypervisor getting support at the hardware level.
- Scanning hardware-level details to assess the integrity of the hypervisor and locate presence of rogue hypervisor. This scanning may include checking the state of the memory as well as registering in the CPU.

6.8   Security Threats of Big Data

Big data is huge volumes of constantly changing data which comes in from a variety of different sources. The constantly changing nature of big data introduces a variety of security threats for big data platforms. Some of the key challenges are summarized in the diagram which is given below:

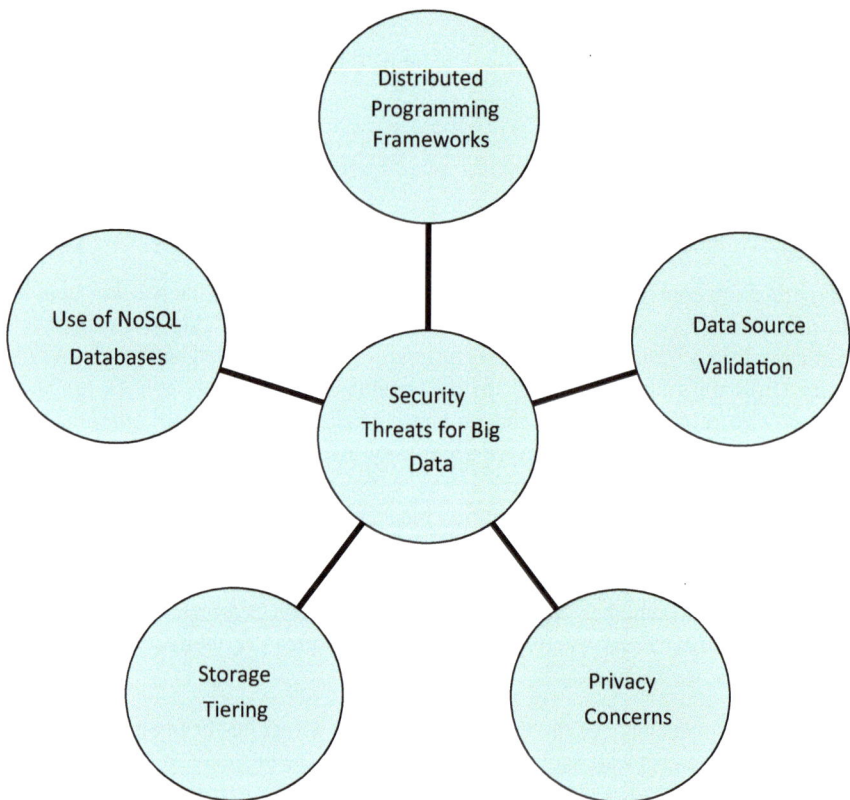

Security Threats for Big Data

6.8.1 Distributed Programming Frameworks

Many programming frameworks which process big data use parallel computation to process huge amounts of data quickly. One such example is the MapReduce framework which is used for processing big data. This framework splits the data into multiple chunks. The mapper then works on each chunk of data and generates key-value pairs for each chunk. In the next step, the reducer component combines values which belong to each key and then generates a final output. In this framework, the main security threat is with regard to mappers. Mappers can be hacked and made to generate incorrect key-value pairs. This in turn will lead to the generation of incorrect final results. Due to vast amounts of big data, it is impossible to detect the mapper which generated the incorrect value. This in turn can affect the accuracy of data which may adversely affect data rich computations. The main solution to this problem is to secure mappers using various algorithms which are available.

6.8.2 Use of NoSQL Databases

NoSQL databases are designed to store big data scale well to store huge amounts of data. But they do not have any security controls/policies embedded in them. The security controls are designed and incorporated into the middleware by the database programmers. There is no provision to include security practices as a part of NoSQL database design. This poses significant threat to the big data which is stored in the NoSQL databases. A solution to this problem is that organizations should review their security policies thoroughly and ensure that appropriate levels of security controls are incorporated into their middleware.

6.8.3 Storage Tiering

Most of the present day organizations have a tiered approach to store data. Tiered approach consists of multiple tiers of heterogeneous storage devices each of which vary in terms of cost, performance, storage capacity, and security policies which are enforced. In normal scenarios, data is stored in different tiers based on their frequency of access, cost, volume, or any other parameter which is of importance for the organization. The tiering of data is done manually. However with the ever increasing volumes of big data, it is becoming very difficult for the storage administrators to do tiering of such huge amounts of data manually. Hence, many organizations now have automatic storage tiering which is done with the help of some preconfigured policies. This might ensure that some data like R&D data which is not frequently used may be stored in the lowest tier as it may not be frequently used as per the policy. But it might be an important data from the context of organizations and storing such data in the lowest tier which has less data security may expose the data to security threats.

6.9 Data Source Validation

As per the 3V's of Big data, i.e., Volume, Velocity, and Variety, input data can be collected from diverse kinds of sources. Some sources may have data validation techniques in place, and some other sources will not have data validation. This is more prominent when the input comes in from mobile devices like tablets and cell phones. Since many of the present-day organizations are promoting bring your own device concept (BYOD), the possibility of threats which are likely to creep in from the mobile devices is still higher. Some examples of mobile device threats are spoofed cell phone ids.

6.9.1 Privacy Concerns

In an attempt to perform analytics to derive insights, a lot of activities of the users are being tracked without their knowledge. This data which is tracked by organizations for deriving various types of insights could prove to be extremely harmful for the users if it gets passed on to some untrusted third party.

Privacy Concern of Big Data Analytics

A recent event which was news recently is an eye opener on how big data analytics could intervene into the privacy of an individual. An analysis which was done by a retail organization for marketing purposes was able to inform a father about his teenage daughter's pregnancy.

6.10 Requirements of Security Management Framework for Big Data

Big data involves data of huge sizes, different types which are constantly changing in nature. In order to design a security management framework for big data, the three key parameters to be kept in mind are summarized in the diagram which is given below:

Security Management Framework for Big Data

6.10.1 Agile Scale-Out Infrastructure

In order to manage huge amounts of constantly changing data, the SDDC infrastructure of organizations should have agility and scale-out capabilities. Apart from storing and managing huge amounts of big data, organizations also use this data to support a plethora of new delivery models like Cloud computing, mobility, outsourcing, and so on. The security management infrastructure should have the capability to adapt quickly to collect and secure this type of data. The underlying security infrastructure should be able to expand and adapt easily to facilitate easy identification of new threats which evolve continually with each new type of data and the associated delivery mechanism.

6.10.2 Security Analytics

Many data analytics and visualization tools exist in the market. They support analytics for wide range of activities and device types. But the number of tools which provide security analytics capabilities is limited in the market. Security management officials require many types of sophisticated analytical tools which can provide them diverse kinds of security analysis insights and visualization capabilities. Security management in enterprises covers a wide range of range of functions which include security analysis of networks, security analysis of databases, and so on. Each type of security analysis requires different type of data. For example in order to perform security analysis of networks, logs and network information pertaining to specific sessions of activity are required. Software which supports the analytical and visualization requirements of diverse types of security personnel in an organization should be present in the organization. For example, in order to perform security analysis of log information, there are a separate category of tools available which come under the broad umbrella called as "Machine to Machine (M2M)" analytics.

IBM Accelerator for Machine Data Analytics

Machines produce large amount of data. This data contains a wealth of actionable insights. However in order to extract and perform analysis on such huge amount of data, tools with large-scale data extraction, transformation, and analysis capabilities are required. IBM® Accelerator for Machine Data Analytics provides a set of diverse applications which helps to import, transform, and analyze this machine data for the purpose of identifying event and pattern correlations and use them to make informed decisions based on the data which is present in the log and data files.

IBM Accelerator for Machine Data Analytics provides the following key capabilities [4]:

- Search within and across multiple log entries using text search, faceted search, or a timeline-based search in order to find specific patterns or events of interest.
- Enrich the context of log data by adding and extracting log types into the existing repository.
- Link and correlate events across systems.

6.10.3 Threat Monitoring and Intelligence

Diverse types of threats for data exist within an organization and outside as well. To add-on to this, new types of threats are evolving everyday. It is very important for organizations to stay updated on the threat environment so that the security analysts can get a clear picture of the various types of threat indicators and the security prejudice which is inflicted by them.

All the mobile applications and use cases of intelligent cities which were discussed in the previous chapter are designed with respect to smartphones. In the next section, we will examine some of the security threats for smartphones and also some mechanisms which can be used to secure smartphones.

6.10.4 Security Threats in SmartPhones

Smartphones have the capability to connect to various types of external systems like internet, GPS, and other different types of mobile devices using wireless networking technology. This is the key feature of smartphone which makes it one of the most widely used and popular devices. Many applications which are run using smartphones store personal data like address book, bank account details, meeting and appointment details, and so on in the smartphones. Proliferation of technologies like NFC for various purposes makes it very critical to ensure security of the smartphone, and the data is stored in the smartphone. A smartphone is exposed to a lot of vulnerabilities which can compromise its security.

The vulnerabilities in smartphones can be classified into two broad categories: internal and external. Internal vulnerabilities exist within the smartphone and external vulnerabilities creep into smartphones from the external systems to which they are connected. Some of the internal vulnerabilities are:

- Operating system implementation error: This error will happen due to the presence of some erroneous code in the operating system of mobile devices. Usually, these types of errors are not introduced by the end users, and they creep into the mobile devices due to fault of the mobile OS owning organizations. It is very common to have such errors in the new version or version upgrades of mobile operating systems. These OS errors can easily provide lot of options to the attackers to hack the operating system and gain illegitimate access to the smartphone or install rogue applications which can track and retrieve the details of the user from the smartphone. One way to avoid this could be by installing only version upgrades which have been fully tested and corrected and to defer from installing beta versions of operating systems.
- End user unawareness error: The smartphone end user can compromise the security by one or all of the following actions which are mainly due to the lack of awareness of the end user. Some of the common errors which are introduced by the end users are the following:

  - Use untrusted wireless networks to connect to Internet
  - Install mobile application from untrusted sources
  - Connect to untrusted Web sites using mobile phones which can inject some malware into the device
  - Improper configuration settings in the mobile device browser
  - Loss of mobile devices which can pose a serious security threat for the user's personal information which is stored in the mobile device.

Some of the external vulnerabilities are the following:

- Wireless network threats: The attacker could hack the wireless network to which the smartphone is connected and thereby gain access into the mobile device of the user.

- External Web sites: If the external Web site to which an end user is connected is hacked by an attacker, it is also possible for the attacker to gain access to the mobile device of the user with the help of the details which are gathered from that specific Web site. It is also possible that a malware which is present in an external Web site can get automatically installed in the mobile device if security mechanisms in the mobile device are not properly configured like unavailability of anti-virus software in the mobile devices.
- Other wireless devices: Smartphones have the capability to connect and communicate with a wide range of other wireless devices. If any of these wireless devices are hacked, then the smart phones can also be hacked easily.

6.11   Security Solutions for Mobile Devices

Many measures can be adopted by the user to enhance the security of the mobile devices. But none of these measures will offer complete security to mobile devices as threats are getting added day on day, and it is impossible to devise solutions at the pace at which threats are being created. Some of the possible security solutions which can be adopted by the users are:

- System add-on: This refers to system updates which are periodically made available to the smartphones. This will include platform updates which will provide enhanced features and in some cases enhanced security as well. It is the responsibility of the user to ensure that the system updates are installed periodically.
- System configuration: This is a very expensive and time-consuming activity as this process involves modification of the mobile OS code in order to add enhanced security features at the kernel level. This approach is rarely adopted by the users because of the huge amount of cost and time involved in it.
- Anti-virus, spam filter: In order to protect the smartphones from virus attacks, anti-virus software is available for specific mobile OS. Also some attacks from rogue Web sites can be prevented by turning on the spam filter in the smartphones.
- Cryptographic security mechanisms: Cryptographic techniques are available to ensure confidentiality and integrity of the data which is stored in the smartphone. Cryptography can be implemented in smartphones in two ways: mobile applications and mobile platform APIs. Cryptographic techniques use various mechanisms to ensure security of data which is stored in the smartphone. One such mechanism is to use encrypt the data which is stored in the smartphone so that even if it is hacked by a third party, the information cannot be deciphered without the availability of the key which will be known only to the smartphone user. Most of the mobile platforms make several APIs for use by the developers. Some of these APIs can be used to access the mobile OS specific security library. This way, the developers can develop specialized mobile security applications for various mobile platforms.

Apart from these methods, several mobile security applications are available in the mobile application store. It is the responsibility of the user to check and install the appropriate applications. In addition to this, in order to protect the information stored in the mobile devices, users can lock the mobile phones using strong passwords. Another option is to make a note of the IMEA number of the mobile device so that if the mobile device is lost/stolen, International Mobile Equipment Identity (IMEA) number can be deactivated which will disable all the functionalities of the mobile device automatically.

6.12   Security Concerns in IoT Components

An IoT platform will contain hundreds of sensors and other different types of devices which are sending data to a public or private Cloud or some big data platform using a wired or wireless network through a gateway as shown in the diagram which is given below. The gateway for some devices will be present within the device itself, and for some other devices, gateway will be present externally.

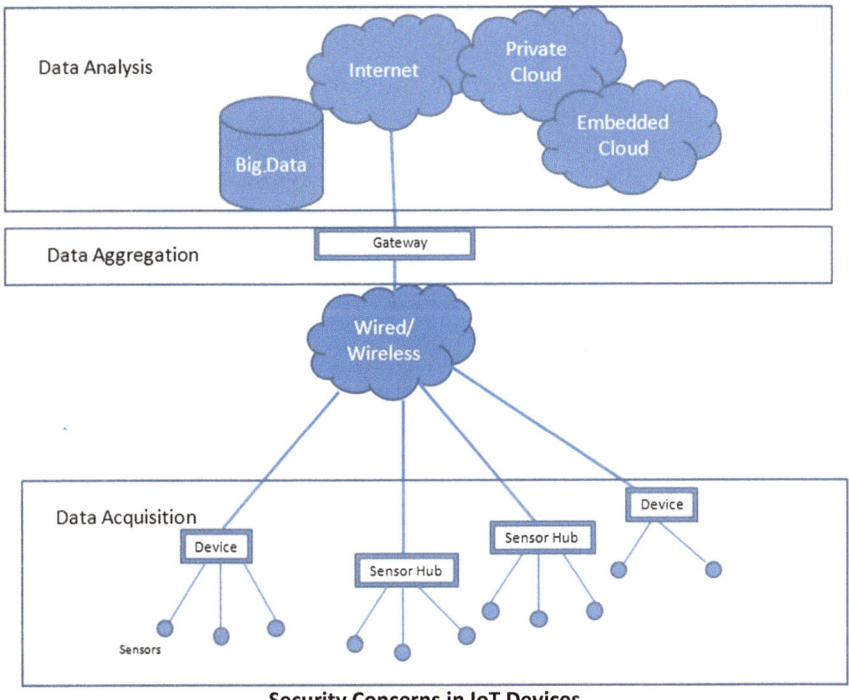

Security Concerns in IoT Devices

In IoT platforms, all types of platforms and technologies which were discussed previously in this chapter are used. So the security concerns which are present in each of them are applicable to IoT platform as well. In addition, because of huge number and types of devices and the plethora of technologies which are used by them for communication, it is necessary to adopt a multifaceted and multilayered approach in order to ensure appropriate security for all components which are part of the IoT platform. The diverse aspects of this multifaceted approach should start right from the booting of the devices and should continue at each phase of the device lifecycle in order to build an IoT ecosystem which cannot be tampered. Some of these security measures are discussed below.

6.13 Security Measures for IoT Platforms/Devices

In order to ensure security of various devices and platforms which are a part of the IoT network, it is essential to ensure adopt a holistic mechanism which spans across all the phases of a device's lifecycle. Some such mechanisms are discussed below:

6.13.1 Secure Booting

When a device powers on, there should be an authentication mechanism to verify that the software which runs on the device is a legitimate one. This is done with the help of cryptographically generated digital signatures. This process ensures that only authentic software which has been designed to run on the devices by the concerned parties will run on the devices. This establishes a trusted computing base for the devices upfront. But the devices still need to be protected from various kinds of run-time threats.

6.13.2 Mandatory Access Control Mechanisms

Mandatory access control mechanisms should be built into the operating system of the devices in order to ensure that the various applications and components will have access only to those resources which they need for their functioning. This will ensure that if an attacker is able to gain access to any of those components/applications, they will be able to gain access only very limited resource. This significantly reduces the attack surface.

6.13.3   Device Authentication for Networks

A device should get connected to some kind of a wired or wireless network in order to begin transmission of data. As a when a device gets connected to a network, it should authenticate itself before it starts data transmission. For some types of embedded devices (which operate without manual intervention), the authentication can be done with the help of credentials which are maintained in a secured storage area of the device.

6.13.4   Device-Specific Firewalls

For each device, there should be some kind of firewall which will filter and examine the data which specifically sends to that device. It is not mandatory for the devices to examine all types of traffic which traverse through the network as that will be taken care of by the network security appliances. This is required also because of the fact that some specific types of embedded devices have custom made protocols which are different from the common IT protocols which are used by organizations for data transmission. One classic example is the smart grid which has its own set of protocols for communication. Hence, it is very essential for the device to have firewalls or some such mechanism in place which is intended to filter the traffic which is intended specifically for that device.

6.13.5   Controlled Mechanism to Ensure Application of Security Patches and Upgrades

Once devices are connected to the networks, they start receiving security patches and upgrades. It so happens that in some situations these patches and upgrades consume a whole lot of network bandwidth making it unavailable for other devices or applications which are a part of the network. Operators need to ensure that patches, upgrades, and authentication of the devices should be planned in such a way that it should involve minimum bandwidth consumption, and it should not impact the functional safety of the device.

In short, for an IoT network's security, the traditional safety measures which are typically adopted are not sufficient. It is mandatory to inject security measures starting from the operating system of the participating devices.

6.13.6   Security Threats in Different Use Cases of IoT

Some of the key IoT use cases are summarized in the diagram which is given below:

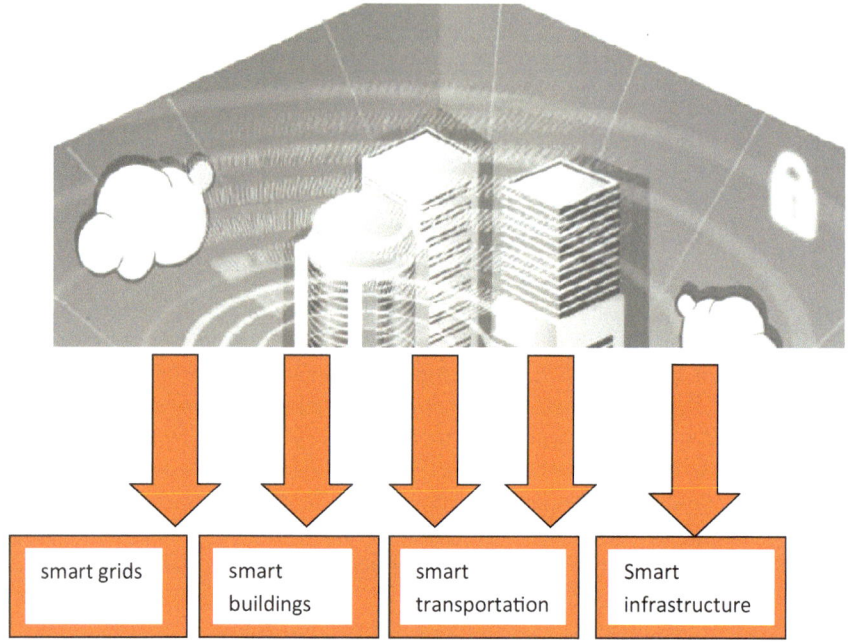

Security Threats in Different IoT Use Cases

Next we identify key security threats which are present in these IT infrastructure components along with some measures to curb them.

6.13.7   Security Threats in Smart Transportation Systems

Smart transportation systems enhance the quality of life by tracking and monitoring the transportation services. Sensors can capture data about the real-time status of transportation services and send the data to a centralized control center or dashboard which can then use the data to coordinate transport services. Tracking and monitoring of transportation services require a highly sophisticated IoT infrastructure and close coordination between the various components in order to avoid disruptions. The different types of security threats which are possible in a smart transportation system are the following:

- Hacking the travel navigation systems to misguide vehicle drivers into wrong routes by providing erroneous information about the traffic volume at various routes.

- The data transmitted to or from mobile devices may be subjected to spoofing.
- Unencrypted traffic reports can be attacked by hackers who can inject incorrect or false traffic-related data or reports into satellite-based navigation devices.

Attack of a Public Transport System in Europe
A teenager in Europe was able to attack the public transport systems with the help of a modified television remote control. He was able to able to cause severe traffic disruption in the city, and he was even able to cause a tram derailment by forcing a vehicle to take an abrupt turn when it was traveling at high speed.

6.13.8 Security Threats in Smart Grids and Other IoT-Based Infrastructure Components

The different components of smart grids are the following:

- Smart meters: Digital meters which can track user consumption in real time and provide alerts to user end point devices.
- Networks with two-way communication capabilities.
- Meter data acquisition and management systems: Software which collects data from the smart meters calculates bill value and analyses usage metrics.

The security of each of these components can be compromised. Smart meters may be hacked to steal energy or to tamper consumption data. Meter data acquisition and management systems can be hacked by the attackers using some of the vulnerabilities which may be present in the system, and this can severely hamper the transmission of data to the end users. White listing techniques which can ensure that only certain applications or processes are active at specific points in time are effective in some situations. However, there are no solutions to zero day-vulnerabilities. Zero-day vulnerabilities are those which no security patches are available.

Networks used by smart grids and other infrastructure components can be hacked by the attackers by installing some malwares which are capable of tracking sensitive network-related information. This sensitive information can be later used by the attackers to create denial of service attacks. These network-related threats can be eliminated to a great extend by using intrusion prevention techniques combined with some robust security practices to handle aspects like browser patches, end-user awareness creation, and network usage tracking.

One of the best possible ways to prevent tampering of smart meters and meter data acquisition and management system is the use of public key infrastructure (PKI). PKIs can be directly implemented on smart meters. This will ensure authentication and validation of meters in a connected network. It is also important to ensure that keys and certificates pertaining to a PKI environment are guarded appropriately using an appropriate management solution.

6.14 Conclusion/Summary

The SDDC infrastructure is a conglomeration of technologies like Cloud, big data, mobile devices, and Internet of things. It is very essential to ensure that each of this component is safe and secure in order to ensure continuous availability of services. The security requirements of the SDDC infrastructure components were examined in detail in the first section of the chapter.

Each component of the SDDC infrastructure is subjected to diverse types of vulnerabilities and threats. The vulnerabilities and threats which exist in each of these platforms were examined in detail. The techniques to safeguard the IT infrastructure components from these threats and vulnerabilities were also discussed in this chapter.

The different smart applications of IoT are smart grids, smart transport systems, smart water systems and smart buildings, and so on. The security concerns of these applications and the different ways to tackle them were also discussed in this lesson.

References

1. http://www.imperva.com/docs/SB_DDoS_Protection_Service.pdf
2. http://www.symantec.com/security_response/publications/threatreport.jsp?inid=us_ghp_thumbnail1_istr-2013
3. http://www-01.ibm.com/support/knowledgecenter/SSPT3X_2.0.0/com.ibm.swg.im.infosphere.biginsights.product.doc/doc/acc_mda.html

Chapter 7
Cloud Service Management

7.1 Introduction

Organizations across the globe are using a combination of on-premise and cloud-based resources for IT service development and delivery. This adds on the complexity of managing the combination of on-premise and Cloud resources. The diagrams given below depict the traditional versus the new approach which depicts the paradigm change which the IT organizations are undergoing:

Traditional model of IT service delivery using only on-premise resources (most services inside the firewall)

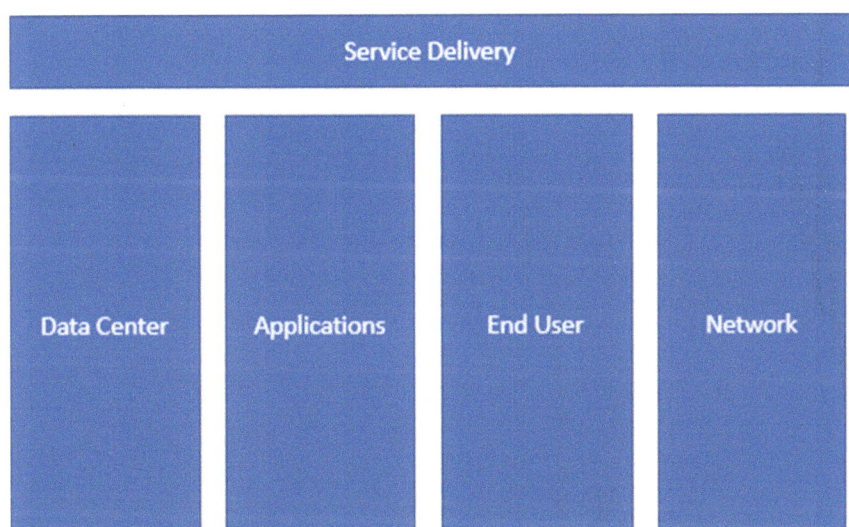

The emerging model of IT service management using a combination of on-premise and cloud-based resources (departmental IT using services outside the firewall)

© Springer International Publishing AG, part of Springer Nature 2018   137
P. Raj and A. Raman, *Software-Defined Cloud Centers*,
Computer Communications and Networks,
https://doi.org/10.1007/978-3-319-78637-7_7

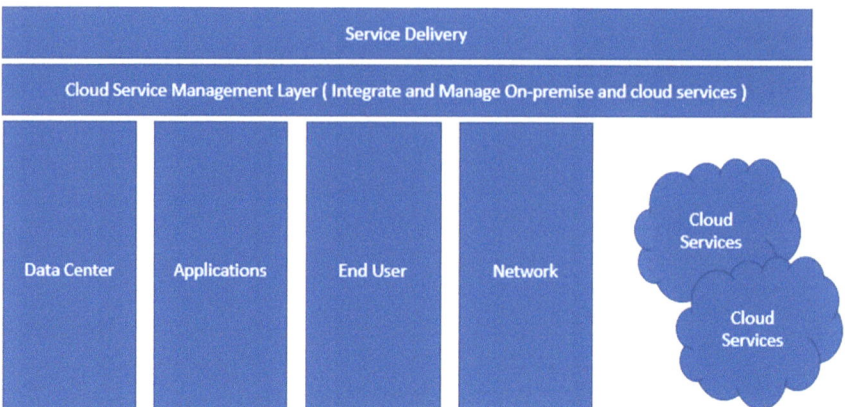

Following are the major challenges that have been identified in this approach:

- Integration—Integration of on-premise and cloud-based services and their seam-less management poses lot of threats and challenges to the IT department of organizations. These issues are a major cause of concern for business leaders and impact the capability of organizations to derive maximum returns out of their investments in cloud-based infrastructure and services.
- Threats—organizations should be equipped to handle several new threats in areas of security, compliance, and service disruption.
- Unified management—IT departments should devise their own frameworks and tools which will help them to develop, deploy, and manage Cloud and on-premise services in a seamless manner.
- Cost control—Effective cost control mechanisms should be in place for managing the usage of on-premise and cloud-based resources in a cost-effective manner for the organizations without compromising on aspects like security and compliance.

For ease of reference, in this chapter, we will refer to this approach as Hybrid IT. This should not be confused with the concept of hybrid Cloud. These two concepts are entirely different. In the next section, we will examine the essential characteristics of Hybrid IT.

7.2 Characteristics of Hybrid IT

Following characteristics should be offered by any Hybrid IT framework to provide actual value for the organization:

(1) Ease of use: The features offered by the Hybrid IT framework should be easily usable by different teams within the organization. This makes adoption much easier within the organization. The Hybrid IT framework should also provide features that will allow new Cloud services to be on-boarded and used within the framework of service delivery.
(2) Complete Visibility: The Hybrid IT framework should have features which provide complete view/visibility of both on-premise and cloud-based services.
(3) Efficient Backup: The Hybrid IT framework should provide backup features that allow backup of the entire data irrespective of whether the data is a part of on-premise service or cloud-based service.
(4) Unified Security: The Hybrid IT framework should be able to provide all levels to security to the services irrespective of whether they are on-premise or on Cloud.
(5) Dashboards: The Hybrid IT framework should provide dashboards which offer various important types of information pertaining to all types of services like usage, cost, performance.

In the next section, we will examine a generic Hybrid IT framework which incorporates all the characteristics which are listed above.

7.3 Framework for Implementing Hybrid IT

The essential features of a Hybrid IT framework are captured in the diagram which is given below:

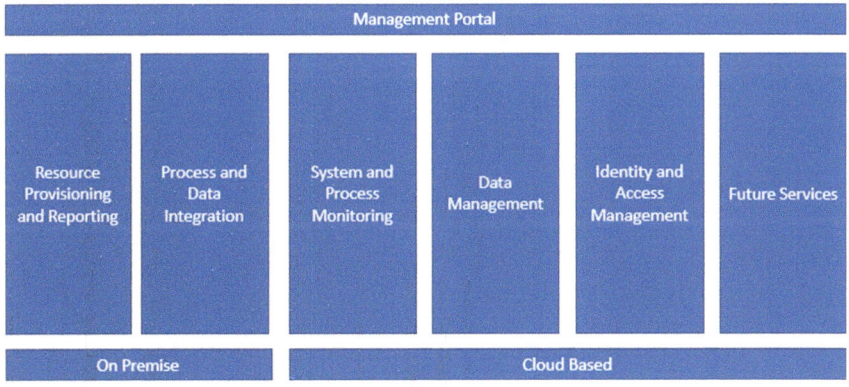

The essential features of the framework are the following:

- Management portal
- Resource provisioning and reporting
- Process and data integration
- System and process monitoring
- Data management
- Identity and access management
- Future Services.

7.4   Management Portal

Following are the main functions of the management portal:

- It provides a single point of entry into the Hybrid IT framework.
- It ensures that on-premise and cloud-based services are managed in a unified and consistent manner.
- It provides easy integration point and offers features to quickly integrate new cloud-based services.

7.5   Resource Provisioning and Reporting

This feature provides the core capability to manage and provision both Cloud and non-Cloud resources as a single entity. Resources in this context include all the components like infrastructure, platform components and software applications. This capability is provided via a service catalog. Through this service catalog, it is possible to access IaaS, PaaS, and SaaS services irrespective of the whether they are accessed from internal private Clouds, external public Clouds, or hybrid Clouds via a service wrap which ensures that both on-premise and cloud-based services are provisioned and provided in a seamless manner. This feature also provides billing based on the usage of services from the catalog.

7.6   Process and Data Integration

This feature provides the capability to integrate processes and data of both cloud-based and on-premise services through a specialized engine. This engine ensures that all systems belonging to both on-premise and cloud-based services are communicated properly with each other. The engine also ensures that critical business processes which may be part of multiple systems are executed in an efficient and seamless manner. The framework provides all components and the user interface which is required to make this happen.

7.7 System and Process Monitoring

This feature provides the capability to get a single, unified view of systems and processes irrespective of the fact whether they run on on-premise or cloud-based systems. This feature offers a single, unified interface which helps to track all the vital resources which are critical for the business. This comprehensive monitoring capability is necessary to ensure that all components of IT function in an optimal manner always.

7.8 Service Management

This feature provides the capability to receive proactive and up-to-date information on various aspects of IT services like performance and availability irrespective of whether the services are on-premise or Cloud based. Most aspects of service management are carried out using ITIL framework-based practices and action-based workflows. The key objective is to increase the service levels by reducing cost and improving efficiency.

7.9 Data Management

This feature provides the capability to take backup and recovery of data across Cloud and on-premise systems using a single portal. This helps to ensure that the organization's storage footprint is reduced. This features also ensures that data is encrypted while at rest and in transition. Vaults are deployed wherever necessary to ensure local backup and restoration of data. It is always recommended to use the cloud-connected data protection system as an add-on or complement to existing data protection approaches to ensure that data is always secure.

7.10 Identity and Access Management

This feature provides a cloud-based federated single sign-on capability to effectively manage access to both on-premise and cloud-based systems. It also provides enhanced security features which reduces risk of inappropriate access and fraud—and avoids potential problems when people join, leave the company, or change roles internally. This feature also makes it possible for users to sign in once and share credentials across domains using advanced identity federation. This features also offers advanced authentication and risk profiling capabilities which works seamlessly across both Cloud and non-Cloud systems.

As per the features which are described in the framework, several vendors have come up with specialized tools/applications which help in the management of Hybrid IT. These tools/applications which are available in the market are called Cloud management platforms (CMP). In the next section, we will examine the various CMP tools.

7.11   CMP Tools

(1) Enterprise Application Store: An Enterprise Application store is a Web portal which provides facilities to the users to download and install diverse types of software applications as per their need. The store can have multiple views as per the roles of the employees or as per the requirements of various business units. The store basically acts as a consumer application market place in the context of an enterprise. Enterprise Application store can be hosted by a service provider like Google, Amazon. Enterprise Application store can be an internal application store which may be a homegrown one or could be adopted from an offering by vendors like BMC, Citrix. The enterprise application store or marketplace developed as a result of a group of Cloud vendors who started providing platform services to their customer in order to offer a storefront/super market experience to IT departments of enterprises. Some popular examples of Enterprise application stores include salesforce.com's AppExchange, Amazon Web Services Marketplace, Heroku, and Life ray Marketplace. All these stores are typical examples of those which are created and maintained by a third-party vendor, but hosted internally with an end-user brand. The survey of some leading enterprises which is depicted below indicates that one-third of enterprises are currently deploying enterprise application store and 20% of others are in several stages of planning. The results of the survey are given in the graphic which is given below [2]

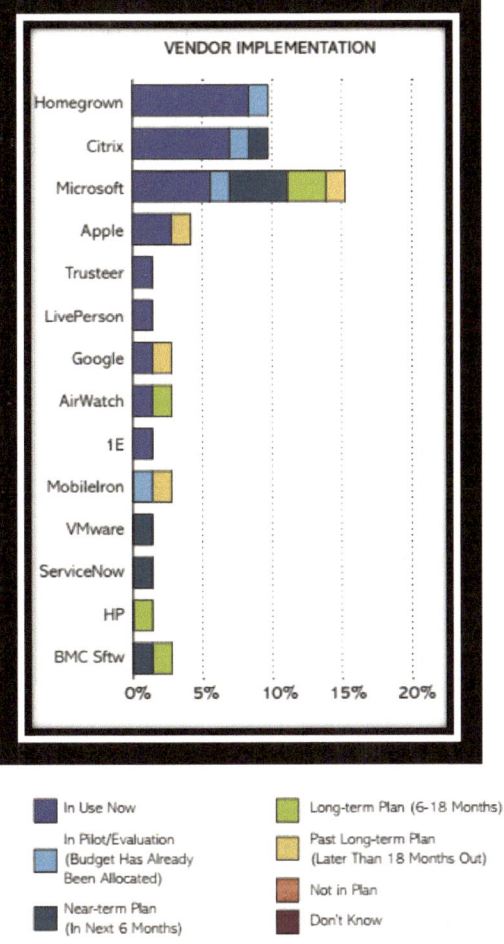

Business application stores provide great opportunities to increase customer engagements by adding lot of value over the existing infrastructure services. Application services can be charged a higher rate than renting a typical infrastructure component like a VM. There are differences in the manner in which different vendors operate their market place. Some vendors provide very capable storefronts to large product portfolios, whereas other vendors act more as aggregator of third-party commercial applications. In short, application stores will offer a plethora of opportunities to various Cloud service providers to sell several enterprise-level software applications on a as-a-service basis. There are several application store owners. Some prominent examples include vendors like Bell Canada, Colt, Deutsche Telekom, Fujitsu. Some of these vendors target enterprises directly, whereas some others have a channel model of offering to reach small and medium businesses.

7.12 Self-service catalog

The self-service catalog provides a catalog of IT services with additional resource provisioning capabilities which includes both internal infrastructure and external infrastructure. It helps the Cloud user to automatically provision the required resources without any manual intervention. Generally, the user interface of self-service catalog is very intuitive and user-friendly. A self-service catalog in most of the cases will also provide workflow management capabilities for the creation, monitoring, and deployment of resources and services. Self-service catalog can be accessed via a portal which in most of the cases is linked to capacity planning and workload automation tools. Most of the Cloud service vendors have either built their own self-service catalog capabilities or acquired them from a third-party vendor. From a study of leading Cloud vendors, most of them have their own self-service catalog as depicted in the graphic which is given below [2]:

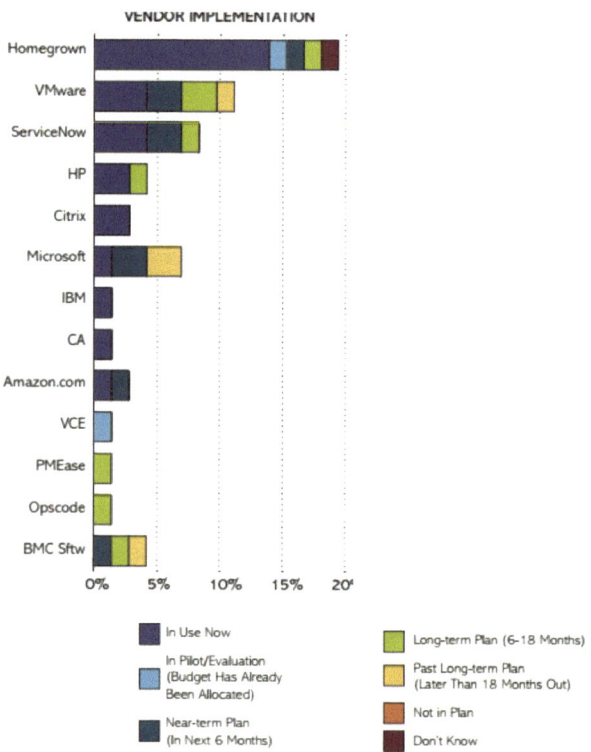

7.13 Unified Cloud Management Console

A unified Cloud management console offers a single window through which a hybrid Cloud ecosystem can be accessed and managed. This console should have the capability to provide a unified view of resource usage across all types of providers and on-premise systems. The survey of the leading Cloud vendors on this capability is depicted in the graphic which is given below [2]:

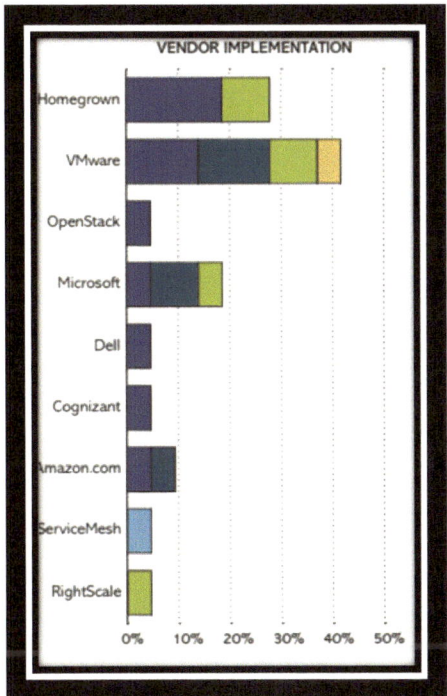

7.14 Cloud Governance

Cloud governance refers to the implementation of policy implementation and resource tracking for managing Cloud cost as well as performance. To implement Cloud governance, the most commonly used mechanism is an orchestration platform which has features to enable dynamic allocation and placement of workloads based on certain pre-defined policies. Orchestration helps to bring together various aspects like:

- Self-service resource provisioning
- On-boarding and management with process
- Policy, security, and governance management.

The graphic given below depicts the level of adoption of Cloud governance mechanisms by some of the leading vendors in the market [2].

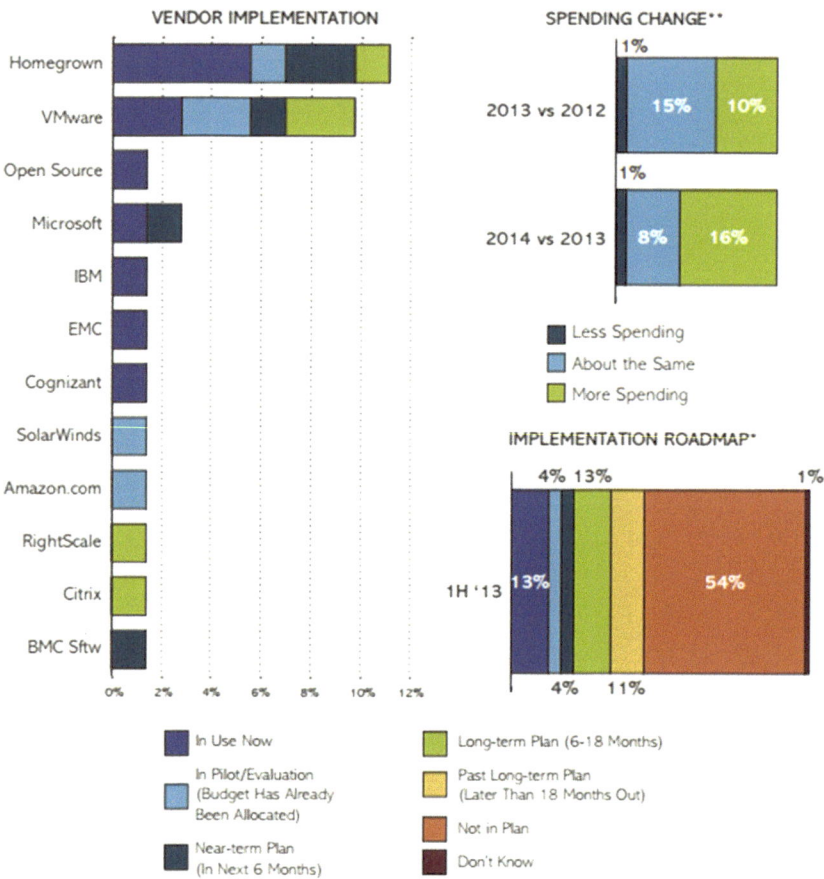

7.15 Metering/Billing

Cost spending on using cloud-based services can be easily tracked and reported. Cloud Management platforms have the capability to provide this data of multiple Cloud providers and on-premise systems using a dashboard view. The capabilities to predict usage based on past data are also present in most of the present-day Cloud management platforms.

- Another use case of cloud-based metering and billing is chargeback based on usage to various departments/business units within an enterprise. Alignment of various IT resources to their cost components can help to define the cost of allocation per department or user. If this mechanism is not in place for an enterprise, it is impossible for an organization to identify cost of using IT resources. And it may also lead to a situation where the correct department or entity is not paying for the services which they are using or which they may need in future to sustain their business-critical operations. Cloud computing alone will not be able to help organizations to exactly streamline the usage of various IT resources. However, it can help organizations to setup an infrastructure design which establishes a chargeback model for metering and billing of resources as per their usage. This use case has led to the emergence of several vendors who have devised and come up with their own tools which will help users to better monitor and plan their Cloud spending. Some of the prominent vendors in this area include:

- Basic6
- Cloudyn
- Apptio
- Cedexis
- Copper.io
- RightScale.

7.16 Infrastructure as a Service Billing and Metering Models

In the past, the cost of provisioning hardware like servers and other associated infrastructure which are required to host applications imposed severe restrictions on the development of software-as-a-service application. For example, in the context of procuring a server, it would have taken several weeks to plan, order, ship, and install new server hardware in a data center. Today, with the evolution of infrastructure-as-a-service concept in Cloud computing, procurement of various infrastructure components can be completed within few minutes or under a minute.

Sample usage of IaaS components is depicted in the graphic which is given below [3]:

Amazon Elastic Compute Cloud		
US East (Northern Virginia) Region		
Amazon EC2 running Linux/UNIX Reserved Instances		
$0.03 per Small Instance (m1.small) instance-hour (or partial hour)	188 Hrs	5.64
Amazon EC2 running Linux/UNIX		
$0.085 per Small Instance (m1.small) instance-hour (or partial hour)	3 Hrs	0.26
Amazon EC2 EBS		
$0.10 per GB-month of provisioned storage	2.978 GB-Mo	0.30
$0.10 per 1 million I/O requests	519.963 IOs	0.05
$0.01 per 10,000 gets (when loading a snapshot)	14,336 Requests	0.01
	Download Usage Report ∞	**6.26**
Amazon Simple Storage Service		
	Download Usage Report ∞	**0.05**
AWS Data Transfer (excluding Amazon CloudFront)		
		0.01

Bill Summary	
Usage charges and monthly recurring fees during this billing cycle † More Info	$6.32
One-time fees during this billing cycle More Info	$0.00
Taxes Estimated Taxes	$0.00
Total new charges this billing cycle	$6.32
No payments received to date.	
Current estimated unpaid balance to be charged for this billing cycle	$6.32

The key components of IaaS pricing are the following:

- Servers which are used per hour based on an on-demand model
- Servers which are reserved for better capacity planning
- Volume-based metering based on the actual number of instances which are consumed
- Prepaid and reserved infrastructure components
- Clustered server resources.

The billing of most of the above components are typically done on a per month basis. Billing charges which are included for a month include the cost of server instances which were running for all the 30 days and the servers which ran only for few minutes. Each server component is charged irrespective of whether it ran for an hour or a minute.

The advanced billing model feature to reserve instances helps to enable lower monthly as well as hourly costs. This feature also helps to make compute resources with necessary baselines and requirements available as needed without any waiting time.

7.17 Platform as a Service (PaaS) and Billing and Metering Services

Billing and metering of PaaS is done as per the actual usage since platform components differ in aggregate- and instance-level usage measures. This also provides flexibility to the PaaS vendors to run code used by multiple vendors on the same hardware based on the granularity of usage monitoring. One example of this aspect could be fact that parameters like CPU utilization, disk usage per transaction, and network bandwidth could determine PaaS cost. Some of the key parameters which define the PaaS billing are the following:

- CPU usage per hour
- High availability
- Monthly service charge
- Incoming and outgoing network bandwidth.

The bandwidth consumed by incoming and outgoing network traffic determines the usage of a single user and can be used as a metric for billing and metering. This metric is also helpful because certain Web applications can consume more traffic depending on the content present in the application. For example, Web application data which contains RESTful payloads may consume very less bandwidth when compared to transactions which include multimedia objects like pictures, audio, and video. Transactions which involve HTTP request-based metering method are generally the most accurate since each transaction can be accurately measured for cost. One issue in PaaS billing is that it is difficult to exactly calculate which transaction user is consuming a specific amount of CPU bandwidth resources per request. One effective way for billing and metering is to calculate the amount of stored data a specific user is consuming and do the billing accordingly. This is a very efficient technique which could be used in storage as service to keep track of the data which is stored across servers.

Some platforms which have limitation in instance-level ability to provide metering and billing often provide generalized flat billing models to run application code. The only criteria is that such platforms typically come with secure code requirements that does not have long-running, CPU-consuming transactions.

7.18 SaaS and Billing and Metering Services

The concept of billing and metering for SaaS-based applications is typically a monthly fixed cost. The number of application users is assigned by the organization based on the IT requirements of specific users/teams. In certain cases, usage above a certain limit is given a discount by the SaaS provider. This discount is given as an incentive to the organization to encourage more users to use the SaaS-based application.

The two concepts included in SaaS billing and metering are:

- Monthly subscription fees
- Per-user monthly fees.

The monthly subscription fee is a typically a fixed cost per month, often fixed for a minimum contracted length of agreement. The per month fee alters the initial investment from an initial software capital cost to a monthly operational expense. This model of usage is especially a lucrative option for small- and medium-sized organizations as this offers them the flexibility to get started with the applications required for their business.

In the next section, we will examine some leading CMP products which are available in the market.

7.19   Leading CMP Vendors in the Market

7.19.1   Cisco Cloud Center

The Cisco Cloud Center solution is a very popular hybrid Cloud management platform which helps to securely provision infrastructure resources and application components across data centers, public and private Cloud environments. Some of the prominent use cases of Cisco Cloud Center are the following:

- Application migration
- DevOps automation across heterogenous Cloud environments
- Dynamic capacity augmentation.

The two core components of Cisco Cloud Center are the following:

- Cisco Cloud Center Manager: The interface through which users' model, deploy, and manage applications which run on or between a data center and a Cloud infrastructure. This component also provides the interface for the administrator to control Clouds, users, and governance rules. One of the key components of Cisco Cloud Center solution is the application profile. This component is a part of Cloud center manager, and it helps to keep track of each application's deployment and management requirements. Each application profile contains a combination of infrastructure automation and application automation layers packaged in a single deployable blueprint. With a specific application profile, one Cisco Cloud Center platform can deploy and manage an application anywhere whether it is a data center or Cloud environment.
- Cisco Cloud Center Orchestrator: This component resides in every data center or Cloud region and helps automate deployment of application along with infrastructure components (computing, storage, and networking). This helps in the provisioning and configuration of infrastructure components as per the application's

requirements. This provisioning is done by the agent component which resides in Cisco Cloud Center orchestrator.

Cisco Cloud Center is an enterprise-class solution which is scalable, secure, extensible, and supports multi-tenancy. It helps organizations to implement IT-as-a Service hybrid delivery strategy. The solution provides very quick RoI for investment and does not involve any complicated deployment methods.

The high-level architecture of Cisco Cloud Center and key functionality offered by each component is depicted in the diagram which is given below:

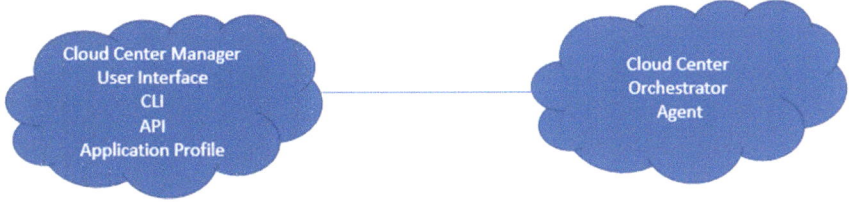

7.19.2 VMware's VCloud Automation Center

VMware vCloud® Automation Center™ helps organizations to accelerate the delivery and management of the following components:

- Personalized, business-relevant infrastructure,
- Application and custom services.

The solution helps to improve overall IT efficiency. The key features of the solution like policy-based governance and logical application modeling ensures that multivendor, multi-Cloud services are delivered at the right size which is aligned to the task that is being done. This solution ensures that resources are maintained at a peak operating efficiency. The release automation feature allows multiple application deployments to be synchronized through the development and deployment process.

vCloud Automation Center provides capabilities which transforms IT into business enablers.

Following are the key capabilities offered by the solution [3]:

- **Comprehensive Purpose-Built Functionality**: vCloud Automation Center is a purpose-built, enterprise-proven solution for the delivery and ongoing management of private and hybrid Cloud services, based on a broad range of deployment use cases from the world's most demanding environments.

- Personalized, Business-Aware Governance Enable IT administrators to apply their own way of doing business to the Cloud without changing organizational processes or policies. Enterprises gain the flexibility needed for business units to have different service levels, policies, and automation processes, as appropriate for their needs.

Provision and Manage Application Services Accelerate application deployment by streamlining the deployment process and by eliminating duplication of work using reusable components and blueprints.

- Infrastructure Delivery and Life-Cycle Management Automates the end-to-end deployment of multi-vendor infrastructure, breaking down internal organizational silos that slow down IT service delivery.
- Extensible by Design vCloud Automation Center provides a full spectrum of extensibility options that empower IT personnel to enable, adapt, and extend their Cloud to work within their existing IT infrastructure and processes, thereby eliminating expensive service engagements while reducing risk.

High-level architecture of VMware's vCloud Automation Center is depicted in the diagram which is given below:

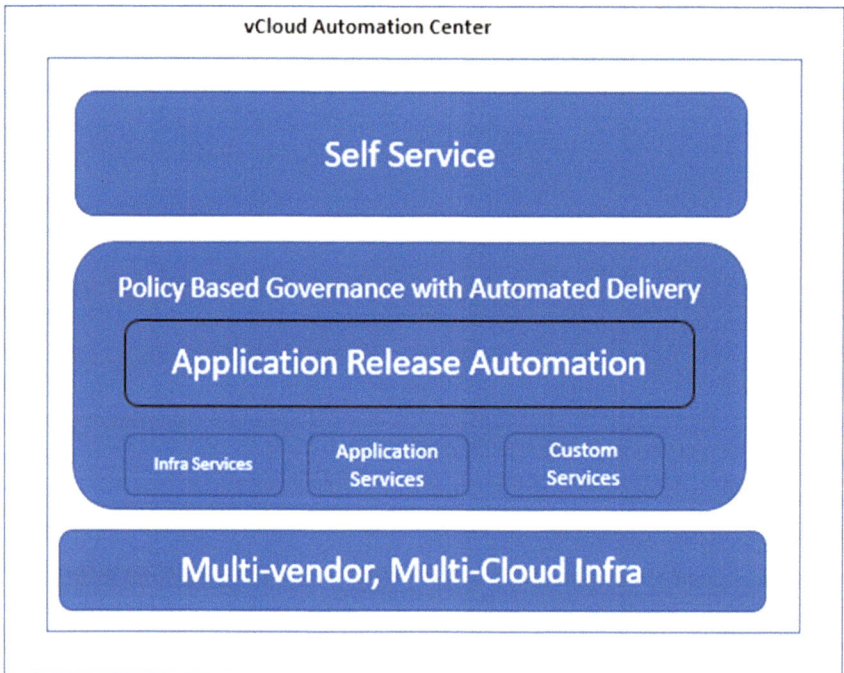

7.20 Summary/Conclusion

In the first half of the chapter, we examined the new trend which is evolving in the enterprises because of the need to use combination of on-premise and Cloud infrastructure and applications. This novel approach is called Hybrid IT. This new trend has forced organizations to adopt and use a new model for managing these components using a single unified framework. Following are the key characteristics of the Hybrid IT approach:

- Ease of use
- Complete visibility
- Efficient backup
- Unified security
- Dashboards.

We then discussed a framework for implementing Hybrid IT. In the second half of the chapter, we introduced the concept of CMPs which are a set of tools used for managing the Hybrid IT infrastructure. Some of the key tools which were discussed in the section are the following:

- Enterprise Application store
- Self-service catalog
- Unified Cloud management console
- Cloud governance
- Metering and billing.

Finally, we concluded the chapter by discussing some prominent vendors in the CMP space and their offerings.

References

1. http://www.cloud-council.org/deliverables/CSCC-Practical-Guide-to-Cloud-Management-Platforms.pdf
2. https://www.ibm.com/developerworks/cloud/library/cl-Cloudmetering/
3. https://www.vmware.com/files/pdf/vcloud/vmware-vcloud-automation-center-datasheet.pdf

Chapter 8
Multi-cloud Brokerage Solutions and Services

8.1 Introduction

Undeniably, the Cloud journey is still at a frenetic pace. The game-changing journey started with server virtualization with the easy availability, the faster maturity, and stability of hypervisors [virtual machine monitors (VMMs)]. This phase is thereafter followed by the arrival of powerful tools and engines to automate and accelerate several manual tasks such as virtual machine (VM) monitoring, measurement, management, load balancing, capacity planning, security, and job scheduling. In addition, the unprecedented acceptance and adoption of Cloud management platforms such as OpenStack, CloudStack have made it easy for decisively and declaratively managing various IT infrastructures such as compute machines, storage appliances, networking solutions, OS images. Further on, there are patterns, manifests, and recipes-centric configuration management tools for appropriately configuring, installing, and sustaining business workloads, IT platforms, databases, and middleware. There are also orchestration tools for templates-enabled infrastructure provisioning, patching, administration, and governance.

There are ITIL-compliant service management tools for servicing all kinds of Cloud infrastructures, resources and applications, operating systems, and application workloads in order to strengthen business continuity, consumability, and customer delight. Thus, the end-to-end lifecycle management of Cloud resources and applications is being taken care of through policy-aware and insights-driven integrated tools. The complicated tasks such as workflow/task scheduling for long-running applications, workload optimization through VM consolidation and placement based on varying parameters, and operational analytics are being got simplified through path-breaking algorithms and patentable techniques. There are promising and proven solutions for business process management (BPM), business rule engines, performance engineering, and enhancement, etc., to take the Cloud enablement to the next level. Now, we are heading toward the realization of software-defined Cloud environments with not only compute machines but also networking as well as storage solutions are also getting fully virtualized. There are hypervisor solutions for enabling network and storage virtualization. The spectacular advancements in the data analytics and

© Springer International Publishing AG, part of Springer Nature 2018   155
P. Raj and A. Raman, *Software-Defined Cloud Centers*,
Computer Communications and Networks,
https://doi.org/10.1007/978-3-319-78637-7_8

machine/deep learning domains will steadily set up and sustain cognitive Clouds in the years ahead.

Thus, the aspect of cloudification is definitely on the right track and direction in order to provide all the originally envisaged business and technical benefits to various stakeholders including Cloud service providers, brokers, procurers, auditors, developers, and consumers. Precisely speaking, these widely debated and discoursed technology-driven advancements have collectively resulted in scores of highly optimized and organized hybrid Cloud environments.

Hybrid Cloud versus multi-cloud

There are some useful differences between these two buzzwords. In a multi-cloud solution, an organization uses multiple different public Cloud services, often from multiple different providers. The different Clouds may be used for various tasks to achieve best-of-breed results or to reduce vendor lock-in. This reflects the growing acknowledgment that not all Clouds are created equal; marketing and sales, for instance, likely have different needs than software development or R&D, and different Cloud solutions can meet those requirements more effectively. Multiple Clouds also give organizations added peace of mind by minimizing dependence on any one provider, often decreasing costs and increasing flexibility. Multiple public Clouds usually operate in combination with on-premise physical, virtual, and private Cloud infrastructure.

Hybrid Cloud, on the other hand, combines private and public Clouds toward the same purpose. This differs from multi-cloud in two main ways.

1. Hybrid always includes private and public, while multi-cloud always includes multiple public Clouds but can also incorporate physical and virtual infrastructure including private Clouds.
2. Unlike a multi-cloud model, in which different Clouds are used for different tasks, the components of a hybrid Cloud typically work together. As a result, data and processes tend to intermingle and intersect in a hybrid environment, while in a multi-cloud situation, usage typically remains in its "own" Cloud's silo.

An application running in a hybrid Cloud framework could use load balancing, Web and application services from a public Cloud, while the database and storage live in a private Cloud. It has compute resources that perform the same function in both a private Cloud and a public Cloud and may swap how much compute is used in either Cloud based on load and cost. An application in a multi-cloud environment that is not hybrid, on the other hand, may run all compute and networking activities in AWS while using database services from Azure. In this multi-cloud environment, some applications leverage resources only in Azure while separate applications use resources only in AWS; or, applications may use resources only in the public Cloud while others leverage resources only in the private Cloud. This is taken from the page (http://www. bmc.com/blogs/hybrid-cloud-vs-multi-cloud-whats-the-difference/).

8.2 The Key Drivers for Cloud Brokerage Solutions and Services

The Cloud technology continues to support and disrupt the realization of digital business. An increasing number of enterprises are realizing the benefits of utilizing multiple Cloud infrastructures and platforms to support employee productivity, collaboration, and business innovation. However, this rapid adoption of Cloud services from multiple Cloud service providers (CSPs) and communication service providers creates a unique set of challenges for IT. More specifically, because enterprise IT teams must now orchestrate onboarding, managing, and delivering IT and business services from multiple portals and vendors. This kind of multiplicity makes it tough in ensuring consistent performance, security, and control within the multi-cloud ecosystem.

That is the reason why Cloud management and brokerage platform solutions are becoming popular. These could help to select the best Cloud services for our organization's needs, support line of business requirements, and meet IT demands across disparate Clouds without jeopardizing performance or security. The availability of different and even same service offerings from different and distributed Cloud environments brings forth a few challenges for institutions, innovators, and individuals in finding and leveraging an increasing number of Cloud services with different SLAs and costs.

Today's business users and application developers now demand immediate availability and unlimited scalability for cloud-based services. The direct procurement of Cloud services by business units leads to the new phenomenon of "shadow IT" because employees could effectively "go around" existing corporate policies and security procedures. This usually occurs because the enterprise IT is not closely aligned with the operational demands of specific lines of business. The expanded use of multi-cloud infrastructures and platforms increases the security risk of the organization. Protecting company data as it moves from on-premise to multiple private and public Clouds and back becomes critical but challenging. IT must manage multiple Cloud environments and services with different capabilities, processes, costs, and performance levels. This not only becomes time-consuming but costs can spiral out of control if not carefully managed.

Cloud brokers have emerged as master orchestrators who can manage the complexity of multiple Cloud ecosystems and transform businesses into digital enterprises. A Cloud broker is a middleware solution that acts as the middle layer or intermediary between Cloud service consumers and Cloud service providers. Typically, there are three types of Cloud brokers:

1. **Cloud aggregator**—An aggregator is a broker that packages and integrates multiple service catalogues into a single user interface. The client then selects as many or as few services that fit their specific business needs but will only pay a single bill to the broker. The Cloud aggregator model is generally seen as a more cost-effective and efficient approach for the client as compared to purchasing each service individually. As part of their function as resellers, aggregators play a critical role in managing Cloud provider relationships and services. The broker may also offer additional services on top of the Cloud including security and governance. Overall, one of the main goals of the aggregator is to curate an actual catalogue of services providing a single pane of glass to all business and IT services empowering agility and portability while saving time and money. **Aggregation** in Cloud Service brokerage creates a virtual service provider, offering normalized data models across Cloud services and enabling data portability and security across a multitude of services. Cloud Service Aggregators should empower flexibility and portability between providers. **Arbitrage** in Cloud Service brokerage is a complementary function of aggregation, wherein flexibility to move between Cloud services and a single point of access enables end users to select the best choice, based on metrics. Offering choice in services is only beneficial with portability to take advantage of performance and cost savings.

2. **Cloud integrators**—Integrators add value by automating workflows across hybrid environments through a single orchestration to improve performance and reduce business risk. Once migration is complete, the integrator can continue to provide support to the organization on an ongoing basis as needed. **Integration** is a function which maintains the data fidelity for organizations using multiple on-demand B2B software services, SaaS, PaaS, or IaaS and the resulting silos they create. Cloud Service Integration can be complex and require effort from not only the brokerage but B2B vendors and infrastructure providers alike.

3. **Cloud customizers**—As the name suggests, customization involves modifying existing Cloud services to meet business needs. In some cases, the broker may even develop additional features to run in the Cloud as required by the organization. This function is critical to building a fully configured Cloud with improved visibility, compliance, and integration of key IT processes. **Intermediation** Cloud Service brokerage provides specific value-added services to enhance the capabilities of existing Cloud services. Examples might include identity or access management to multi-cloud services.

Cloud service brokers provide solutions that turn IT into a growth accelerator for end customers. Additional benefits of Cloud services brokerage include:

- Cloud service brokers serve to reduce the barriers to adopting, managing, and customizing services in the Cloud because they fill in gaps in knowledge and skills. Brokerage service providers and their consultancy team members are often hired to evaluate services from different vendors and provide the customer with information about how to use Cloud services to power digital innovation. Once the research is complete, the broker presents the customer with a list of recommended vendors along with a comparison of service features, cost breakdowns, SLAs, and other criteria. In this way, the broker's toolkit and expertise foster objective, accurate, and informed decision-making.

- Cloud brokers may sometimes be given the rights to negotiate contracts with Cloud service providers on behalf of the client. In such cases, the broker is given the authority to contract services across several vendors which can be an excellent strategy to keep costs low. In addition, CSBs typically have preexisting relationships with a number of vendors, and in some cases even have predetermined contracts, which help to speed up the vendor acquisition process. This benefit is usually most common in the case of Cloud aggregators.
- Cloud service brokerage (CSB) providers can help eliminate redundancies, optimize resource utilization, and allow the IT organization to gain control of Cloud consumption costs. Furthermore, having a real-time unified view of on-premise and public Cloud resources also helps the organization to cut down on errors relating to managing multiple Cloud platforms across the organization.
- With the faster and wider adoption of Cloud services, the IT spending at a company occurs without the knowledge or approval of the centralized IT department; that is, the shadow IT is growing steadily. However, since Cloud service brokers provide a unified Cloud strategy, they can help to align lines of business with IT capabilities and improve the responsiveness of IT to the operational demands of the organization. IT can then transition from providing reactive support to delivering proactive solutions.
- Cloud brokers could reduce the risk of migrating security services to the Cloud by vetting vendors to ensure they meet robust security standards. This is especially critical in highly regulated industries such as healthcare and financial services where data protection is paramount. Here, the broker automates Cloud governance and compliance along with a single view to manage risk across the enterprise environment.

Overall, CSBs enable the secure migration of data, applications, and infrastructure components between public and private Clouds. The traditional IT environments also can get the benefit of Cloud brokers in order to participate in the growing Cloud space. A trusted Cloud services broker should enable governing Cloud environments without disrupting the much-needed innovation by:

- Streamlining tracking of changes and configurations through integration with service management processes
- Providing users with upfront visibility into the cost of their Cloud service choices
- Reporting on usage and then managing the budget
- Monitoring performance of Cloud services to prevent downtime
- Separating departments or users with fine-grained multi-tenancy and role-based access control.

As worldwide organizations get ready for the next-generation Cloud, there is no better time to leverage the benefits of Cloud service brokerage to remove complexity, boost productivity, and reduce the risk of shadow IT. These enhanced business outcomes will allow any organization to keep pace with the demands of rapidly changing business requirements and ensure agile delivery of innovative services (http://www.bmc.com/blogs/cloud-service-brokerages-how-csbs-fit-in-a-multi-cloud-world/).

The following are the prominent and dominant drivers for the huge success of the brokerage concept:

1. Tending toward multi-cloud environment
2. Transforming to Hybrid IT
3. Delivering the ideals of "IT as a service"
4. Planning smooth transition to Cloud
5. Empowering self-service IT
6. Incorporating shadow IT
7. Setting and sustaining multi-cloud environments
8. Streamlining multi-cloud governance and control

IBM Cloud brokerage is the prime ingredient for enabling Hybrid IT—When a data center nears the end of life, an important decision has to be made on how to replace it and increasingly enterprises are opting to replace their inflexible and complicated data centers with a mix of Cloud and physical assets, called Hybrid IT. Enterprises are recognizing the need to be more competitive in their dealings, decisions, and deeds. Some of the basic problems they need to solve for are the capital and operational costs, the time to value, the lack of automation, the chargeback accuracy, etc. Hybrid IT helps solve these perpetual problems and increases competitiveness, as long as the right expertise and tools are being leveraged.

1. **Ongoing cost**—The cost of operating, maintaining, and extending application services within the physical data center environments, especially across political and geographic boundaries, would continue to increase.
2. **Speed**—Internal and technology requests for services, on average, took four to six weeks for review and approval, often leading to frustration and a lack of agility for business units.
3. **Lack of automation**—Fulfilling application service requests took too many manual steps, exacerbated by required technology skill sets.
4. **Chargeback accuracy**—Business units were being charged a percentage of IT costs without consideration of usage.
5. **Capital expenditure**—There is a large upfront cost associated with building and deploying new data centers.

The Hybrid IT is definitely a long-term, strategic approach and move for any enterprise IT. The Hybrid IT typically comprises private Cloud, public Cloud, and traditional IT. There are some game-changing advantages of Hybrid IT. The first and foremost is that it never ask to rip-and-replace the current system. Any Hybrid IT solution would need to continue to interoperate with the existing service management system and work with ticket management where appropriate. The most crucial tool for realizing painless and risk-free Hybrid IT is a highly competitive and comprehensive Cloud brokerage solution. A complete Cloud brokerage solution would tie planning, consumption, delivery, and management seamlessly across public, private, virtual, hosted and on-premises and off-premises solutions. IBM Cloud brokerage is widely recognized as the best-in-class Cloud brokerage solution. I have given its unique capabilities in comfortably fulfilling the various.

IBM Cloud brokerage provides the following features:

- A seeded catalogue of the industry's leading Cloud infrastructure providers, out of the box without the overhead of custom integration
- A marketplace where consumers can select and compare provider services, or add their own IT-approved services for purchasing and provisioning. Consumers can use a common workflow with approval processes that are executed in terms of minutes not weeks
- Reporting and monitoring that includes multi-provider consolidated billing estimates, actuals, and usage projections for accuracy and cost assignment
- A visual designer that includes sync-and-discover capabilities to pull assets (VMs) into a single, architectural view and management standard.
- Integration with service management and ticketing systems through an API framework.

Creating Hybrid IT environments—As we all know, hybrid Cloud is typically a kind of dynamic combination of private and one or two public Cloud environments. However, Hybrid IT represents a multi-cloud environment by seamlessly integrating geographically distributed and disparate Cloud environments in order to gain the strategic advantages of the location, performance, capability, and cost in order to elegantly fulfill the workload requirements and granular business objectives. There are definitely challenges and concerns in the form of multiple locations, application/workload features, governance models, proprietary technologies, etc., to achieve the elusive Hybrid IT goal. In the recent past, there came a number of enabling Cloud connectors, integrators, adaptors, APIs, and brokers to realize the Hybrid IT vision.

Devising and delivering a successful Hybrid IT implementation come down to evaluating and managing both traditional and Cloud IT, balancing various on-premises and off-premises suppliers, and making dynamic choices about technology on the fly as business requires new capabilities. All of these tasks must be done simultaneously and in tandem to achieve three fundamental aims for success:

1. Providing users and customers with the right service levels for each application and user
2. Optimizing application delivery, streamlining, simplifying, and automating IT operations

3. Enabling service-centric IT that accelerates business responsiveness now and ongoing

But these aims require new approaches. Solutions are no longer wholly contained in the house, on-premises. Technology becomes an ecosystem of providers, resources, and tools. Interactions between old and new IT have to be devised, modeled, tested, implemented, and improved. Many sources of technology have to be managed, integrated, and directed on-demand toward business agility. This extended scope requires IT to connect the company with a variety of suppliers and customers—all of which must be juggled effectively to avoid risks or organizational impact. Actually, Hybrid IT infrastructure cannot be achieved unless IT operates more like a business—managing vendor selection, packaging, pricing, delivery, and billing in a multi-sourced model. Considering all these correctly, there is an expressed need for enterprise-class, context-aware, highly synchronized, and sophisticated software solution for fulfilling the Hybrid IT vision.

Journeying toward the "IT-as-a-service (ITaaS)" days—This is definitely service era. The excitement and elegance associated with service-oriented architecture (SOA) have paid well in formulating and firming up the journey toward the days of "everything as a service (XaaS)." The service paradigm is to the heightened growth. The varied tasks such as service conceptualization, concretization, composition, deployment, delivery, management, and enhancement are getting extremely simplified and accelerated through a variety of automated tools. All kinds of IT capabilities are being expressed and exposed as easily identifiable, network-accessible, distinctively interoperable, smartly composable, quickly recoverable, and replaceable services. With such kinds of service enablement, all kinds of closed, monolithic, and inflexible IT infrastructures are being tuned and turned into open, remotely consumable, easily maneuverable, and managed components. With the arrival and acceptance of IT service monitoring, measurement, and management tools, engines and platforms, the IT assets and applications are being readied for the era of ITaaS.

Further on, microservices architecture (MSA), which is an offshoot of SOA, is gaining a lot of ground these days and hence the days of "as a service" are bound to see a litany of powerful innovations, transformations, and even a few disruptions. Cloud broker solutions are being recognized as the best fit for ensuring this greatly expressed need of ITaaS.

Embracing the Cloud idea—The raging Cloud paradigm is acquiring a lot of attention and attraction because of its direct and decisive contribution toward highly optimized and organized IT environments. However, Cloud embarkation journey is beset with innumerable barriers. For jumping on the Cloud bandwagon, especially identifying which application workloads give better results in which Cloud environments is a tedious and tough job indeed. Herein, a full-fledged Cloud broker plays a very vital role in shaping up the Cloud strategy and implementation.

Ticking toward self-service IT—It is being insisted that IT has to be business- and people-friendly. For working with IT solutions and availing IT-enabled services, the interfaces have to be very informative, intuitive, and intelligent for giving a simplified and streamlined experience to various users. Automation has to be an inherent and important tenet and trait of Cloud offerings. Cloud brokers are being positioned as the principal instrument to have quick and easy servicing of Cloud infrastructures, platforms, and applications.

Enabling the Shadow IT requirements—The IT organizations of worldwide enterprises literally struggle to provide the required capabilities with the same level of agility and flexibility as being provided by public Clouds. Even their own on-premise private Clouds with all the cloud-enabled IT infrastructures do not provide the mandated variety, simplicity, and consumability of public Clouds because legacy workflows, manual interpretation and intervention, and business procurement requirements often reduce the accelerated realization. These challenges increasingly drive business users to search for and procure various IT capabilities without involving the core IT team of their organizations; that is, different departments and users within a corporate on their own fulfill their IT requirements from various public Clouds. They circumvent the core IT team, and this industry trend is being called as the shadow IT. Users use a shadow IT model because public Clouds guarantee on-demand resources and this, in turn, lays a stimulating foundation for accelerating innovation and improving time-to-market for newer and premium offerings.

However, the shadow IT is beset with risks and challenges and there is an intense pressure on IT divisions of business houses to address this in a structured and smart manner. Many IT organizations do not know what Cloud services their employees are using because users are keeping IT abreast of their Cloud activities. The IT team does not know where data resides, whether data sets are safeguarded accordingly, whether data and applications are backed up to support data and disaster recovery, whether the capabilities will scale in line with fast-evolving business sentiments, and what the costs are. Thus, it is becoming mandatory for business behemoths to address this issue of shadow IT by offering a compelling alternative. The traditional IT centers and even private Clouds need to be empowered to give all that is being ensured by public Clouds that are very famous for on-demand, online, off-premise, consolidated, shared, automated, virtualized, and containerized IT services. In effect, IT organizations have to offer shadow IT capabilities and benefits without the identified risks. Herein, the celebrated role and responsibility of Cloud brokerage solutions are vividly prescribed to provide shadow IT capabilities yet without the articulated risks. With IBM Cloud Brokerage, IT organizations can devise a pragmatic approach to discover existing resources, provide visibility to new resources, and offer an equivalent alternative to shadow IT. Organizations can start small and then extend capabilities and functionality as desired.

Establishing and managing multi-cloud environments—There are integration engines enabling distributed and different Clouds to find, bind, and leverage one another's unique feats and features. Clouds are increasingly federated to accomplish special business needs. Clouds are being made interoperable through technology-centric standardization so that the vision of the InterCloud is to see the reality sooner than later. There are a few interesting new nomenclatures such as open, delta, and interoperable Clouds. Apart from the virtualization dogma, the era of containerization paradigm is to flourish with the industry-strength standards for containerization are being worked out. The Docker-enabled containerization is to have containerized applications that are very famous for portability for fulfilling the mantra of "make once and run everywhere." Developing, shipping, deploying, managing, and enhancing containerized workloads are made simple and faster with the open-source Docker platform. All these clearly indicate that disparate and distributed Cloud environments are being integrated at different levels in order to set everything right for the ensuing days of people-centric and knowledge-filled services for achieving varying personal, social, and professional needs of the total human society. There are several business imperatives vehemently insisting for the onset of hybrid and multi-cloud environments. It is visualized that geographically distributed and different Cloud environments (on-premise Clouds, traditional IT environments, online, on-demand, and off-premise Clouds) need to be integrated with one another in order to fulfill varying business requirements.

Having watched and analyzed the market sentiments and business environments, it is safely predicted that multi-cloud environments will become the new normal in the days to unfurl. We need industry-strength and standardized integration and orchestration engines, multi-cloud management platforms, and a host of other associated empowerments in order to make multi-cloud environments a worthy addition for next-generation business behemoths. Clouds bring in IT agility, adaptivity, and affordability that in turn make business more easily and expediently attuned to be right and relevant for their constituents, customers, and consumers. Cloud brokerage solution is being touted as the most significant entity for presenting a synchronized, simplified, and smart front end for a growing array of heterogeneous generic as well as specific Clouds; that is, Cloud consumers need not interact with multiple and differently enabled Clouds. Instead, users at any point in time from anywhere just interact with the Cloud broker portal to get things done smoothly and in time with just clicks.

In concluding, the role of a Cloud broker is to significantly transform IT service delivery while ensuring the much-demanded IT agility and control. A Cloud broker enables Cloud consumers to access and use multiple Cloud service providers (CSPs) and their distinct services. Further on, a Cloud broker can also take care of the service delivery, fulfillment, API handling, configuration management, resource behavior differences, and other complex tasks. The broker facilitates users to make informed decisions for selecting Cloud infrastructures, platforms, processes, and applications. This typically includes the cost, compliance, utility, governance, auditability. Cloud brokers simplify the procedures and precipitate the Cloud adoption and adaption. The IT operating model is bound to go through a number of transformations and disruptions through the smart leverage of Cloud brokerage solution. The Cloud complexity gets nullified through Cloud brokerage solution. In short, the digital, API, idea and insightful economy and era are bound to go through a radical transformation through Cloud services and brokerage solutions.

A Cloud service broker operationalizes best execution venue (BEV) strategies, which is based on the notion that every class of IT-related business need has an environment where it will best balance performance and cost, and that the IT organization should be able to select that environment (or even have the application select it automatically). Brokers thus enable any organization to create the "right mix" of resources for its Hybrid IT environment. The strategic goal of more with less is to get accentuated with all the accomplishments in the Cloud space. Cloud users expect to be able to make decisions about how and where to run applications and from where to source services based upon workload profile, policies, and SLA requirements. As the worlds of outsourcing, hosting, managed services, and Cloud converge, the options are growing exponentially. BEV strategies enable users to find the most suitable services to meet their needs. The Cloud broker is the key element toward operationalizing this approach.

We have detailed how next-generation Cloud broker solutions are to do justice to the above-mentioned Hybrid IT requirements. In the following sections, we are to detail how IBM Cloud brokerage is emerging as the strategic software suite for the Cloud brokerage needs.

Benefits of having a Cloud Broker:

- **Reduce the costs of Cloud services** (30–40% estimated savings by using Cloud brokers)
- **Integrate multiple IT environments—existing and Cloud environments**…e.g., establish hybridity—as well as integrate services from multiple Cloud providers
- **Understand what public Cloud services are available** via a catalogue
- **Policy-based services catalogue** populated with only the Cloud services that an enterprise wants their employees to purchase
- **Unified purchase Cloud services** (broker) and helps those services selected (by clients) better together
- **Assess current applications for Cloud readiness**
- Ensure Cloud services **meet enterprise policies**
- **Ensure data sovereignty** laws are followed
- Cloud Brokers

  - **Cover all layers of the Cloud stack** (IaaS, PaaS, and SaaS)
  - **Offer multiple deployment models**: on-premises (local); off-premises (dedicated or shared). IBM supports all of these "as a service" deployment models but does not currently offer a traditionally licensed software product.

8.3 Elucidating the IBM Cloud Brokerage Solution

The IBM Cloud brokerage solution was identified as one of the only purpose-built solutions for Hybrid IT. IBM Cloud brokerage enabled the enterprise to transform its IT services model from a high-cost, inflexible physical data center model into a next-generation, pay-per-use model. IBM Cloud brokerage provides an automated and self-service view of many Cloud providers. It has a distinctive feature that reviews and audits each Cloud provider. It assesses strengths and weaknesses of each of the Cloud service providers. It clarifies cost structures and contractual complexities to give your organization a clear understanding of upside, downside, and long-term value. IBM Cloud brokerage even gives you a framework for rapidly integrating your existing contractual relationships with Cloud vendors. IBM Cloud brokerage was designed to enable Hybrid IT while addressing the challenges Cloud brings to the IT value chain. By addressing the multiple steps in the process with the support of a dynamic marketplace, IBM Cloud brokerage can:

- Support accurate and timely access to service providers and delivery environments you choose
- Facilitate delivery of a multi-sourced solution using existing service management tools through open APIs
- Provide a single system of record that tracks an order from design through billing, enables centralized governance and cost management by application, virtual data center, and business unit

The real benefit of IBM Cloud brokerage is that it helps organizations abstract away from Cloud complexity toward Cloud value. Rather than getting bogged down in vendor RFPs and technology comparisons, IBM Cloud brokerage offers quick choices based on short-term and long-term objectives. IBM Cloud brokerage lets your organization and your users make informed choices in minutes instead of weeks. You're no longer vetting suppliers and managing technology integrations—instead IBM Cloud brokerage streamlines that complexity for you, as per your requirements and objectives.

IBM Cloud brokerage is a Cloud brokerage SaaS offering to facilitate you to plan, buy, and manage software and Cloud services from multiple suppliers from a single dashboard in an exceedingly simple manner as pictorially illustrated below.

Plan

- Assess workloads to determine which will benefit from Cloud
- Compare IT resources from multiple providers side-by-side
- Create custom, reusable solutions, or blueprints that include managed services

Buy

- Explore the service store powered by a dynamic catalogue
- Find the best solutions for your business needs

Manage

- Aggregate bills and navigate payment processes with centralized billing management solution
- Better manage compliance with enterprise policies

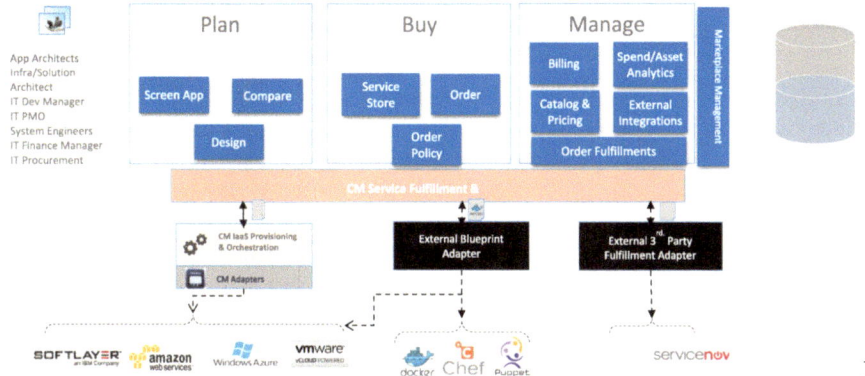

Cloud brokerage helps organizations with a solution for delivering public cloud-like agility. The IBM Cloud brokerage solution delivers an evidence-based approach that limits guesswork. It can map your interdependencies, create a dynamic decision tree, and assign weights to various parameters, giving you a framework for delivering consistent and more accurate results. The functional component architecture is given below.

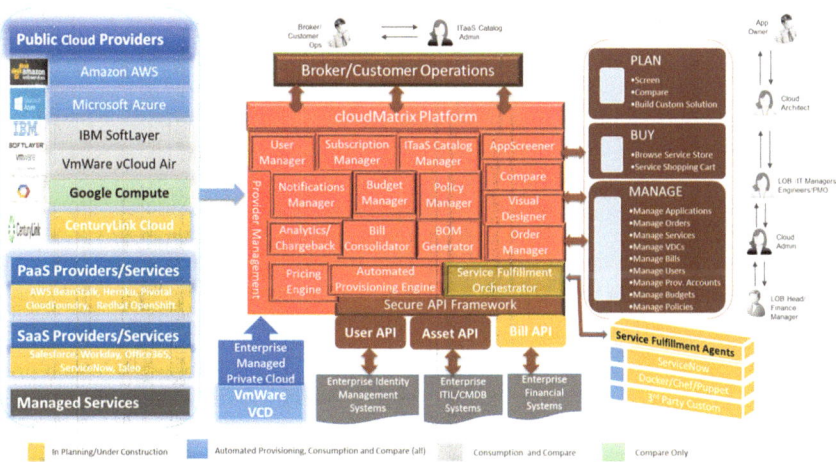

8.4   The Key Components of IBM Cloud Brokerage

Application screener—Using patented analytics, based on unbiased analysis from many deployments and a rich set of current workload data, the IBM Cloud brokerage application screener helps planners to more quickly determine project fit, feasibility, and benefits of migrations. Does it address a basic set of questions: 1. Which workloads? 2. In what order? 3. Readiness? 4. Benefits? 5. What infrastructure? The application screening wizard provides two key recommendations: a matrix of benefits and a Cloud readiness assessment. The benefits are measures of improvement (total cost of ownership and performance gains) gained by operating in the Cloud. Readiness is a measure of an application's ease to move and run in the Cloud, driven by architectural feasibility, platform portability, and application complexity. The application screener also provides insights into the ideal infrastructure for a particular application.

Cloud compare—Before, choosing a Cloud provider has involved some guesswork, because varying pricing and packaging models make it almost impossible to get to a clear comparison. IBM Cloud brokerage uses the patented Gravitant Capacity Unit (GCU) to normalize the costs of various providers. A GCU is the capacity to compute at a speed of 4.0 GHz with random access memory of 4 GB and local storage of 100 GB through 1 Mbps of bandwidth. IBM uses mathematical modeling to normalize the service provider offerings across price, SLAs, and capabilities. IBM Cloud brokerage provides pre-sized packages for comparison. These are standardized packages. It is a starting point to understand the cost, capacity, and SLAs for a particular sized Cloud service—to facilitate cost projections and longer-term planning. Having said that, you can also customize a package to more closely match your business needs and drive more accurate comparisons.

IBM Cloud brokerage helps you make informed trade-offs between match index and cost. You can either select a small number of expensive providers with extensive offerings (higher match index) each or a larger set of providers with more specific offerings (lower match index) each.

Visual solution designer—With IBM Cloud Brokerage, you can design virtual data centers (VDCs) from a robust IT-as-a-service catalogue that includes public, private, and virtual resources, as well as associated, managed services. The IBM Cloud brokerage multilayered, multi-environment design tool allows you to design complete (infrastructure plus managed services) IT solutions in a fraction of the time. Plus, you can save these designs as solution blueprint templates—decreasing design time and increasing standardization to confirm adherence to security, compliance, and budget standards.

The IBM Cloud brokerage visual solution designer helps you easily collaborate to make sure interdependencies are managed and the architecture meets the needs of IT and the business. Perhaps most importantly, you'll be able to build application architectures across multiple VDCs—on-premises or off-premises—mapping relationships to help ensure that migration and evolution do not compromise capability.

The visual solution designer helps you to identify, manage, and orchestrate organizational requirements to help ensure that transformation happens in a predictable, successful way. With this tool, you'll end up with a design that enables tracking and reporting of components in the context of the architecture and solution design. Because context is retained throughout the life cycle, it is easier to determine the return on investment and total cost of ownership at the VDC and architecture level.

Estimated bill of IT—Know your complete cost before you order. A detailed view of costs, mapped to the solution design, provides users with an estimated bill of IT as the last step before you order.

In short, IBM's aim is to help you deliver breakthrough results by:

- Identifying the impactful workloads to move, and what is needed to make the migration successful
- Select the best-fit solution across a wide variety of deployment options
- Design a multi-tiered application architecture that produces a bill of IT before you order.

8.5   The Distinct Capabilities of IBM Cloud Brokerage

IBM Cloud brokerage is a Cloud brokering software suite that addresses the entire IT value chain: assess, compare, design, procure, provision, operate, and control as well as the new area of broker operations. The consolidation of virtualized resources, public and private Clouds and the integration of managed services through the entire life cycle make Cloud brokerage the only software that supports an IT-as-a-service model. Cloud brokerage offers Cloud service broker as a SaaS platform to systems integrators and large enterprises. The other noteworthy features are:

IBM Cloud brokerage planning—enables the enterprise to assess an existing application's benefit from and readiness for the Cloud with its analytics-based workload characterization, automated Cloud service brokerage capabilities, and Cloud management. Workload characterization with sophisticated analytics defines the potential workload using an interactive, research-based questionnaire. The customer chooses what to assess, e.g., application readiness, comparison of Cloud providers or a custom-designed solution or blueprint. Using additional analytics and user priorities, it makes recommendations on where the workload best fits from among Cloud provider and in-house options. Out-of-the-box comparisons cover AWS, Azure, IBM Bluemix, Google Compute, VMware vCloud Director 5.1 and 5.5. It delivers information for essential purchasing decisions, such as estimated costs and operational requirements. The below table lists the public Clouds with which the Cloud brokerage solution currently interacts to give a multi-cloud environment for consumers.

Providers	Summary	Types
AWS	Order, Discovery synch, Provisioning, Billing automation	Public Cloud
Azure	Order, Discovery synch, Provisioning, Billing automation	Public Cloud
VMware VCD	Order, Discovery synch, Provisioning, Estimated charges	Private Cloud
IBM Bluemix	Order, Estimated charges (Discovery synch, Provisioning, Billing automation)	Public Cloud
OpenStack	(Order, Discovery synch, Provisioning, etc.)	Private Cloud
vCloud air	Order, Estimated charges	Public Cloud

Application assessment—Considers both technical readiness and business benefit when selecting the most appropriate target infrastructure.

Workload placement—With IBM Cloud Brokerage, you can feel confident in the placement and prioritization of applications to the Cloud. The IBM Cloud brokerage solution helps you to identify the relative readiness and benefit of moving a given application to the Cloud. It then recommends the ideal target infrastructure for your organization. In the end, you will have a map of all your workloads and their relative readiness and benefit. You'll also know what additional work or investment is needed to prepare these workloads for their new target infrastructure.

Provider matching and selection—Simple side-by-side comparison of provider services to more easily match capabilities with requirements. Most often a single provider will not match all your requirements, so a set of providers may be needed to design a multi-cloud solution. This step includes the cost normalization across Cloud providers with side-by-side comparisons of cost, SLA, provisioning, and support.

Multi-cloud solution design—Once you have selected your provider or providers, then you need to design a multi-tiered, multilayered application architecture to get a clear understanding of the interdependencies and costs associated with the solution.

Discover and sync existing resources—It starts with knowing what resources are currently in the Cloud. IBM Cloud brokerage helps enable IT organizations to discover and sync up existing assets from major Cloud providers. Bringing these once hidden resources into a centralized location provides IT with a detailed view of existing resources that can be tagged and utilized in future application architectures. This capability allows IT team and users to more easily discover resources under existing provider accounts and sync those resources so they display in IBM Cloud Brokerage. By centralizing resources into a single place, IBM Cloud brokerage helps IT to extensively review security procedures. IT can learn more about how the users are using the public Cloud, to facilitate cost controls and future planning.

Track new public Cloud deployments—IBM Cloud brokerage enables organizations to offer public Cloud offerings through a centralized store, giving IT a new way to track assets and monitor spend as users consume public Cloud capacity. With IBM Cloud Brokerage, the enterprise IT team can have greater visibility and insight while starting to direct users toward using IT's catalogue, reducing shadow IT demand

and utilization. IBM Cloud brokerage helps organizations get started with a pre-populated catalogue with the major providers, using standard list prices or applying contact pricing. IT admins can even customize what appears in the catalogue.

Create incentives to use approved resources—Use IBM Cloud brokerage to build a robust marketplace that includes prepackaged and vetted solutions from a variety of public, private, and virtual deployment options and provide automated deployment across on and off-premises resources to speed delivery.

Visual solution design—Categorize and view Cloud resources by application, application layer, virtual data center, or environment.

Solution blueprint—Design a solution—including managed services—and make it available as a standard, predefined architecture.

ITaaS catalogue—Collection of public, private, virtual, and managed services.

Fulfillment and integrations—Open architecture that can be customized to match the services and delivery ecosystem you define.

Billing and cost management—View bills and cost dashboards by VDC, organization, or application.

Bill of IT—View estimated and actual bill of IT for your complete Cloud service.

Governance—Workflow-based approval flow and integration with identity management SW.

The other noteworthy technical capabilities include:

- **Open architecture (extensible and open)**
  - APIs providing extensibility
  - Build your own blueprints, bring your own technology
  - Build your own fulfillment agents—pluggable into Cloud Brokerage
  - Build your own IT solutions/services—BOM, catalogue, design, etc.

- **Reference adapters and blueprints**
  - Interoperation with DevOps technologies such as Chef, Puppet, Docker, Jenkins, Bamboo
  - Reference blueprints using Docker, and Chef—Hadoop cluster, WordPress, SharePoint
  - Reference adapters—ServiceNow CMDB Integration, ServiceNow Ticket Integration

- **Scalability and reliability**
  - Clustered, failover, no single point of failure
  - Scale each layer to handle large and increasing number of transactions and providers

- **Multiple deployment architecture models (onsite, Cloud, provider neutral, single stack, clustered, etc.)**
- **Collect marketplace intelligence**
- **Cloud brokerage managed public Cloud content and integrations**

  - Pricing, catalogue content, provisioning API integrations, billing API integrations

IBM Cloud brokerage makes it easier to build solution blueprints, incorporate governance policies, and automate approval processes. Cloud brokerage offers varied options and a bevy of tools to select the best Cloud venue for your organization and nonintrusive governance. Finally, it provides users with the single point of contact, speed, and smartness to fulfill the varying IT needs with all the visibility and maneuverability. IBM Cloud brokerage is a highly automated, more easily tunable, multi-environment orchestration and management engine. It lets IT operations orchestrate simple or complex, new or existing applications, across various environments, infrastructures, and providers. IBM Cloud brokerage manages the implementation of infrastructure resources as well as the deployment and configuration of the bottom-to-top application stack and security settings.

From a different perspective, Cloud brokerage is a tool that exists to turn IT operations into an innovation engine. It helps IT operations shift from a manual, pain-filled existence toward an automated, self-service model of IT procurement, with standardized blueprints and frameworks that users can rely on for faster provisioning.

Let us explore a scenario to illustrate how this works.
A user is utilizing AWS without IT engagement or visibility, resulting in hidden costs to the organization. Once IBM Cloud brokerage has been implemented, the user can then go to the IBM Cloud brokerage marketplace for AWS capacity. The user accesses a consolidated storefront for public Cloud procurement, prepackaged solutions, and internal resources. In other words, both on-premises and off-premises resources are available from the same internal portal.

When purchasing public Cloud resources through the marketplace, tags are added to the virtual data center and business unit, allowing for quick identification. It is easier to tie utilization to the user.

IT can easily set spend alerts, review security settings, and track usage. As use patterns highlight problems, IT has the ability to proactively fix deficiencies to provide a high level of service for the user.

IBM Cloud brokerage automatically synchronizes the bills of major providers. It will compare actuals with the estimated bill of IT. If the spend is out of range, IBM Cloud brokerage will trigger an alert and work with the user to resolve the issue. When situations happen, organizations can limit their exposure by monitoring spend and identifying anomalies.

With IBM Cloud Brokerage, auditing expenditures and assessing risks are as simple as one, two, three:

- Discover and sync at the virtual data center (VDC) level to determine if there have been additional resources added that could account for the spend.
- Use the security audit in IBM Cloud brokerage to quickly view if there are risks that need to be mitigated.
- Take the resource offline if the security threat warrants.

8.6   The High-Level Cloud Brokerage Service Fulfillment Bridge (SFB) Architecture

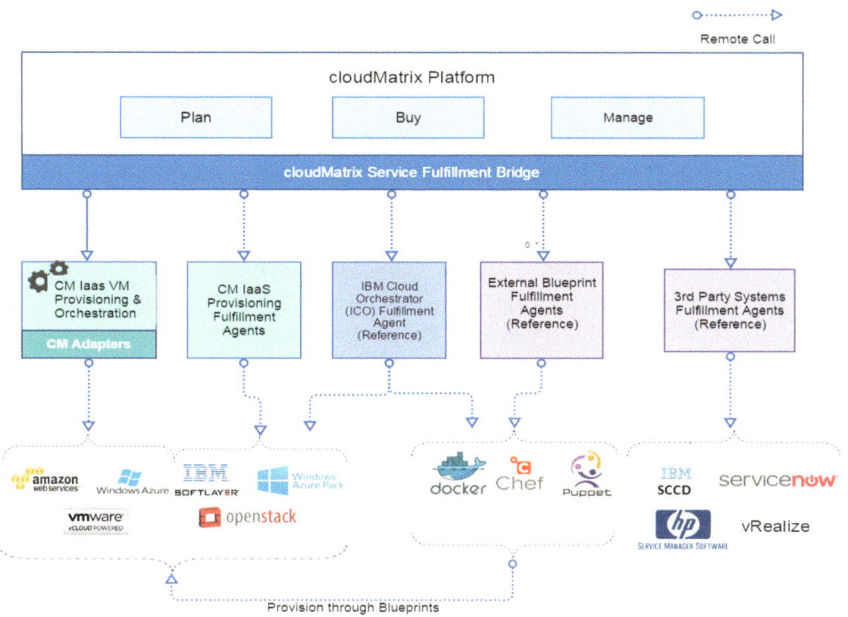

8.7   The Integration Benefits of Cloud Brokerage and IBM Cloud Orchestrator (ICO)

IBM Cloud orchestrator accelerates the delivery of software and infrastructure. Based on open standards, it reduces the number of steps to manage public, private, and hybrid Clouds by using an easy-to-use interface. ICO gives you access to ready-to-use patterns and content packs helping to speed up the configuration, provisioning, and deployment activities. It integrates management tools such as metering, usage, accounting, monitoring, and capacity management into your Cloud services. Precisely speaking, go live as quickly as you develop and test applications. IBM Cloud orchestrator helps you:

• Quickly deploy and scale on-premise and off-premise Cloud services
• Provision and scale Cloud resources
• Reduce administrator workloads and error-prone manual IT administrative tasks
• Integrate with existing environments using application program interfaces and tooling extensions
• Deliver services with IBM Bluemix, existing OpenStack platforms, PowerVM, IBM System z, VMware, or Amazon EC2.

Combine the best of both worlds where Cloud brokerage can be used as the end-to-end catalogue and store for service design and consumption with pricing/billing, and ICO is used for advanced orchestration for OpenStack-based private Clouds and some blueprint-based provisioning into IBM Bluemix and other supported Clouds. Provisioning for AWS/Azure/VCD would use Cloud brokerage provisioning/orchestration and other OpenStack private Clouds can be done via ICO. Cloud brokerage integrates with ICO via a service fulfillment bus (SFB) agent (called the Services Fulfillment Bridge) design that exposes the services of ICO into the Cloud brokerage catalogue and can be automatically provisioned via an SFB agent that invokes ICO.

   IBM Cloud brokerage could work with any orchestrator via a blueprint fulfillment-based architecture where the orchestrator exposes the blueprints/orchestrations it supports and it is added to the Cloud brokerage catalogue for consumption via a service store with price/cost and billing. Once ordered with an order approval process, the automated provisioning can be invoked on the external orchestrator using a REST-based microservice that integrates with the Service Fulfillment Bus of Cloud Brokerage.

8.8   IBM Cloud Brokerage Solution Use Cases and Benefits

Full Brokerage	Customers that are undergoing signification IT transformation or renovation, such as vacating data centers and are moving core workloads to cloud environments.
Self-Service IT	Directed at CIOs that are seeking a means to enable Hybrid IT with a common, self-service user experience.
Continuous Delivery	Directed at Developers, QA staff and Production Operations Administrators who want a common, automated process using tools of their choice.
Service Marketplace	Sourcing/Procurement Managers and consumers that want to establish and manage contractual terms beyond IT capabilities – Dynamic Pricing, Service Levels
Multi-Cloud Solution	Architects that design solutions that include services from more than one service provider, including multi-cloud IaaS, PaaS and/or SaaS.
Shadow IT	Infrastructure & Operations leaders looking to adopt the benefits of self-service IT, while ensuring organizational security and cost management.
Cost Management	IT & Business Financial Controllers looking to manage spend across multiple technology service providers and pro-actively alert on spend deviations.
Workload Placement	CIOs/Architects that are in the initial stages of determining a cloud strategy and examining workloads for fit/feasibility readiness.

The Distinct Benefits

- **Assess current applications for Cloud readiness and benefit**—Huge client pain point! Should I migrate this workload to the Cloud? What benefit will get realize? Is it ready to move to the Cloud?
- **30–40% reduced costs of Cloud services**—Visibility of shadow IT and idle services; centralized IT supply chain, chargeback, and financial reports, purchasing power, estimated bill, etc.
- **Enable self-service ITaaS across the IT supply chain**—Plan (assess, compare, design, and estimate); buy; and manage Cloud services on-prem and off-prem across IaaS, PaaS, and SaaS
- **Policy-based services catalogue**—Pre-seeded AWS, Azure, and IBM Bluemix. Can be customized to include only the Cloud services that an enterprise wants their employees to purchase. Enables enterprise compliance
- **Integrate multiple IT environments—existing and Cloud environments**…e.g., establish hybridity—as well as integrate SaaS from multiple Cloud providers.

8.9   The Industry Pain Points, Cloud Brokerage Targets, and Fitment Questions

Pain Points

- **Enabling ITaaS:** Inability to integrate dozens of required multi-sourced tools. Cannot track consumption and delivery of services

- **Planning and deploying workloads:** Struggling to find the best mix of deployment models and assess migration requirements while developing a Hybrid IT strategy
- **Offering self-service IT:** Users procuring their own IT (unmanaged shadow IT) to find the speed, agility, and freedom they need. Need to offer LOBs a unified, self-service IT experience
- **Overseeing a service marketplace:** Trying to augment a traditional service catalogue to add public Cloud, but the Cloud has a different, a dynamic pricing model that catalogues are not designed for
- **Shadow IT:** Third-party Cloud services posing security risks and cost management challenges. Organizations want shadow IT, in accordance with an approved version and security standards, with self-service.
- **Continuous delivery:** Lack of DevOps automation and integrated order-to-delivery process between DevOps and the infrastructure and operations team.

IBM Cloud Brokerage, the most comprehensive yet compact Cloud brokerage solution, is a great value-add for any enterprise to plan and embark on the Cloud journey. The targets enterprises include:

1. **System integrators (SIs) and managed service providers (MSPs)**: Often these companies want to become Cloud service providers (CSPs) or else they wish to deliver IT services to their clients through an online portal. Typically, they negotiate volume discounts with the Cloud providers and pass the discount on to their clients, with a margin, and adding their own unique services. This can add up to tens of millions of dollars in revenue for them.
2. **Communication service providers** such as Vodafone, Telefonica, and Ericsson want to become Cloud service providers.
3. **Multinational companies** want to centralize the management and control of IT services to provide ITaaS; for example, Unilever and Nestle.

The Decision-enabling Questions

- How do you decide whether to use AWS, Azure, IBM Bluemix, or your own internal data center?
- How do you determine which platform to use for an application? How long does it take to decide?
- Do you run regular RFPs to keep up-to-date with pricing trends and SLA changes for those vendors?
- We see cases where the price of the lowest and second lowest providers differs by 25%. How would a potential 25% cost reductions benefit your business?
- Does your organization have a process defined for application development and infrastructure team projects?
- How are application architectures designed/approved? Is there a PMO managing these processes?
- How do you currently manage all of your ITaaS providers? Do you have a defined IT service catalogue in place already? If so, how often do you update the offerings?

- Do you have thresholds that a group is approved to go out and provision on their own? (USD 1 K/month, USD 1 M a month?)
- Have you implemented a "no-cloud" policy due to concern about compliance? Or have you implemented an "if you want Cloud, get it yourself" policy because of the strain on IT? Is shadow IT an issue?
- What percentage of public Cloud usage run through IT today?
- Can IBM Cloud brokerage provide a self-service framework that enables your users to utilize IT as a service?
- Can IBM Cloud brokerage provide multi-sourcing of IT that is dynamic and consumption-driven?
- Can IBM Cloud brokerage quickly drive a shift from mainly CapEx to CapEx + OpEx?
- Can IBM Cloud brokerage automate order fulfillment by coordinating internal and external providers?
- Can IBM Cloud brokerage help your IT organization transition toward Hybrid IT, not just a hybrid Cloud?

The Unique Value Propositions

1. **Reduce shadow IT**—flexibility of choice for end users within the organization's compliance framework
2. **Rapid financial decision-making** for the CIO by consolidating all Cloud service costs on a single dashboard
3. **Negotiate better T's and C's** with Cloud providers based on performance visibility
4. **Enforce organizational policy compliance** for service selection—based on cost, location, workload, or performance requirements
5. **Integrated service management** across traditional and Cloud IT services—enabling the virtual data center.

8.10   IBM Cloud Brokerage Case Studies

Case Study 1

When a leading, Fortune 500 nutrition, health and Wellness Company needed to migrate applications from two end-of-life data centers, they took the opportunity to evaluate how they could increase competitiveness through IT. The enterprise found that moving to a Hybrid IT model—a mix of private Cloud, public Cloud, and physical assets—would help them solve problems hindering competitiveness.

The need—Two existing global data centers were closing, creating the need to find new hosting environments for over 250 business application workloads, including mission-critical transactional systems. The enterprise also needed to increase business competitiveness through IT.

The Problem Areas

- **Ongoing cost**—The cost of operating, maintaining, and extending application services within the physical data center environments, especially across political and geographic boundaries, would continue to increase.
- **Speed**—Internal and technology requests for services, on average, took four to six weeks for review and approval, often leading to frustration and a lack of agility for business units.
- **Lack of automation**—Fulfilling application service requests took too many manual steps, exacerbated by required technology skill sets.
- **Chargeback accuracy**—Business units were being charged a percentage of IT costs without consideration of usage.
- **Capital expenditure**—There is a large upfront cost associated with building and deploying new data centers.

The solution—The enterprise took a long-term, strategic approach and adopted a Hybrid IT model that included implementing IBM Cloud Brokerage, managed by a top system integrator.

Solution components software—IBM Cloud Brokerage

IBM Cloud brokerage provided:

- A seeded catalogue of the industry's leading Cloud infrastructure providers, out of the box without the overhead of custom integration
- A marketplace where consumers can select and compare provider services, or add their own IT-approved services for purchasing and provisioning. Consumers can use a common workflow with approval processes that are executed in terms of minutes, not weeks
- Reporting and monitoring that includes multi-provider consolidated billing estimates, actuals, and usage projections for accuracy and cost assignment
- A visual designer that includes sync-and-discover capabilities to pull assets (VMs) into a single, architectural view and management standard
- Integration with service management and ticketing systems through an API framework

The benefits—By quickly moving to a Hybrid IT delivery model, this company increased their speed and agility by providing self-service IT to their business units; created cost and usage transparency from day one; and increased their competitiveness by establishing an IT services delivery model.

Case Study 2

A multinational enterprise with over 100 years of history providing value to legal, tax, finance, healthcare organizations on a global scale has undergone a transformation. Their value is created by combining information, deep expertise, and technology to provide their customers with solutions that improve their quality and effectiveness.

The need—The enterprise needed to retake control of their IT services supply chain in order to offer their customers a one-stop consumption experience, independent of supplier, and provide greater value by building on technological innovations.

The primary goals in mind were:

- Retaking control of IT service supply and creating mechanisms to enable them to retain control independent of current suppliers
- Enabling users with a one-stop shop for all their IT service needs
- Offering consumers a ubiquitous consumption experience, independent of underlying supplier
- Enabling market management techniques that enable shared services to learn from market dynamics, consumption patterns, and develop and publish solution patterns for new consumption
- Reducing cost and inefficiencies

The solution—The leadership of the enterprise chose to employ IBM® Cloud brokerage Cloud service brokering technology platform as the platform of choice to enable its shared services organization to become a Cloud service broker.

Solution components software—IBM Cloud Brokerage

IBM Cloud brokerage provided:

1. A seeded catalogue of the leading Cloud infrastructure providers
2. A marketplace for consumers to search, compare, select, and procure provider services with a common workflow approval process facilitated by global business services group
3. A marketplace for global business services group to add their own IT-approved services for consumer purchasing as well as the ability to glean consumption patterns, develop, and publish new solution patterns for new consumers
4. Reporting and monitoring that includes multi-provider consolidated billing estimates, actuals, and usage projections for accuracy and cost assignment
5. A visual designer that includes sync-and-discover capabilities to pull existing Cloud service assets (VMs) into a single, architectural view and management standard

The benefit—By quickly moving to a Hybrid IT delivery model, the enterprise increased its speed and agility by providing self-service IT to their business units; created cost and usage transparency from day one; and established a long-term IT services delivery model with IT-approved resources.

Case Study 3

A leading company is in the production of long steels in the Americas and one of the major suppliers of speciality long steel in the world. More than a century ago, it began its expansion path and now has a presence in 14 countries: Argentina, Brazil, Canada, Chile, Colombia, Dominican Republic, Guatemala, India, Mexico, Peru, Spain, USA, Uruguay, and Venezuela. It has to focus on reduction of costs and increased flexibility (thinking in digital environment).

Type	Gerdau requirements
Public Cloud service providers Existing/planned	AWS and IBM Bluemix existing, Azure planned
Private Clouds existing/planned	VMware existing farms vRealize-based private Cloud planned
Identity management	Existing Gerdau IDM services based on MS Active Directory (for user validation)
Service management	ISM Maximo tool
Approval management	Cloud Brokerage
CMDB	ISM Maximo tool
Financial Mgmt./billing	Extract metering and billing info from CSPs monthly basis; Cloud brokerage standards Billing reports Broker consumptions report being provided back to GTS financial management teams; using tags to provide reports

It requires a single platform to unify the planning, consumption, delivery, and management of Cloud services within it.

- Cloud services should include all major suppliers with the current traditional environment.
- Integrates and composes Cloud services by orchestrating the Cloud resources and services across various Cloud domains and Cloud service providers, and offers guaranteed Cloud services to consumers with SLA. The service integration architecture is as follows.

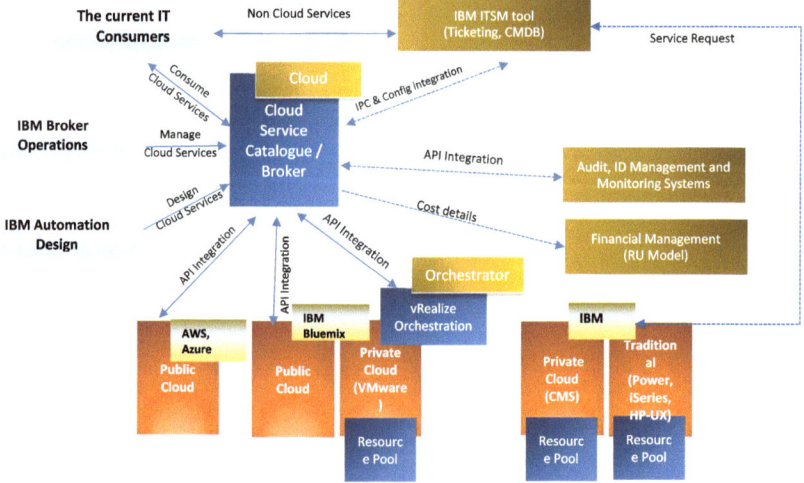

8.11   The Capabilities to Be Incorporated

Roadmap capability	Description
OpenStack support	Cloud brokerage native integration with OpenStack IaaS for: 1. Consumption (catalogue and pricing information) 2. Automated provisioning 3. Asset sync and discover 4. Note: Billing is not included b/c OpenStack is a private Cloud play. Also, OpenStack support can be achieved through IBM orchestrator as well
IBM smart Cloud control desk (SCCD) integration	Integration with IBM's Help Desk/Ticketing System—SCCD
Globalization	Staged support for single-byte/double-byte language translation, date/time conversion, and currency conversion
New cost analytics tool	New capability targeted at IT and Business Financial Controllers looking to manage to spend across multiple technology service providers, identify and optimize spend based on policy and prioritization and proactively alert on spending deviations. Includes reporting integration and enhancements by linking cost analytics output to existing/enhanced reports. Translates OpEx into CapEx within appropriate systems
Enhanced catalogue provider management	Additional automation to enable faster onboarding of external service provider services, including bulk uploads and enhanced user interfaces
ServiceNow Integration	Integration with popular third-party helpdesk product, ServiceNow
Continuous delivery: bring your own tools	New capability directed at developers, QA staff, and production operations administrators who want a common, automated process using tools of their choice. Allows users to "bring their own tools" but enables control and management at scale across the enterprise. Streamlined "buy" experience for existing client tools like Docker, Chef, Puppet.
Enhanced services marketplace	Added capability to existing store-based ordering, enables users to order and provision VMs directly from the Cloud brokerage store
IBM Bluemix integration	Integration into IBM's platform as a service (Paas) (Bluemix)
Enhanced application screening	Next-generation (v2.0) application screening tool provides additional application patterns, reporting export, enhanced usability for customization of screening questions/weights, and enhanced user interface
Enhanced provider comparison	Next-generation (v2.0) Cloud provider comparison tool provides additional application templates for fast comparison, reporting exports to support business case development, and enhanced the user interface. Adds additional comparison information for IBM Bluemix

Roadmap capability	Description
Enhanced provider account sharing	Extension to current subscription management capability. Allows users to "share" service provider account information across Cloud brokerage groups, such as business units (exclusive vs. share capability). (MS Azure only)
IBM Cloud orchestrator integration	Integration with IBM's Cloud orchestration system, especially for immediate full IBM Bluemix and OpenStack support for existing customers; includes workflow orchestration for Cloud brokerage blueprints
Enhanced IBM Bluemix support	Cloud brokerage native integration with IBM Bluemix IaaS for: 1. Automated provisioning 2. Billing information 3. Asset sync and discover
Enhanced Integration Hub	Next-generation Integration Hub (called Services Fulfillment Bridge 2.0) enables the ability to: 1. Provision VMs through the Services Fulfillment Bridge (SFB) 2. Sync and provision tags to/from service providers for enhanced tracking and reporting 3. Asset sync and discover through SFB 4. Enhancement Agent Management (fire/forget, polling, callback, custom actions)
Enhanced provisioning capabilities	Enables users, especially fulfillment users to define additional provisioning information (e.g., boot scripts) to be executed pre-post- and during boot-sequences of VM provision processes
Enhanced Azure Support (ARM)—MS Azure private Cloud	Cloud brokerage native integration with MS Azure ARM 2.0—IaaS (e.g., Azure private Cloud) for: 1. Consumption (catalogue and pricing information) 2. Automated provisioning 3. Billing information 4. Asset sync and discover
Enhanced application screening	Next-generation (v2.0) application screening tool provides additional application patterns, reporting export, enhanced usability for customization of screening questions/weights, and enhanced user interface
Enhanced provider comparison	Next-generation (v2.0) Cloud provider comparison tool provides additional application templates for fast comparison, reporting exports to support business case development, and enhanced the user interface. Adds additional comparison information for IBM Bluemix

8.12　Other Cloud brokerage Solutions and Services

Jamcracker—The Jamcracker platform is a comprehensive Cloud services broker, Cloud management, and governance platform, including risk and policy compliance management, spend management, and operations management. Jamcracker enables organizations to create, deliver, and manage multi-cloud services and implement a cloud-enabled business model for offering, delivering, supporting, and billing for Cloud services. The platform ensures global flexibility and scalability, with a multi-tiered, multi-tenant architecture, RESTful APIs, and integration frameworks while supporting multiple currencies and languages. Jamcracker allows service providers, technology providers, system integrators, IT distributors, and enterprise/government IT organizations to unify delivery and management of private and public Cloud application/services and distribute them to customers, partners, and employees through a customer-facing self-service/App Store.

Jamcracker has added full support for infrastructure as a service (IaaS) Cloud management platform (CMP) functionality for multi-cloud and hybrid Cloud services environments. Hence, Jamcracker unifies Cloud services management needs for SaaS, PaaS, and now IaaS, offering a holistic Cloud services enablement solution across all flavors of Cloud services.

With the enterprise organizations transforming traditional IT to cloud-based IT-as-a-service (ITaaS) model, there is a critical need to unify many of the Cloud services management functions such as aggregation, onboarding, catalogue, self-service fulfillment, access management, billing, invoicing, settlements, SLA monitoring, reporting, and services analytics. Offering a single pane of glass and consistent user experience in managing Cloud services of all flavors is important to make IT productive. Driven by customer needs, Jamcracker platform has evolved from being a Cloud broker to now a complete Cloud services lifecycle manager. Jamcracker platform addressed these by adding following key CMP features to existing Cloud brokerage platform:

Access management

- Multi-tiered marketplaces
- Self-service portal
- Multi-tenancy and user management
- Identity platform integration
- Governance (RBAC, budgets, approval workflow)

Service management

- Services catalogue
- Service onboarding
- Usage analytics
- Financial management
- Compute, network, storage across public and private CSPs
- Image management, VPC, volumes, and snapshots support

Service optimization

- Cost control
- Policy control
- Multi-cloud, Intercloud support
- AppStack orchestrator

Cognizant Cloud Integration brokerage (CCIB) is a holistic solution that provides B2B platform as a service with in-built scalable infrastructure on the Cloud. It comes with preconfigured B2B software that has multi-tenant features and a managed services team packaged together. This helps provide our customers with the ability to leverage service provider advantages, the scalability to grow in tandem with the organization's growth, and the flexibility to customize the solution and services to suit their needs.

8.13   Conclusion

As the technology landscape is ever-changing, the role of enterprise IT is in a constant state of evolution. Cloud service providers have created a new and agile model for IT procurement by providing offerings that are scalable, and on-demand in nature. This has created a challenge for enterprise IT with the widespread adoption of Cloud, which is not always approved or monitored. Choosing the right set of Cloud services fulfilling a few important expectations (business and technical) can be a really difficult proposition especially for organizations procuring services from multiple IT providers. Manually comparing services and providers is a tedious and error-prone task and often forces IT staff into guessing games. To understand which services best align with business goals and which offer the best value in terms of location, cost, dependability, security, etc., organizations need to accurately compare service costs, capacity requirements, etc. A Cloud service brokerage solution comes handy in addressing these challenges quite easily and precisely.

Chapter 9
Automated Multi-cloud Operations and Container Orchestration

9.1 The Introduction

The pivotal and paramount Cloud idea is being presented as the most crucial concept in sustaining IT to fulfill the evolving needs of businesses. The much-touted IT optimization and organization is being accomplished through Cloud technologies and tools. As the IT budget is seeing gradual reduction year after year, the challenge before IT professionals and professors is to do more with less. Thus, the technology-sponsored optimization solutions are given much importance these days. The Cloud idea was born and has gained a lot due to the persistent pressure on IT teams by businesses. Various lines of business (LOB) needed specific types of support that the centralized IT could not give them. The IT budget is primarily spent on IT operations. To bring forth newer business capabilities, the IT budget allocated falls short. This scenario prompted and pushed IT pundits and pioneers to unearth ways and means of bringing more deeper and decisive automation in order to bring down IT operational costs. Not only automation but also the grandiose aspect of orchestration is being introduced and involved in order to realize extreme and elegant IT optimization. IT simplification, rationalization, consolidation, centralization, federation, compartmentalization (virtualization and containerization), policy-based manipulation, and other sustainable and smart measures are being enacted and enforced in order to make IT lean, green, and clean.

There are divisions and departments focusing on sales force automation (SFA), customer relationship management, marketing, and supply chain management services. The LOBs needed to enable or improve the automation of these operations to stay competitive in the increasingly cutthroat competitive market. Many LOBs, therefore, are forced to use their own budgets to take control of the matter by turning to various software-as-a-service (SaaS) offerings. Further on, they approach integrationplatform-as-a-service (iPaaS) providers to link the selected SaaS offerings with their own on-premise data sources. This is typically called shadow IT, and this pattern of ad hoc outsourcing accelerated the trend toward multi-cloud environments.

© Springer International Publishing AG, part of Springer Nature 2018   185
P. Raj and A. Raman, *Software-Defined Cloud Centers*,
Computer Communications and Networks,
https://doi.org/10.1007/978-3-319-78637-7_9

IT organizations also inadvertently created the climate for multi-cloud infrastructure. They began spinning up compute and storage services from infrastructure-as-a-service (IaaS) providers and explored PaaS offerings to accelerate cloud-based software development and testing. Provisioning servers and other infrastructure services in a full-fledged Cloud center compared to traditional IT infrastructure is quite easy and quick.

9.2   A Brief of Cloud Automation and Orchestration

Traditional IT administrators use sequential scripts to perform a series of tasks (e.g., software installation or configuration). Orchestration differs from automation in that it does not rely entirely on static sequential scripts but rather sophisticated workflows. The orchestration and automation market has evolved from mere task automation, which was performed via simple virtualization management tools, to process and workflow automation, which is increasingly done through orchestrators. The creation of virtual machines (VMs) which are not application ready is creating a need for workload automation. Even with an orchestrator in place, organizations have a need to integrate with service management tools. There have been lot of piecemeal solutions, but organizations need an end-to-end, highly synchronized, and holistic orchestration and automation solution which can

- Help automate delivery of infrastructure, application, and custom IT services
- Support direct integration of service management capabilities
- Deploy application workloads across on-premise and off-premise Cloud environments
- Provide policy-based governance and logical application modeling to help ensure that multi-vendor and multi-cloud services are delivered at the right size and service level for each task performed
- Include both build/deployment and delivery/support orchestration and automation services
- Enable intelligent orchestration and smart automation with cognitive functions

> **Automation versus Orchestration**—is for automating a single task such as launching a Web server, configuring a Web server, stopping a service. Orchestration, on the other hand, is concerned with automating multiple automated tasks together. Typically a process comprises multiple tasks and systems. The tasks inscribed in a process need to be executed in a sequence in order to be fruitful. That is, a process starts with an appropriate workflow representation and ends with the workflow execution. Thus, a process or workflow execution is simply termed as orchestration. As articulated above, in a Cloud environment, there are multiple jobs to be executed in a preferred fashion in order to complete business or operational processes. And the domain of orchestration has become the keystone for the survival and sustenance of the Cloud paradigm. In short, automation and orchestration are the top two ingredients for the Cloud idea to be a highly preferred mechanism for IT optimization and organization.
>
> Cloud orchestration is actually a more complex affair. Automation usually focuses on a single task, while orchestration deals with the end-to-end process, including management of all related services, taking care of high availability (HA), post-deployment, failure recovery, scaling, and more. Automation is usually discussed in the context of specific tasks, whereas orchestration refers to the automation of processes and workflows. Basically, orchestration *automates the automation*—specifically, the order that tasks take place across specific machines, especially where there are diverse dependencies.

Thus, the orchestration of processes (which are formally represented as workflows) is an essential part of Cloud computing. Without orchestration, many of the benefits and characteristics of Cloud computing cannot be achieved at the price point that Cloud services should be offered. Any failure to automate as many processes as possible results in higher personnel labor costs, slower time to deliver the new service to customers, and ultimately higher cost with less reliability.

9.3 Setting the Context

With Cloud adoption and adaptation is growing steadily, there came a number of Cloud services with different quality attributes and prices. Experts are of the opinion that policies are the key for efficiently and intelligently moderating the rising complexities of Cloud bloat. Thus, policy-based Cloud strategies were born. Organizations began enacting policies that determined the circumstances under which certain workloads (applications, databases, repositories, etc.) would be deployed in different environments such as public, private, and hybrid Clouds. Most of the policies were based on the value or risk associated with each workload. High-value/high-risk workloads might be required to run on a private Cloud, while customer-facing and Web-scale applications are put up at public Clouds. Inevitably, multi-cloud Cloud scenarios emerged as each workload is migrated to its best runtime environment.

For certain workloads, the hybrid Cloud strategy is insisted. The process/application/service orchestration across different and distributed Cloud environments started to gain preference and importance. There are integration services and tools for enabling public Cloud applications to connect and fetch highly secured data at private Clouds. Thus, enterprises started to embrace the hybrid Cloud concept in order to be beneficial for their customers, clients, and consumers. Workloads are made to interoperate across heterogeneous Cloud environments through API calls, message queues and brokers, enterprise service bus, etc. Production-grade applications are partitioned into a dynamic set of microservices, which are spread across many Cloud environments. Thus, Hybrid IT especially hybrid Cloud started to flourish. Big data and large-scale application processing mandated for availing the distributed computing model.

Hybrid Cloud management tools come handy in enabling the realization of hybrid Cloud setup and sustenance. Figure 9.1 shows some of the complexity involved in managing a true hybrid Cloud environment.

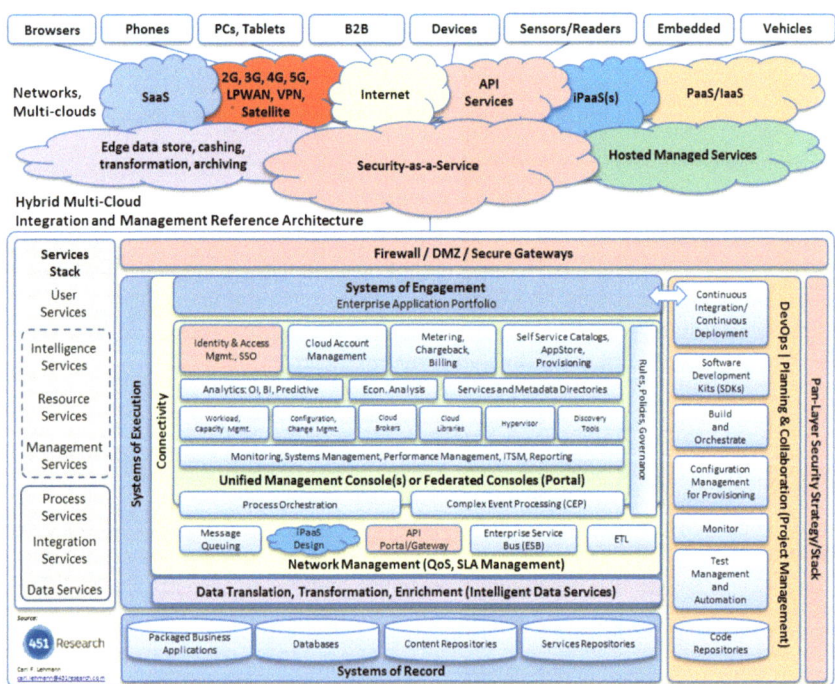

Fig. 9.1 Reference architecture for hybrid Clouds

9.4 The Emergence of Multi-cloud Environments

Businesses increasingly prefer the multi-cloud approach in order to be extremely safe in their operations, offerings, and outputs. There are other benefits of embracing the multi-cloud strategy. The market research and analyst groups say that three out of four companies today have deployed their software applications more than one Cloud. The enterprise IT teams have to have the required skills to build and manage multi-cloud environments with speed and security. The quality of service (QoS) attributes need to be ensured while monitoring, measuring, managing, and maintaining multi-cloud environments. There are powerful management platforms for managing uniform Cloud environments with all the astuteness, alacrity, and authenticity. But, for managing multiple and disparate Cloud environments, the conventional Cloud management platforms are found insufficient and obsolete. Thus, product vendors in the Cloud space have come out with multi-cloud management solutions and services.

A multi-cloud management solution enables automatic deployment and management of multi-cloud environments. At the same time, it provides an easy access for developers to rapidly and securely create applications. Multi-cloud management solutions typically provide an automatic provisioning capability and workflow management. They also accelerate application deployment and automate manual or scripted tasks to request, change, or deploy standardized Cloud services. They also facilitate the execution of these tasks across a range of Cloud platforms, often leveraging other automation tools like configuration management. In the Cloud arena, there are several automation tools for automating different tasks associated with Cloud enablement.

It is estimated that around 85 percent of business workloads are to run on Cloud environments by 2020. Thus, the Cloud adoption by worldwide corporates is on the fast track. Starting with a single Cloud, the business establishments and enterprises are tending toward multi-cloud environments. Business behemoths already have multiple tools to manage their own on-premise private and off-premise public Cloud environments. The piecemeal approach is common while embracing new technologies and tools, but this is not competent enough to give the desired results for enterprises. The story, in short, is that the automation has been the cornerstone for the abundant success of the Cloud paradigm. There are a bunch of automation tools empowering different aspects of the Cloud idea.

Figure 9.2 pictorially illustrates how a multi-cloud environment is being formed and operated. There are multiple public Clouds. Similarly, there are private Clouds and traditional IT environments. It is all about employing two or more public Clouds for running the IT portion of any business. Further on, the other brewing option is that private Clouds are integrated with public Clouds. There are Cloud connectors, adapters, brokers, and other middleware solutions in plenty in order to establish and sustain a kind of linkage between multiple and geographically distributed Cloud environments. Every Cloud exposes competent interfaces in order to enable other Cloud environments to connect and get benefited immensely.

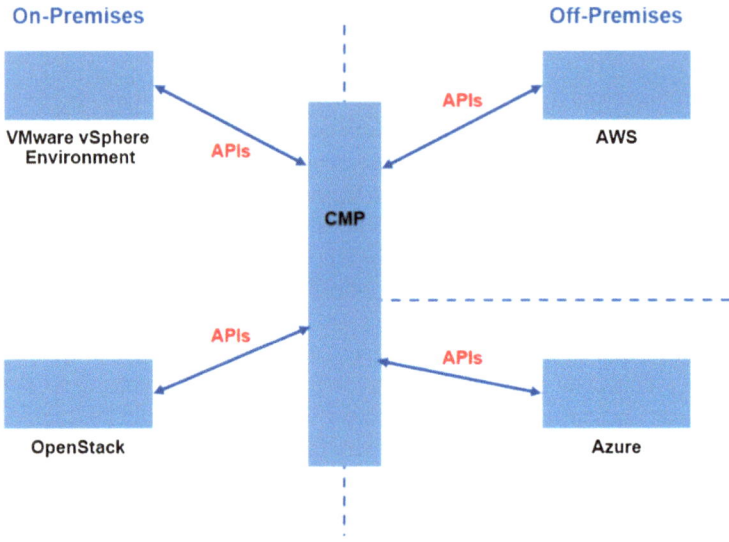

Fig. 9.2 Clustered orchestration

9.5   The Next-Gen DevOps Solutions for Multi-cloud Environment

There are several interesting and inspiring trends and transitions happening in Cloud computing. The concept of DevOps is flourishing. This is a promising and popular mechanism to build and deploy applications in multiple Cloud environments. That is, continuous integration, deployment and delivery of software applications across different and distributed Cloud environments are being speeded up by the powerful tools in the DevOps space. Organizations that are driving a new DevOps strategy need to account for the multi-cloud application deployment. We need DevOps tools that can swiftly and reliably deploy application code to private, public, and hybrid Clouds. In the multi-cloud era, there are several problems that need to be identified and solved.

- We have primarily cloud-enabled and native applications. Also, multiple Cloud environments are being leveraged by enterprises to host and run various software packages. The futuristic and flexible DevOps tools need to innately recognize and leverage the various advantages of cloud-native applications to bring forth the originally envisaged benefits of Cloud computing for businesses.
- The Cloud platforms and infrastructures are undergoing several innovative, transformative, and disruptive movements. Therefore DevOps tools need to dynamically adjust to those changes without human intervention.

Fig. 9.3 DevOps process for multi-cloud environments

- Finally, security and governance must be part of this process. Thus, logging, tagging, and other cloud governance concepts need to be considered in the tools, the applications, and the target Cloud platforms.

Thus, DevOps processes and tools need to be accordingly enhanced to contribute to multi-cloud deployment and delivery.

Platform-specific testing for multi-cloud deployment—In multi-cloud deployments, it is important to remember that we are taking the same code set, typically coupled with data, and marking it for a target platform at the point of staging. Next, the application runs through platform-specific testing as illustrated in Fig. 9.3. This tool/process checks the application for issues that it may have when using some of the native features of each Cloud platform. For example, provisioning is different from Cloud to Cloud, so this testing engine would look for provisioning issues. The engine would also look for other issues that would make the application not work on the target platform or, more likely, cause suboptimal performance.

A good system should automate the correction of issues where it makes sense, and if they cannot be corrected, they should be returned to the developer for manual correction. Once that is complete, the application needs to go through the platform-specific testing step again.

Monitoring and governance for multi-cloud deployment—Once all of the platform-specific test findings are resolved, the application moves to the next step "deploy to production." Within this automated task, the application is packaged up for deployment to each target Cloud platform. This means it is placed on a machine instance within a private or public Cloud and enters into a "continuous operations" process. This includes several components.

- Monitoring
- Management
- Resource Governance (CMPs)
- Service Governance/Service Catalogue
- Security (IAM)

The proper use of these components is vital to the success of multi-cloud DevOps automated solution. Once placed into production, the ability to effectively provide application and data services to the end users is really where the rubber meets the road.

Monitoring refers to the ability to monitor the application during execution. This process looks at performance and stability issues and includes setting thresholds for these subsystems. If the readings exceed these thresholds, the DevOps system is alerted.

Management refers to the ability to manage the applications, or take action based on interpretation of the monitoring data. This means resource management, including using a CMP (Cloud management platform), and the overall management of all major application components and subsystems, including security and governance.

Resource Governance refers to the use of a CMP or other similar tools. The idea is to abstract those who manage the cloud-based applications on the target platforms by using a single console to manage applications and resources from multiple Clouds on a single Cloud. This allows setting user policies that span across all of the Clouds where the applications are deployed on. These policies should also work well with the application-level security and governance of each Cloud.

Service Governance refers to the ability to create policies around the use of APIs and services, and even the use of services between Clouds. This means that we can create common services in any Cloud and have those services leveraged by applications running on any Cloud. Those services, either infrastructure- or application-level services, are tracked using the *Service Catalogue*.

Security—In a multi-cloud model, we do not want to deploy and manage too many different security services because that increases the complexity and the cost of deploying applications. In Cloud environments, administrators typically are dealing with identity and access management, which has the ability to track all applications, resources, services, data, humans, etc., and define access and authentication policies and rules for each.

Thus, the hugely used DevOps techniques, tips, and tools are being modernized and enabled to facilitate multi-cloud application integration, deployment, and delivery.

Today, we have a number of Web-scale applications such as social and professional sites, e-commerce, e-auction, and e-business systems. They have been designed to be distributed across multiple Cloud environments. So if a problem crops up in one Cloud center, it does not hurt them badly. This is, naturally, the most recommended way to use Cloud services. There data and disaster recovery Cloud centers. Data loss is avoided through this mechanism if there is an outage. The goal of cloud-enabled business continuity is being achieved through the multiple Cloud strategy. Cloud applications generate a lot of data, which is carefully captured, cleansed, and crunched in order to extricate actionable insights in time. Thus, next-generation corporates prefer and proceed with the multi-cloud paradigm. That is, data stores are one or more Clouds, applications and their components are hosted and run in other Clouds, data analytics is enabled in a different Cloud, etc.

Organizations have since started looking for different means to avoid data loss and downtime and to better support different applications, not to mention resilient application support, customer management, and data analytics. This is where multi-cloud computing can help solve the challenges and which focuses provisioning, managing, and monitoring workload across many Clouds.

9.6   The Multi-cloud: The Opportunities and Possibilities

When the IaaS Cloud computing first picked up steam, the manual tasks of cobbling together things like CPU, memory, OS, storage, middleware solutions, network, and databases to support a multi-tier application were simply part of the long process. For many just getting started with the Cloud, flexibility and scalability benefits trumped ease of deployment and management. Not much thought really went into streamlining and speeding up the deployment and delivery processes. That is not the scenario now. We have enterprise-scale IaaS and PaaS Cloud environments across the globe. The application scale and complexity are also on the climb. Therefore, management of Cloud infrastructure to fulfill Cloud service users becomes a tremendous challenge for Cloud IT teams. This is precisely why the concept of Cloud orchestration has become a hot trend these days. The established product vendors built orchestration tools in order to empower Cloud IT, administrators and operators, in quickly provisioning and preparing appropriate Cloud infrastructure instances to install and run software applications. Cloud orchestration tools provide added visibility into Cloud resources and processes. Orchestration software combines all the possible Cloud resources and then provides a mechanism to link and automate the provisioning for various services your organization requires. The following advantages are being quoted in order to embrace Cloud orchestration and its distinct tools.

- **Achieve disaster resilience** with continuous service availability during Cloud center failures and disasters.
- **Anytime, Anywhere, Any network, Any device, Any application and content access** with low latency guarantees for mobile users, branch offices, and backbone Cloud centers.
- **Integrate and automate business processes** across the organization's vendor/partner/customer ecosystem.
- **Maintain data sovereignty and meet data privacy** requirements across multiple legal jurisdictions.
- **Provide operational flexibility** to run workloads wherever makes the most sense for financial, workload balancing, maintenance, or convenience reasons. Companies can deploy to public, private, and hybrid Clouds using a range of services.

- **Reduce the expenditure**—Competitive prices and services from different Cloud providers enable companies to achieve optimum cost expenditure.
- **Enhance the IT autonomy**—Companies avoid keeping all their IT workloads in one Cloud provider's basket.
- **Embark on Customization toward enhanced IT performance**—Customization leverages the best-of-breed capabilities from multiple Cloud vendors.
- **Hardware diversity**—Relying on multiple locations and multiple providers significantly reduces the chances of impacting QoS.

9.7 Multi-cloud Deployment Models

Cloud deployment models are steadily expanding. With hybrid and multi-cloud approaches for enabling full-fledged distributed computing are gaining a lot of momentum these days, there came a few new Cloud deployment scenarios in order to meet up the evolving business requirements. The other well-known options include keeping multiple Cloud centers in different states: active–passive and active–active. Today, organizations desire the sophisticated active–active approach that can keep costs, complexity, and management efforts to a minimum. The following is a description of the spectrum of multi-cloud deployment scenarios.

Multi-cloud Deployment Scenarios

- Cold Standby
- Warm Standby
- Hot Standby
- Hot Standby with Read Replicas
- Active–Active: Partitioned Data and Access
- Active–Active: Transactional Consistency
- Active–Active: Conflict Resolution

All workload and business requirements are not the same. It is therefore very paramount to find the suitable Cloud environment to run specific workloads to produce the best performance and the least cost. The other considerations include vendor lock-in, the network latency, etc.

9.8 Challenges of Managing Multi-cloud Environments

Having understood both the tactical and strategic benefits, worldwide organizations are keenly contemplating to embrace the multi-cloud approach. However, there are a few challenges coming in the way of adopting the powerful multi-cloud idea. Cloud environments are emboldened with several measures in order to exhibit the smartness and sagacity to put an end to data lock-in. But the issue at hand is that every

Cloud service and resource provider comes with different access interfaces. The core Cloud platforms are different. The processes to obtain and activate runtimes (bare metal servers, virtual machines, and containers) are varying. The ways and means of attaching storage with applications are also different. We have several business, technical, and user challenges as far as integrating and orchestrating several Clouds.

The Technical challenges

- **API**—No single model of integration or infrastructure automation can work, as each Cloud provider provides a different API to access different Cloud services.
- **Behavior**—There are many differences in how Clouds behave for common actions or under certain circumstances. For example, some Clouds automatically provision storage upon launch of a server or instance, while others do not.
- **Resource sizes and types**—Each Cloud provider offers different sizes and types of compute, storage, and network resources. Hence, the IT team must work carefully about provisioning with optimum resource size and type needed for their workloads.
- **Operating system images**—Each Cloud provider provides a unique set of operating system (OS) images. This makes it difficult to run the workload using the same image in other Clouds.
- **Hypervisors**—Each Cloud provider leverages different and sometimes proprietary, hypervisor options.
- **Application stacks**—Some Cloud providers provide a selection of common and pre-configured application stacks (such as LAMP or Java or .NET).
- **Add-on services and features**—Each Cloud provider offers extra add-on services and proprietary features beyond the common compute, network, and storage resources. These may include load balancing, application servers, analysis tools, or databases.
- **Security capabilities**—The access control capabilities vary across Cloud providers. This becomes more complex if different providers demand different password complexities or authentication measures.
- **Network Capabilities**—Each Cloud offers different ways to define subnets, security groups, and network gateways, increasing difficulty in network planning.

The Operational Challenges

- **Testing**—Deploying applications to multiple Clouds requires platform-specific testing, and this needs separate and several automated tests targeting multiple Cloud platforms.
- **Tool diversity**—DevOps tools have to keep pace with the rapid changes being made to the platforms.
- **Maintaining security and governance**—Companies have to need to go through the rules and regulations of each Cloud service provider to fully adhere to security compliance.
- **Managing applications and infrastructure configurations across multiple Cloud stacks**—This can be difficult since the Cloud platforms do not share a common API, which exposes different service definitions and billing models.

- **Technical support and expertise**—Extra administrative work and research are required to determine the best provider and whether its services are compatible.

The Business Challenges

- **Cloud brokers**—This is a software solution for choosing the appropriate Cloud service providers and having a Cloud broker is an additional cost (capital as well as operational) while using multiple Clouds.
- **Billing and Pricing**—Each Cloud provider offers different pricing models for services with different quality of service (QoS) attributes. The multiple billing and pricing factor is definitely a challenge for businesses for leveraging multiple Clouds. There has to be one single dashboard with all the Clouds' service charges.
- **Skill sets and training**—Different technologies and tools are being used by Cloud service providers. Therefore, the lack of education, experience, and expertise of different Clouds in the organization can lead to outages of workloads and increase cost/effort.
- **Planning and execution**—It can be difficult to choose the services that match a company's business needs, pricing, governance, and team's expertise.

9.9   How Multi-cloud Orchestrator Helps?

Cloud orchestration refers to the arrangement and coordination of automated tasks resulting in a consolidated process or workflow. Many IT operations organizations implement automation in an ad hoc and opportunistic fashion that yields islands of automation with low operational agility and high costs. Cloud orchestration offers a systematic approach that maximizes automation benefits of agility and reduces cost. Cloud Orchestration allows businesses to accelerate delivery of new innovations, applications, and hybrid infrastructure by orchestrating processes across domains, systems, and teams. IT also leverages a unified portal and cloud-inspired IT service model with full-stack automation and monitoring. This improves the customer experience and provides error-free delivery and continuous compliance.

Cloud orchestration is the end-to-end automation of the deployment of services in a Cloud environment. It is the automated arrangement, coordination, and management of complex server systems, network solutions, storage appliances and arrays, middleware, and services. It is used to manage Cloud infrastructures, which supply and assign required Cloud resources to the customer like the creation of VMs and containers, allocation of storage capacity, management of network resources, and granting access to Cloud software. By using the appropriate orchestration mechanisms, users can deploy and start using services on servers or on any Cloud platforms. There are three aspects to Cloud orchestration.

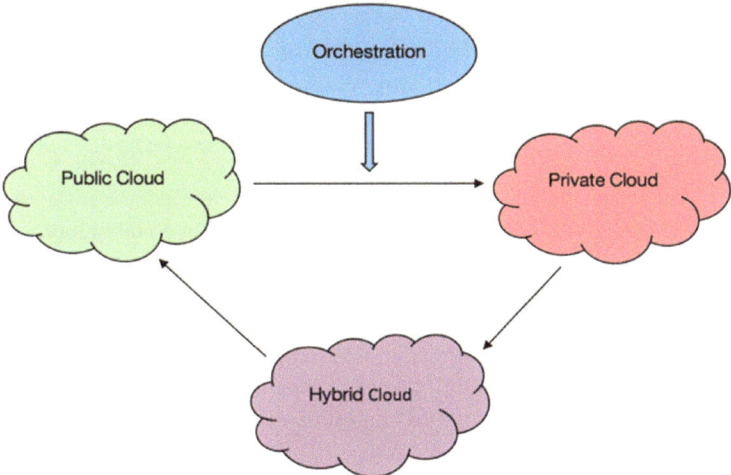

Fig. 9.4 Role of Cloud orchestration in forming multi-cloud environments

- **Resource orchestration**, where resources are identified and allocated
- **Workload orchestration**, where workloads are shared among the resources
- **Service orchestration**, where services are deployed on servers or Cloud environments.

Figure 9.4 illustrates how Cloud orchestration automates the services in all types of Clouds—public, private, and hybrid.

Regardless of the challenges enumerated above, multi-cloud environments are steadily growing with the ready availability of multi-cloud orchestration tools, which can prove to be a right fit to address above-discussed challenges. These orchestration tools have the innate capability to make multiple Cloud providers look like a single provider. They can ensure the configuration of all Cloud dependencies within one configuration model. These tools enable companies to automatically deploy and manage multi-cloud environments. Some of the big players in this segment are RightScale, Cloudify, VMware vRealize Orchestrator, and IBM Cloud orchestrator, which provide a standard set of interfaces and capabilities across a multi-cloud environment. The distinct capabilities of these multi-cloud management platforms are

- **Planning and Execution** of an application from design to transition to deployment.
- **Installation and configuration** of infrastructure packages and services in an automated way.
- **Provisioning** of the application environment.
- **Deployment** plan and execution.
- **Cost Management**—This capability suggests cost-effective Cloud services and a single dashboard track the cost associated with different Cloud services.

- **Monitoring** of entire application stack.
- **Security and Governance** as to who can view, create, execute environment-related activities.
- **Blueprint** Templates which can be easily reused to create a new environment.
- **Reporting**—These can give a consolidated report of instances that are consumed by the organization across multiple Clouds.

Multi-cloud orchestrator tools help address the challenges to configure, provision, and deploy several Cloud environments, as well as integrate service management from a single, self-service interface. Additional competencies will be embedded in the orchestration software solutions in order to cater to the advanced needs of multi-cloud setup, automation, management, security, synchronization, and operations. Workflow execution capability will be a critical requirement, and there is still a scope for insightful, integrated, multifaceted, and state-of-the-art multi-cloud orchestration tools to build more secure, easy-to-set-up standardized workflows across different Cloud providers to moderate the challenges which multi-cloud computing era offers.

9.10 Multi-cloud Brokerage, Management, and Orchestration Solutions

We have talked about Cloud brokerage solutions and services in another chapter in detail. For the emerging multi-cloud era, the need for pioneering Cloud brokers is going up. Besides brokers, we need a variety of middleware solutions in the form of message queues and brokers in order to provide data integration across different Clouds. Similarly, we need Cloud integrators, connectors, drivers, adapters, etc., in order to fulfill the needs of application and process integration. Cloud services spread across Cloud environments need to be integrated on demand in order to produce a composite, business-aware, process-centric, enterprise-class, and production-grade Cloud applications.

9.11 The Leading Cloud Orchestration Tools

The Chef is a powerful automation platform that transforms complex infrastructures into the code, bringing both servers and services to life. Chef automates configuration, deployment, and management of applications across the network. Chef uses **cookbooks** to determine how each node should be configured. Cookbooks consist of multiple **recipes**; a recipe is an automation script for a particular service that is written using the Ruby language. The **Chef client** is an agent that runs on a node and performs the actual tasks that configure it. The Chef can manage anything that can run the Chef client, like physical machines, virtual machines, containers, or cloud-based instances. The **Chef server** is the central repository for all configuration data.

Both the Chef client and Chef server communicate in a secure manner using a combination of public and private keys, which ensure that the Chef server responds only to requests made by the Chef client. There is also an option to install stand-alone client called **Chef-solo**.

Puppet requires the installation of a master server and client agent in target nodes and includes an option for a stand-alone client, which is equivalent to Chef-solo. We can download and install deployment modules using Puppet commands. Like Chef, Puppet comes with a paid Enterprise edition that provides additional features like reporting and orchestration/push deployment. However, while both Chef and Puppet perform the same basic functions, they differ in their approach. The Chef seems to be significantly more integrated and monolithic, whereas Puppet consists of multiple services. This can make Chef somewhat easier to get up and run and manage. Both have their pros and cons, so we need to evaluate which one makes the most sense for our operation teams and infrastructure development workflow.

OpenStack is a free and open-source Cloud computing software platform that is primarily used as an infrastructure-as-a-service (IaaS) solution. It consists of a series of interrelated projects that control pools of processing, storage, and networking resources throughout a Cloud center. Users manage all of them through a Web-based dashboard, command-line tools, or a RESTful API. Figure 9.5 conveys the key components of the OpenStack platform.

The main components of OpenStack include Nova (compute), Cinder (block storage), Glance (image library), Swift (object storage), Neutron (network), Keystone (identity), and Heat (orchestration tool).

Heat is a pattern-based orchestration mechanism from OpenStack and provides a template-based orchestration for describing a Cloud application by executing appropriate OpenStack API calls that generate running Cloud applications. The software integrates other core components of OpenStack into a one-file template system. The templates allow for the creation of most OpenStack resource types (such as instances,

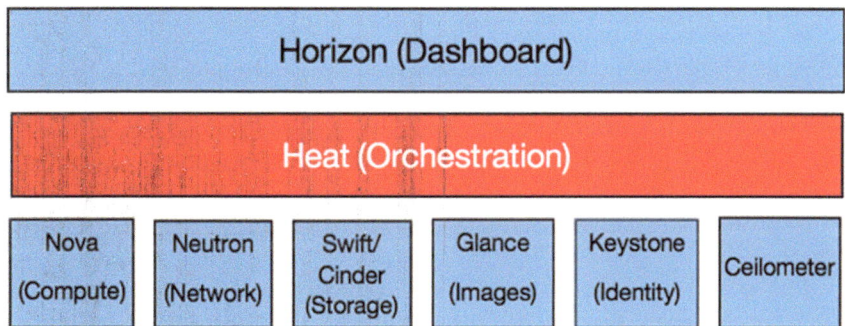

Fig. 9.5 OpenStack components

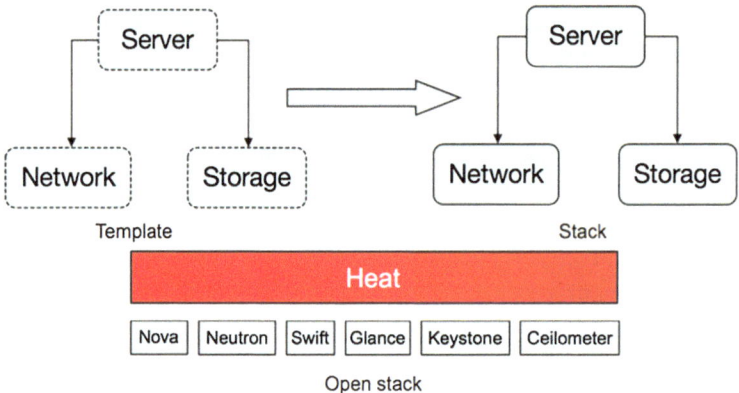

Fig. 9.6 How heat works

floating IPs, volumes, security groups, and users) as well as more advanced functionality such as for instance high availability, instance auto-scaling, and nested stacks.

We can use Heat instead of writing a script that manages all of the software in OpenStack (like setting up the servers, adding volumes, managing networks, etc.). To do this, we create a Heat template that specifies what infrastructure we need. If any further changes to the existing service are required, later on, we just modify the Heat template and the Heat engine will make the necessary changes when we rerun the template. When it is finished, we can clean up and release the resources, and they can be used by anyone else who needs them.

As you can see in Fig. 9.6, passing a Heat template through the Heat engine creates a stack of resources that are specified in the Heat template. Heat sits on top of all the other OpenStack services in the orchestration layer and talks to the IPs of all the other components. A Heat template generates a **stack**, which is the fundamental unit of currency in Heat. We write a Heat template with a number of resources in it, and each resource is an object in OpenStack with an object ID. Heat creates those objects and keeps track of their IDs.

We can also use a **nested stack**, which is a resource in a Heat stack that points to another Heat stack. This is like a tree of stacks, where the objects are related and their relationships can be inferred from the Heat template. This nested feature enables independent teams to work on Heat stacks and later merge them together. The main component of Heat is the Heat engine, which provides the orchestration functionality.

Heat Orchestration Templates (HOT) are native to Heat and are expressed in YAML.

Juju is an open-source automatic service orchestration management tool and enables us to deploy, manage, and scale software and services on a wide variety of Cloud services and servers. Juju can significantly reduce the workload for deploying and configuring a product's services.

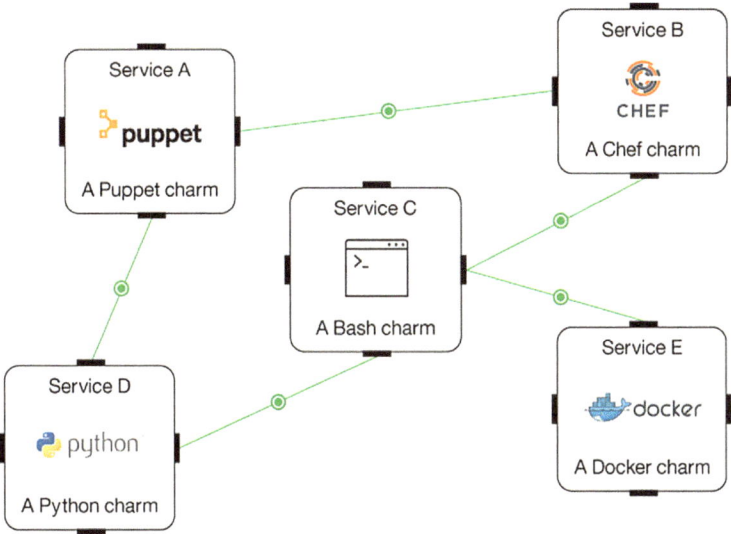

Fig. 9.7 Services deployed using Juju

Juju is the fastest way to model and deploy applications or solutions on all major public Clouds and containers. It helps to reduce deployment time from days to minutes. Juju works (Fig. 9.7) with existing configuration management tools and can scale workloads up or down very easily. Juju includes providers for all major public Clouds, such as Amazon Web Services, Azure, OpenStack, and LXC containers. It also offers a quick and easy environment for testing deployments on a local machine. Users can deploy entire Cloud environments in seconds using bundles, which can save a lot of time and effort.

Juju utilizes **charms**, which are open-source tools that simplify specific deployment and management tasks. A charm is a set of scripts that can be written in any language that fire off hooks based on certain things. After a service is deployed, Juju can define relationships between services and expose some services to the outside world. Charms give Juju its power. They encapsulate application configurations and define how services are deployed, how they connect to other services, and how they are scaled. Charms define how services integrate, and how their service units react to events in the distributed environment, as orchestrated by Juju.

A Juju charm usually includes all of the intelligence needed to scale a service horizontally by adding machines to the cluster, preserving relationships with all of the services that depend on that service. This enables to build out (and scale up and down) the service we want, especially in the Cloud. Juju provides both a command-line interface and an intuitive Web application for designing, building, configuring, deploying, and managing Cloud infrastructure.

Docker is an open and containerization-enabling platform for developing, shipping, running, and delivering applications quickly. Containerization is an OS-level virtualization. The software portability is being achieved through this newly introduced abstraction. The impact on the software industry has been tremendous. It improved the speed of software delivery. It did away with manual handovers between development and operational teams. It made the deployment process 100% reproducible. Once an application is containerized, then it can run anywhere without any twists and tweaks. We give some reasons (https://articles.xebia.com/the-effect-of-containers-on-the-software-delivery-process), why container technology is a fundamental and foundational building block for establishing and ensuring a multi-cloud strategy.

Accelerated Software Installation—In the olden days, we need to manually install the software, configure the operating system, etc., in order to give the distinct capabilities of the software to its users. Today, we can create a Docker image for any application, database, and middleware readily and from there, with a single command, the image gets transitioned into a container that can run in any environment.

Security through Isolation—Through the various kernel-level features, containers are separated from other containers as well as from the underlying Docker host. Application inside the container cannot see other containerized applications, data, and network details. It is possible to restrict the amount of CPU, memory, and disk space they use. Besides this isolation, there are other approaches to supply unbreakable and impenetrable containers. The Docker Hub allows only verified and validated Docker images for applications.

Run Anywhere—Creating highly portable software has been the crucial challenge for the IT experts. Several concepts and abstractions were tried, but they failed. For the first time in the IT history, the arrival of the Docker-enabled containerization paradigm has led to the realization of portable software, which can run on any environment (local or remote, small or big, etc.)

Facilitating the DevOps features—Once an application is containerized, then the application deployment is simpler and faster. The containerization movement guarantees 100% reproducibility. The age-old frictions between development and operation teams get eliminated through containers.

Rock-solid version control—Once an application gets containerized, it is easy to version and sign the application. When the application is running on a machine, Docker will tell which image version it is. This obviates the need for maintaining a configuration management database. Just querying the runtime gives an accurate inventory.

Real-time Horizontal Scalability—Containers are very lightweight, and hence, provisioning containers are very fast (in the range of a few seconds). Therefore, accomplishing the scale-out (horizontal scalability) task in time is guaranteed in the containerization age.

Delivering high availability is a breeze—Starting containers in the same machine or in adjacent machines is quick. Also, many containers can be provisioned concurrently. All these clearly point out that the application availability is very high.

Disaster recovery built-in—Container images form the basic building block for immutable infrastructures. All the images are curated and stored in a repository. In a disaster situation, reproducing application and data containers can be accelerated and automated.

The summary of container benefits

- **Agile application creation and deployment**—Increased ease and efficiency of container image creation compared to VM image use is achieved.
- **Continuous development, integration, and deployment**—This provides for reliable and frequent container image build and deployment with quick and easy rollbacks due to image immutability.
- **Dev and Ops separation of concerns**—This capability creates application container images at build/release time rather than deployment time, thereby decoupling applications from infrastructure.
- **Application-centric management**—Containers raise the level of abstraction from running an OS on virtual hardware to run an application on an OS using logical resources.
- **Loosely coupled, distributed, elastic, and liberated microservices**—Applications are broken into smaller, independent pieces and can be deployed and managed dynamically—not a fat monolithic stack running on one big single-purpose machine.
- **Resource isolation**—This guarantees predictable application performance.
- **Resource utilization**—This ensures higher efficiency and density.

The containerization technology has brought in a series of paradigm shifts for the field of software engineering, and the IT operations see a lot of decisive and deeper automation, augmentation, and acceleration.

9.12 Container Management Tasks and Tools

The fast proliferation of containers in our Cloud environments has brought in the additional operational complexity of Cloud operational teams. Also, the density of containers in physical machines also contributed to the heightened complexity. The lifecycle management of containers, therefore, becomes a tedious affair. We need solid automation here. There are a few container management solutions on the market. This section is to throw some light on that aspect. There are container operation monitoring and measurement tools. Monitoring solutions that are host-centric, rather than role-centric, quickly become unusable in the containerization era. There are orchestration tools that enable clustering and scheduling containers. The container management tools handle the administration tasks for containerized applications and application components. The various features and functionalities of containerization management tools are

- **Provisioning**—These tools can provision or schedule containers within a container cluster and launch them. Ideally, they spin up containers in the best VM or bare metal (BM) servers depending on the requirements, such as resources and geographical location.
- **Configuration Scripting**—Scripting permits loading the specific application configurations into containers in the same way we do by using Juju Charms, Puppet Manifests, or Chef Recipes. Typically, these are written in YAML or JSON.
- **Monitoring**—The container management tools track and monitor containers' health and hosts in the cluster. If they do their job, the monitoring tool spins up a new instance when a container crashes. If a server fails, the tool restarts the containers on another host. The tools also run system health checks and report irregularities with the containers, the VMs they live in, and the servers on which they run. The container performance and operational status are being minutely monitored and measured. If there is any threshold break-in, any state change, or any noteworthy event, then the concerned modules are being given the sufficient details to take appropriate actions immediately with all the clarity and confidence.
- **Rolling Upgrades and Rollback**—When we deploy a new version of the container, or the applications running within the containers, the container management tools automatically update them across the container cluster. If something goes wrong, they enable in rolling back to known good configurations.
- **Service Discovery**—Containers use service discovery to find their appropriate services in an automated manner. It is all about dynamically discovering other relevant services and processes to complete the business task initiated. For example, these tools help front-end applications, say WordPress, to dynamically discover its corresponding backend service such as a SQL database instance via DNS or a proxy.
- **Container policy management**—Policies are becoming an important ingredient for activating and accelerating container usages in multiple contexts. The policy establishment and enforcement are important to bring in the much-desired automation in the container era. Policies prescribe the tools how, when, and where to launch containers. There are configuration pointers such as "how many cores ought to be assigned to each container," and these are getting automated through well-intended and defined policies, which turn out to be a vital factor to speed up and simplify container management, security, orchestration, and governance.

There are three leading container management tools, and each of them is being explained below.

Docker swarm—As discussed above, containers have recently become a very popular delivery mechanism for software applications. This is partly due to the surging popularity of the microservices architecture (MDA), which encourages and enables delivering applications as a set of loosely and lightly coupled, horizontally scalable, independently deployable, easily manageable, publicly discoverable, and API-enabled services. A microservice is an ideal payload for containers to contribute as the most optimal runtime resource. Working with containers on a single Docker host for development purposes is a relatively straightforward experience. However, we need additional capabilities when we want to deploy our application into a production environment? We need resilience, the ability to scale our services, and to update them "in flight," etc. This is literally difficult to achieve on a single Docker host and has given rise to the notion of container orchestration.

In order to provide a suitable environment for running containers at scale, we require an orchestration platform, or cluster, to host the containers. Swarm, just like the other peer orchestration tools, requires a cluster of compute nodes in order to function. In the case of Swarm, these nodes all run the Docker Engine and cooperate together as a tightly coupled unit, for deploying containerized workloads. The nodes in the cluster will be delegated a role—a manager or a worker. Manager nodes take part in the management of the cluster, maintaining its state and scheduling container workloads, while the workers are recipients of the container workloads. Unless directed otherwise, a manager will also perform the worker role and will host container workloads as well as perform management functions.

Docker Swarm is the Docker platform's stand-alone orchestrator. Swarm gives users control over the full application lifecycle, not just container clustering and scheduling. Docker Swarm is an older stand-alone product, which used to be used to cluster multiple Docker hosts. Swarm mode is Docker's built-in cluster manager. With Docker 1.12, swarm mode is part of the Docker Engine. Scaling, container discovery, and security are all included with minimal setup.

Swarm mode includes the support for rolling updates, transport layer security encryption between nodes, load balancing, and easy service abstraction. In short, Docker swarm mode spreads a container load across multiple hosts, and it permits setting up a swarm (that is, a cluster), on multiple host platforms. It also requires having a few things on the host platform, including integration (this is because containers running on different nodes have to communicate with each other) and segregation (this helps to isolate and secure different container workloads).

Kubernetes is an open-source system for automating deployment, scaling, and management of containerized applications. It groups containers that make up an application into logical units for easy management and discovery. Kubernetes offers a high degree of interoperability, as well as self-healing, automated rollouts and rollbacks, and storage orchestration. Kubernetes excels at automatically fixing problems. This is good at it that containers can crash and be restarted so fast we do not notice our containers are crashing. Some of the self-declared features of Kubernetes are:

- **Automatic bin-packing**—With that, we can specify how much CPU or RAM each container needs. Also, we can add a specified limit.
- **Horizontal scaling**—We can scale our application with a simple command or automatically based on CPU usage.
- **Self-healing**—Restarts the containers that fail, replaces, and reschedules containers when nodes die.

- **Service discovery and load balancing**—Kubernetes gives containers their own IP addresses and a single DNS name for a set of containers and can load-balance across them.
- **Automated rollouts and rollbacks**—With this feature, Kubernetes does progressively roll out changes and it ensures it does not kill all our instances at the same time.
- **Storage orchestration**—Automatically mount the storage system of our choice, whether from local storage, a public Cloud provider such as GCP or AWS, or a network storage system such as NFS, iSCSI, Gluster, Ceph, Cinder, or Flocker.
- **Batch execution**—Kubernetes can manage our batch and CI workloads using jobs.

Why do you need Kubernetes?—Real production applications span multiple containers. Those containers must be deployed across multiple server hosts. Kubernetes gives the orchestration and management capabilities required to deploy containers, at scale, for these workloads. Kubernetes orchestration allows building application services that span multiple containers, schedule those containers across a cluster, scale those containers, and manage the health of those containers over time.

Kubernetes also needs to integrate with networking, storage, security, telemetry, and other services to provide a comprehensive container infrastructure.

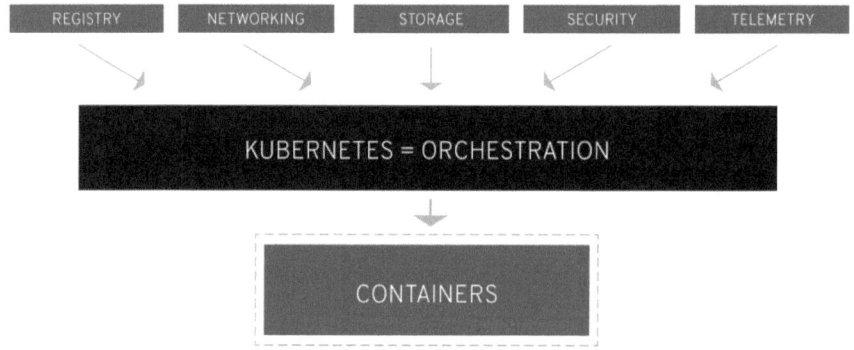

Kubernetes fixes a lot of common problems with container proliferation—sorting containers together into a "pod." Pods add a layer of abstraction to grouped containers, which helps scheduling workloads and provides necessary services (like networking and storage) to those containers. Other parts of Kubernetes help load-balance across these pods and ensure that we have the right number of containers running to support our workloads.

What can you do with Kubernetes?—The primary advantage of using Kubernetes in our environment is that it gives the ability to schedule and run containers on clusters of physical or virtual machines. More broadly, it helps to have a competent container-based infrastructure in production environments. And because Kubernetes is all about the automation of operational tasks, we can do many of the same things that other application platforms or management systems let us do. With Kubernetes, it is easy to

- Orchestrate containers across multiple hosts.
- Make better use of hardware to maximize resources needed to run our enterprise applications.
- Control and automate application deployments and updates.
- Mount and add storage to run stateful applications.
- Scale containerized applications and their resources on the fly.
- Declaratively manage services, which guarantees the deployed applications are always running how we deployed them.
- Health-check and self-heal applications with auto-placement, auto-restart, auto-replication, and auto-scaling.

The Key Terms—Let us break down some of the common terms to understand Kubernetes better.

1. **Master**—The machine that controls Kubernetes nodes. This is where all task assignments originate.
2. **Node**—These machines perform the requested, assigned tasks. The Kubernetes master controls them.
3. **Pod**—A group of one or more containers deployed to a single node. All containers in a pod share an IP address, IPC, hostname, and other resources. Pods abstract network and storage away from the underlying container. This lets moving containers around the cluster more easily.
4. **Replication controller**—This controls how many identical copies of a pod should be running somewhere on the cluster.
5. **Service**—This decouples work definitions from the pods. Kubernetes service proxies automatically get service requests to the right pod—no matter where it moves to in the cluster or even if it has been replaced.
6. **Kubelet**—This service runs on nodes and reads the container manifests and ensures the defined containers are started and running.
7. **Kubectl**—This is the command-line configuration tool for Kubernetes.

A look at how Kubernetes fits into our infrastructure.

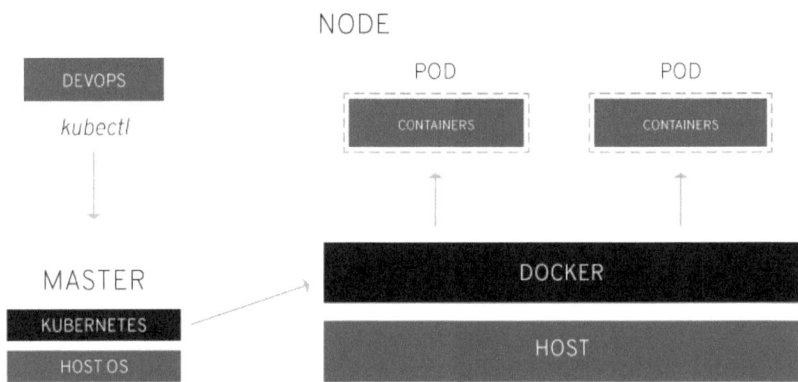

Kubernetes runs on top of an operating system and interacts with pods of containers running on the nodes. The Kubernetes master takes the commands from an administrator (or DevOps team) and relays those instructions to the subservient nodes. This handoff works with a multitude of services to automatically decide which node is best suited for the task. It then allocates resources and assigns the pods in that node to fulfill the requested work.

9.13 Mesosphere Marathon

Marathon is a container orchestration platform for Mesosphere's DC/OS and Apache Mesos. DC/OS is a distributed operating system based on the Mesos distributed systems kernel. Mesos, in turn, is an open-source cluster management system. Marathon via its partner program, Chronos, a fault-tolerant job scheduler provides management integration between our existing stateful applications and container-based stateless applications. Marathon boasts many features, including high availability, service discovery, and load balancing. If we run it on DC/OS, our applications also get virtual IP routing. However, Marathon can run only on a software stack with Mesos. In addition, certain features (such as authentication) are only available with Marathon on top of DC/OS.

Features

- **High Availability**—Marathon runs as an active/passive cluster with leader election for 100% uptime.
- **Multiple container runtimes**—Marathon has first-class support for both Mesos containers (using cgroups) and Docker.
- **Stateful applications**—Marathon can bind persistent storage volumes to your application. You can run databases like MySQL and Postgres and have storage accounted for by Mesos.
- **Constraints**—Only one instance of an application per rack, node, etc.
- **Service Discovery and Load Balancing**—Several methods available.
- **Health Checks**—Evaluate application's health using HTTP or TCP checks.
- **Event Subscription**—Supply an HTTP endpoint to receive notifications—for example to integrate with an external load balancer.
- **Metrics**—Query them at/metrics in JSON format or push them to systems like graphite, statsd, and Datadog.
- Complete REST API for easy integration and scriptability.

DC/OS features

Running on DC/OS, Marathon gains the following additional features
- **Virtual IP routing**—Marathon allocates a dedicated, virtual address to our application. The application is now reachable anywhere in the cluster, wherever it might be scheduled. Load balancing and rerouting around failures are done automatically.
- **Authorization (DC/OS Enterprise Edition only)**—True multi-tenancy with each user or group having access to their own applications and groups.

In summary, compared with previous technologies designed to improve operational and developmental efficiency, containers really do deliver the goods through better resource utilization, easier configuration, faster deployment, and more flexible development processes.

However, the real benefit of containerization is the realization of multi-container applications. Therefore, a container orchestration platform is required to deploy and manage even a moderate amount of containers in production. A modern application using a microservices architecture might consist of dozens or even hundreds of containers spread across dozens of physical nodes and interdependent containerized services. For combining multiple components with a continuous integration and delivery system, a cluster has to spin up and then kill millions of containers per day in order to test code. The role and responsibility of container orchestration and cluster management tools are on the climb for the ensuring era of containers and microservices.

9.14 Cloud Orchestration Solutions

1. **Micro Focus Cloud Orchestration solutions** (https://www.microfocus.com/) offer greater flexibility and simplified operations to securely create, deploy, and operate applications and services across hybrid Clouds and increase the speed of delivery. Micro Focus offers a variety of Cloud orchestration solutions including:

   - **Cloud services**—Cloud management software that makes it easy for our business to benefit from secure, compliant Cloud services
   - **Continuous deployment**—Solution that provides automation and releases management of complex applications across application lifecycle
   - **DevOps**—Solutions that unify development and operations to accelerate innovation and meet market demands
   - **Enterprise architecture**—Solution that helps identify waste and redundancies and drive transformation
   - **API management**—Software that manages the lifecycle of APIs, applications, and integrations within heterogeneous environments and SOA

2. **The RightScale Multi-cloud Platform**—This helps to mix and match public Clouds, private Clouds, and virtualized environments to meet any Cloud portfolio strategy. In addition to Clouds, this platform supports a portfolio of hypervisors—KVM, Xen, and vSphere—as well as operating systems—CentOS, RHEL, SUSE, Ubuntu, and Windows. A portfolio approach gives any enterprise the ability to future-proof the drawn-up Cloud strategy, optimize cost and performance, access a global footprint with best-of-breed capabilities, and gain financial flexibility and negotiating leverage.

3. **Cloudify** is an open-source Cloud orchestration platform, designed to automate the deployment, configuration and remediation of application and network services across hybrid Cloud and stack environments. Cloudify uses a declarative approach based on the Topology and Orchestration Specification for Cloud Applications (TOSCA) specification, in which users focus on defining the desired state of the application through simple and readable terms, and Cloudify takes care of reaching the desired state all while continuously monitoring the application to ensure that it maintains the desired SLAs in the case of failure or capacity shortage.

   The Cloudify pure-play orchestration platform provides a generic automation engine that spans the diversity of tools used in production environments from the applications through the networking services, databases, and infrastructures. Through the role-based access control and fine-grained multi-tenancy, developers can have access to their applications, while IT remains in control of the resources and data.

4. **IBM Cloud Orchestrator**—Componentized applications present challenges for operations lifecycle management, particularly with deployment and redeployment. This only gets more challenging when you move beyond a single Cloud. Multi-cloud projects, including hybrid and public Clouds from multiple providers, compound these difficulties because they use different hosting models. Automating deployment through DevOps tools can ease complications but is predominately designed for data center usage and lacks the ability to deal with the elasticity and portability of Cloud. Additionally, DevOps tools are not aimed at end-to-end, full-scale, operational automation; most are deployment-centric, and the Cloud needs more than that. That is where IBM Cloud Orchestrator, a Cloud management platform for operations automation, comes in.

IBM Cloud Orchestrator reflects the need for more complex application lifecycle management to deal with complicated IT and business frameworks. The Cloud management platform organizes and manages applications to support business goals, not just deployment rules. IBM Cloud Orchestrator puts three elements of Cloud deployment into templates for order and control: infrastructure services, application platforms, and governance. The graphical interface enables users to define the control structures for each template and import third-party elements for them. All of the elements are integrated through IBM's Business Process Manager (BPM), which ties back to the root business activities.

The applications, infrastructure, and platform descriptions are highly abstract patterns, which means users can define a deployment in general terms and then describe how that general approach applies to any Cloud or private IT platform. Patterns, which are various steps melded together to create a predefined form, can also reference DevOps tools already in use. This way, the administrator can connect islands of DevOps deployment with end-to-end orchestration. You can use IBM Cloud Orchestrator to harmonize differences among orchestration tools the Cloud provider offers, as well as the deployment differences between containers and VMs.

IBM's Cloud management platform is event-driven, which makes it well-suited to control multi-cloud environments—in which conditions in all the Clouds and components hosted there are completely asynchronous. Events trigger operations defined by either the users or third-party suppliers, and these operations are analogous to lifecycle processes. With IBM Cloud Orchestrator, multi-cloud users can import, deploy, and export Topology and Orchestration Specification for Cloud Applications (TOSCA) service templates as patterns for platform and infrastructure elements. Because TOSCA acceptance is growing, it is a critical resource to incorporate Cloud descriptions from multiple providers. TOSCA models include three plans: structural, build, and management. Patterns native to the Cloud management platform take this general approach and seem to draw strongly on TOSCA lessons.

The first step to use IBM's Cloud management platform is to define the application's operations lifecycle as a set of business processes with BPM. This outlines the abstract set of steps to complete for deployment and the events that could arise during the operation, such as failure or scaling. The IBM Cloud Orchestrator console uses simple drag-and-drop steps to simplify this process.

Next, define patterns for each application and its hosting environment. Patterns can describe individual deployments and cluster, pod, or group deployments; users can describe a different pattern for each Cloud in the multi-cloud environment. Remember to define the structure—the workflow-linked map of components—as well as the management events, rules, and the process descriptions associated with each event, including the deployment requests. If all of this is done properly, IBM Cloud Orchestrator will manage the entire application lifecycle automatically. It can balance work among multiple Clouds, shift between public Cloud and data center, back up one facility with another, and so forth. In short, IBM's Cloud management platform organizes an environment that deals with multiple Clouds.

- **Application-aware monitoring across SDDC and multiple Clouds**—This infrastructure software solution centralizes IT operations management of SDDC and multi-cloud environments, accelerates time to value and troubleshoot smarter with native integrations, and ensures unified visibility from applications to infrastructure health and actionable insights combining metrics and logs.
- **Unified Performance Management**—This automation solution gets a unified IT operations view into applications and infrastructure health with an easy-to-use, highly scalable, and extensible platform. It can visualize key performance indicators and infrastructure component dependencies. It can get actionable out-of-the-box persona-based dashboards that explain underlying problems and recommend corrective actions. Further on, it troubleshoots quickly with an easy and intuitive UI. It also enables proactive remediation of performance problems through predictive analytics and smart alerts besides monitoring applications and operating systems in one place. Customizable dashboards, reports, and views enable role-based access and enable better collaboration across infrastructure, operations, and applications teams.
- **360 Degree Troubleshooting**—This product troubleshoots smarter with 360-degree troubleshooting using metrics and logs side-by-side and in context. The seamless integration of vRealize Operations and vRealize Log Insight brings structured data (such as metrics and key performance indicators) and unstructured data (such as log files) together, for faster root-cause analysis. It saves time and improves return on investment by using a central log management solution to analyze data across the IT environment, including virtual, physical, and Cloud environments.
- **Native SDDC Integrations**—This platform operationalizes and scales VMware SDDC components such as vCenter, vSAN, and VMware Cloud Foundation, with native integrations. Native vSAN management provides vSAN-specific capacity monitoring, including capacity and time remaining, deduplication and compression savings and reclamation opportunities. It enables centralized management of multi-site and stretched clusters with advanced troubleshooting, proactive alerting, and visibility from virtual machines to disk.

- **Open and Extensible Platform**—This platform solution manages large and complex heterogeneous and hybrid environments with an open and extensible architecture with scalability and resilience to support highly complex environments. It deploys domain-specific Management Packs from VMware and third-party hardware and application vendors.

- **Application-Aware Infrastructure Management**—This gains insight into application-to-infrastructure dependencies through a centralized operations view. It also visualizes infrastructure components dependencies for applications, simplifying change impact analysis and troubleshooting. In addition, it can assess and analyze dependencies and uncover overlooked relationships between virtual machines and critical connections that may be missing from your disaster recovery plan.

- **Automated and proactive workloads management**—This simplifies and streamlines IT operations with fully automated management of infrastructure and applications performance, while retaining full control. Further on, it automatically balance workloads, avoid contention, and enable proactive detection and automatic remediation of issues and anomalies before end users are impacted.

- **Automated Workload Balancing**—This automatically and continuously moves and balances workloads across hosts and clusters based on business requirements. It controls at the level of automation, what automated actions are taken and when these occur. It selects business imperatives, such as optimizing for cost, performance, or utilization and then automates and schedules workload balancing, or even continues to perform manual rebalancing.

- **Predictive Distributed Resource Scheduling**—This helps to avoid contention by combining predictive analytics from vRealize Operations with VMware Distributed Resource Scheduler (DRS), to calculate future contention and proactively move workloads to avoid the issue. This also uses predictive analytics to analyze hourly, daily, and monthly patterns for every metric associated with an object, predict future demand, and proactively prepare for increased demand by triggering move actions by DRS.

- **Predictive Analytics and Remediation**—This enables proactive remediation of performance problems through predictive analytics and smart alerts, which innately correlate multiple symptoms into meaningful warnings and notifications. Also it supplies simple actionable explanations of underlying problems and recommended corrective actions. Remediation alerts and issues are issued well before they impact end users. This accomplishes everything with just one click and comprises scores of fully automated actions.

Thus, multi-cloud management and orchestration solutions are indispensable for enterprises to get benefited immensely out of multi-cloud projects.

9.15   The Security Aspects of Multi-cloud Environments

Cloud computing refers to the method of computing in which an interconnected network of remote servers is utilized for the execution of the operations such as storage, management, and processing of information. The business units in the current era are making use of multiple Cloud computing services and techniques in an integrated architecture. There are various deployment and delivery models of the Cloud which are amalgamated as one unit for the execution of business processes and activities. However, with the expansion of such practices, there are some security issues that have been observed. The security issues and occurrences are primarily associated with network-based security risks, availability, confidentiality threats, and integrity risks. Events such as Denial of Service (DoS) attacks, malware attacks, message/media alteration attacks, spoofing and phishing attacks, man-in-the-middle attacks, and eavesdropping attacks are common in the multi-cloud environment. Organizations are required to follow certain steps toward security to make sure that the security risks and occurrences are prevented, detected, and controlled. The following security measures and steps shall be included in for achieving a secure multi-cloud environment (https://www.fingent.com/blog/how-secure-is-your-business-in-a-multicloud-environment).

- **Prioritization of Visibility**—The business organizations in the multi-cloud environment must ensure that they have completed visibility across all the Cloud instances. Behavior-based monitoring shall be adopted for enhancing the visibility. Objectionable modifications and malevolent activities will also be highlighted with this process.
- **Adherence to the Best Practices**—In the case of the multi-cloud environment, there are various systems, devices, and networks that are involved. Each of these entities has a set of guiding principles and standards. The Cloud security team must analyze and understand the best practices that are associated with each entity. For instance, in case of NoSQL databases present in the multi-cloud environment, it would be best to meet the compliance requirements, install advanced access control and authentication measures, and promote database security for the overall security of the Cloud.
- **Flexible and Secure Governance**—Governance is a critical element in any of the organizations. It is possible to establish trust and security across the organization only with the aid of well-governed systems. In association with the multi-cloud environment, the processes such as identity management, scheduling activities, and resource allocation must be securely governed.
- **Encryption of the Data at Rest**—It is often witnessed that the business organizations enforce and implement the encryption of the information that is in-transit. However, the encryption of the information at rest is often not paid due attention. Such loopholes in security provide the attackers with an opportunity to get hold of the information at rest and misuse the same. It is, therefore, extremely necessary to encrypt the information at rest using advanced encryption algorithms.

- **Advanced Shared Responsibility Model**—Sharing of resources is one of the prime features of Cloud computing, which gets enhanced in the multi-cloud environment. There are overlapping responsibilities and ideas that are often observed which may lead to the occurrences of loopholes in the security. Every entity that is present in a multi-cloud environment must make sure that complete justice is done to the shared responsibility model of the Cloud. The allocation of roles and responsibilities shall be done in such a manner that there are complete transparency and ease of execution that is involved.
- **Network-based Security Controls**—Most of the security issues that occur in the multi-Cloud environment have networks as the prime agents of the threats. It adds to the requirement of implementing automated and advanced network security tools and controls to ensure that such risks are avoided and controlled. Some of these tools include network monitoring tools, intrusion detection systems, intrusion prevention systems, anti-malware tools, and anti-denial tools.

Cloud strategy and planning has provided the organizations with the ability to enhance the performance, speed, and quality of their respective business operations and activities. With the occurrence of the security risks and threats, there is a poor impact on the business continuity and customer engagement. It is, therefore, required to include the basic and advanced steps to security to deal with the security issues and problems. These steps shall combine administrative, physical, logical, and technical controls.

The use of security solutions that are available in the market will allow the organizations to achieve and maintain security in the multi-Cloud environment. These solutions will provide an integrated security mechanism and will eliminate the need to deploy security measures for each of the Cloud model and elements. Security concepts and requirements, such as information security, network security, and database security are now provided in a single package by the leading software solution providers while entrusting them for your digital transformations.

9.16 Twelve-Factor Multi-Cloud DevOps Pipeline

This section explains the twelve steps of a build in a CI/CD DevOps pipeline (https://dzone.com/articles/twelve-factor-multiCloud-devops-pipeline) that employs multiple Cloud environments, from source code to monitoring.

1. **Source Code Management**—The continuous delivery pipeline starts when the developer commits the code related to the microservice, configuration files (Ansible playbook, Chef cookbooks, or shell scripts), or infrastructure as a code such as CFT, ARM, GCP, or Terraform. Based on organization policy, post-merge to the build branch, it will trigger the build.
2. **Build Management**—The pipeline defines the entire lifecycle of an application as code. This can be achieved in many ways, including a Jenkins or Spinnaker pipeline. Spinnaker is a Cloud agnostic that can target any Cloud platform

and is YAML file based. The entire stages of an application are written in a JenkinsFile and are executed automatically. There can be N number of Jenkins masters and a pool of executors or agents in order to manage it efficiently. CloudBees JOC Enterprise manages shared slaves quite efficiently. Another way to scale Jenkins is by using DC OS and Marathon, which allow multiple Jenkins masters to share a single pool of resources to run builds. The dynamic destruction or creation of Jenkins agents is directly related to the demand.

3. **Quality Management**—SonarQube can analyze 20 + different languages. The outcome of this analysis includes quality measures and issues (instances where coding rules were broken). However, the software that is analyzed will vary depending on the language.

4. **Repository Management**—Artifacts built by Jenkins are pushed to the repository manager and can be tagged based on environments.

5. **Docker Registry**—The Docker daemon running on the CI server is going to build an image based on the DockerFile as a source code and will push it to the Docker registry. It can be DockerHub, AWS ECR, Google Container Registry, Azure Container Registry, or even a private registry.

6. **Deployment Management**—Here, artifacts are going to pass all the stages starting from dev to prod. We have to ensure that it passes each stage gate as per organization standards and is promoted to a higher environment using the proper tag(s).

7. **Build Infrastructure in the Cloud**—If it is a single Cloud provider, based on the provider, we can use templates; for AWS, we have Cloud Formation Template, for Azure, we can use Azure Resource Manager, and for Google, it will be Google Cloud Platform Template. We have CLI in build tools agent, which will help us trigger it automatically and create the infrastructure for the target environment.

   Terraform is Cloud-agnostic and allows a single configuration to be used to manage multiple providers. It can even handle cross-Cloud dependencies. This simplifies the management and orchestration of the infrastructure, helping operators build large-scale multi-Cloud infrastructures.

   If you use Docker or Packer, you would not require configuration management tools to configure the server because these tools already have that ability; all you need is a server to run the container. To provide multiple servers, Terraform is the ideal orchestration tool.

8. **Container Configuration**—It is advisable to have the *same* container for all environments. There are multiple ways of configuring it. Here is a list of a few of them below:

   - Set the application configuration dynamically via environment variables.
   - Map the config files via Docker Volumes.
   - Bake configuration into the container.
   - If provided as service, then fetch it from Config Server.

9. **Test Automation**—A fast User Acceptance Test [UAT] feedback cycle is critical for continuous delivery to be successful. Automated Test-Driven Development [ATDD] is a necessity to establish a speedy feedback loop. With ecosystems like Docker and Cloud infrastructure, automated tests that require compute, storage, and network environments get easier. For ATDD, we can use Mockito, Cucumber, or Selenium Grid.

10. **Container Cluster Management**—Using the microservices architecture, you can easily deploy containers and run your application. These containers are lightweight in comparison with virtual machines [VM] and more efficiently use the underlying infrastructure. They can be scaled up or down depending on the demand. In addition, they make it easier to add or remove applications between different environments. The orchestration tools should have the following capabilities.

- Provisioning
- Monitoring
- Service Discovery
- Rolling Upgrades and Rollback
- Configuration-as-text
- Policies for Placement, Scalability, etc.
- Administration.

We have already discussed about a few popular Cloud orchestration tools such as Kubernetes, Docker Swarm, Mesos + Marathon.

11. **Log Management**—There is a plethora of log management tools available in the market, and Docker has introduced plug-ins for them. These can be installed as binaries. Listed below are the various drivers for log management:

- Fluentd—supporting TCP or Unix socket connections to fluentd
- Journald—storing container logs in the system journal
- Splunk—HTTP/HTTPS forwarding to Splunk server
- Syslog Driver—supporting UDP, TCP, TLS
- Gelf—UDP log forwarding to Graylog2.

For a complete log management solution, additional tools need to be involved.

- Log parser to structure logs, typically part of log shippers
- Log indexing, visualization, and alerting
- Elasticsearch and Kibana
- Graylog OSS/Enterprise
- Splunk.

12. **Monitoring Management**—The Agent collects metrics and events from our systems and applications. You can install at least one Agent in the container, and then it can generate the metrics and publish them. The user can see the number of containers over time and information across instances such as CPU usage, the operating system usage, and container usage.

9.17 Conclusion

The Cloud journey is enjoying the roller-coaster ride. Cloud environments represent the IT industrialization, centralization, consumerization, federation, etc. Cloud environments, especially public Clouds, are stuffed with massive number of server machines, storage appliances and arrays and network components. This necessity-induced transformation is leading to heightened operational complexities. The other noteworthy trend is that business houses and behemoths are keen on embracing the proven and potential multi-Cloud strategy toward off several internal as well as external challenges. This chapter is specially prepared and presented in this book to tell all about the role and responsibility of Cloud orchestration platforms in lessening the rising Cloud complexity.

Chapter 10
Multi-cloud Management: Technologies, Tools, and Techniques

10.1 Introduction

The digitization technologies and tools are becoming pervasive and persuasive. Nations across the globe are competing with one another in observing and absorbing the digitization processes, platforms, patterns, products, practices, and procedures in order to be smartly sensitive and really responsive to their constituents. All kinds of business establishments and corporates are eagerly strategizing to be elegantly digitized in their operations, offerings, and outputs. Human societies are being made aware of the significant impacts of digitization technologies. IT organizations are equally keen on bringing forth an arsenal of digitization-enablement solutions and services. Academic institutions, innovators, and individuals are overwhelmingly convinced about the tactic as well as strategic implications of digitization. The awareness and articulation of digitization movement is definitely on the climb with the enhanced understanding of the business, technical, and user benefits of digitization technologies such as Cloud computing, data analytics (big, real-time, streaming, and IoT), enterprise mobility, Web 2.0 (social Web) and Web 3.0 (Semantic Web), artificial intelligence (AI).

Not only our computers, but also our everyday devices, handhelds, wearables, healthcare instruments, flying drones, industrial robots, consumer electronics, defense equipment, manufacturing machines, household wares and utensils, personal mobiles, and implantables such as sensors, actuators are also being systematically connected with one another and also with remotely held software applications, services, and databases. There are a bevy of connectors, drivers, adapters, and other middleware solutions to enable the smart linkage among digitized artifacts, connected devices, and cloud-based applications. There is a close tie-up with the physical and the cyber worlds. This deeper and decisive connectivity results in highly integrated and insightful systems, networks, applications, and environments. All the anticipated and unanticipated interacts among all the participants and constituents generate a massive amount of multi-structured data. That is, the data speed, structure, schema, scope, and size lay a stimulating foundation for better, bigger, and brighter possibilities and opportunities. This chapter details the various characteristics, challenges, and competencies of multi-cloud environments.

© Springer International Publishing AG, part of Springer Nature 2018 219
P. Raj and A. Raman, *Software-Defined Cloud Centers*,
Computer Communications and Networks,
https://doi.org/10.1007/978-3-319-78637-7_10

10.2   Entering into the Digital Era

The projected digital era, therefore, involves and invokes a number of innovative, disruptive, and transformative technologies. Besides the growing family of technologies, we need more polished and fine-tuned processes. The traditional processes need to be subjected to a variety of enhancements, rationalizations, and optimizations. Development, deployment, and delivery processes need to be lean, green, and clean. Besides the highly synchronized and refined processes, we need competent architectures for applications and data. Microservices architecture (MSA) is being projected as the next-generation architectural style for designing modular applications. Monolithic and massive applications are being meticulously segmented into a dynamic pool of interoperable, publicly discoverable, network-accessible, and automatically assessable, portable and composable microservices. Distributed and decentralized applications are going to be realized with ease through the smart application of the proven and potential MSA pattern. There are a number of maturing and stabilizing design patterns for developing microservices-centric applications.

Finally, it is about the digital applications, platforms, and infrastructures. As articulated above, MSA is the chosen architecture paradigm for modernizing conventional and current legacy applications. New applications are being produced from the scratch using the MSA patterns, processes, and platforms. Further on, on the platform front, we have a variety of development, deployment, delivery, automation, integration, orchestration, governance, and management platforms in order to speed up the process of realizing and running scores of microservices in bare metal (BM) servers, virtual machines (VMs), and containers. The digital infrastructures typically include commodity servers, high-end enterprise-grade servers, hyper converged infrastructures, hardware appliances, and hybrid Clouds. The advancements and accomplishments in the digital IT space have brought in a number of delectable transformations. Digital transformation is accelerating as more and more enterprises work to create and innovate by taking advantage of pioneering digital technologies.

10.3   The Emergence of Multi-cloud Environments

The Cloud idea, which is being celebrated as the most significant technology for succinctly enabling the dreamt digital transformation, is gaining a lot of momentum these days with the arrival and articulation of an assortment of powerful Cloud realization technologies and tools. The cloudification era has definitely kicked in positively and is on the right track toward to be an influencing and important factor and facet for the endearing and ensuring smart IT era. Business organizations, IT teams, and Cloud service providers (CSPs) collaborate to have a variety of business-specific and generic Cloud environments by leveraging the well-defined and designed cloud-enabling processes, products, and patterns. The high-priority limitations and issues are being identified and surmounted by a host of technological solutions. The acclaimed market analyst and research groups have predicted that around 80% of the currently running business applications is to get formally modernized and moved to Cloud environments by the year 2020. Clouds emerge as the most optimized and organized IT environment for residing and running a growing array of personal, social, and professional applications. The brewing trends in the IT space clearly tell us that the Cloud acceptance and adoption rates are picking up fast. One desirable movement is that worldwide business enterprises are tying up their own IT environments/traditional data centers with one or more public Clouds to get the distinct and direct benefits of the Cloud paradigm. Thus, there is a close linkage being established and sustained between the traditional IT and the modern IT, which is overwhelmingly represented by the Cloud paradigm. This aspect is being termed as Hybrid IT. This new and combined operating model brings forth the needed agility, flexibility, and innovation to drive any business forward. A Hybrid IT model enables IT to deliver on key business goals:

- Increase the customer engagement, share of wallet, satisfaction, and loyalty
- Create new areas of profitable growth and differentiation
- Reduce risk and lower operational costs by accelerating and driving efficiency.

Another exciting phenomenon is hybrid Clouds. That is, integrating private Clouds with one or more public Clouds is being touted as the hybrid cloud. There are a number of strategically sound advantages being bandied about for this new phenomenon. In short, we are steadily trekking and tending toward the multi-cloud era. With the distributed computing model is being projected as the viable and venerable model for the forthcoming era of knowledge services and smarter applications, the embrace of hybrid Cloud technologies cannot be delayed any further. With the availability of standardized Cloud integration and orchestration products and platforms in the market, the days of hybrid Clouds involving and leveraging multiple and geographically distributed and disparate Clouds are at hand. For establishing digitally disrupted and transformed businesses and societies, the role and the responsibility of multi-cloud environments are bound to climb up in the days ahead.

10.4 The Multi-cloud Management Platform Solutions

For establishing and supporting multi-cloud environments, there are a few important requirements. As indicated above, multi-cloud architectures frequently include some mix of on-premises or off-premise private Clouds and one or more public IaaS, PaaS, and/or SaaS Clouds. That is, private and public Clouds coming together in bringing forth additional capacities and capabilities for business organizations is the talking point here. Cloud environments are being stuffed with bare metal servers, virtual machines, and containers. Thus, the number of moving parts within any Cloud environment is growing steadily and hence the challenge of managing Cloud environments is growing. The Cloud management platform market is flooded with a number of open source as well as commercial-grade solutions in order to substantially lessen the workloads of Cloud operational teams. Another noteworthy point is that Cloud applications are increasingly microservices-centric. Enterprise applications are being made out of hundreds of interacting microservices. There are several instances for a particular microservice in order to ensure high availability. Also, there are many Cloud environments working together to achieve the identified business goals. Precisely speaking, the management complexity of multi-cloud environments and the applications running on them is climbing up consistently.

These extremely complex environments present IT operations and DevOps teams with new types of management challenges. Traditional IT management strategies and tools were designed for stateful applications that were tightly coupled to the underlying infrastructure. However, virtualized and containerized Cloud environments no longer maintain such a stable relationship with applications. Virtualization and containerization add an additional layer of abstraction, and hence, applications are not tightly coupled with the underlying infrastructure. Virtual machines and containers inside a host are dynamic in the sense that they can be provisioned and decommissioned frequently. There are other pertinent challenges and concerns in Cloud center operations. Businesses invariably expect to get more out of IT. Especially, the Cloud computing is being projected and pronounced as the smart marriage between the age-old mainframe and the modern computing models. That means all the non-functional requirements/quality of service attributes of Cloud systems and services can be fulfilled with ease at scale.

The ability to deliver service levels and satisfy business demands for on-demand access to IT infrastructures and business applications mandates that the operations teams need to be able to proactively monitor infrastructural components, resources, and applications by using unified and automation tools. The data collected by monitoring tools has to be subjected to a variety of investigations to extricate actionable insights in time in order to ponder about the next course of corrective actions. The insights also help the team members in pinpointing and remediating the root cause of any problems. The performance, scalability, security, availability, and other aspects of Cloud systems can be measured and managed in time. The matured operational and log analytics tasks are capable of maintaining the Cloud environment up and running. The tools-supported, policy-based, templates-centric, and process-optimized automation is the futuristic and flexible way forward for keeping up increasingly complicated multi-cloud environments.

Enterprises across the globe are geared up toward embracing the multi-cloud concept for various reasons. With the Cloud management tooling market is steadily expanding with the availability of new and enhanced management platforms, enterprises are keen to be blessed with the multi-cloud strategy and implementation. Enterprises with technical expertise, matured processes, and centralized governance can be hugely successful in having and managing multi-cloud deployments. That is, it is all about the distributed deployments of IT resources and business applications while ensuring centralized monitoring, measurement, and management.

As per the Gartner report, Cloud management platforms (CMPs) typically address the following five requirements: service request management; provisioning, orchestration, and automation; governance and policy; monitoring and metering; and multi-cloud brokering. The key value proposition of a CMP is enabling multi-cloud management to apply policy and to orchestrate and automate across public and private Cloud services in a uniform way. The tangible benefits of a CMP are threefold:

- Assist Cloud service subscribers—which provider to use and what applications can be consumed by that provider.
- Offer a single view and implementation across multiple Cloud providers through abstracting Cloud providers' proprietary APIs.
- Reduce the lock-in of any Cloud infrastructure services provider.

Cloud service providers expose their own APIs in order for any Cloud consumers, clients, and customers to facilitate the required access to their capabilities and capacities. For multi-cloud setup and sustenance, Cloud users have to go via a CMP, which has the inherent ability to compare, collaborate, correlate, and corroborate with multiple Cloud services to arrive at the deft decisions that enable both tactical and strategical requirements of Cloud subscribers. CMPs are being stuffed with policy-aware and based management capabilities in order to reduce any kind of human intervention, instruction, and interpretation. Some CMPs have responded by lessening the level of abstraction that they provide, leaning more toward tagging to allow visibility within public Cloud environments. Some have added reactive governance—the continuous monitoring of the environment for compliance with policies and retroactive enforcement of those policies. Fresh functionalities are being continuously incorporated in order to bring in a bevy of full-fledged automation capabilities toward the goals of accelerated cloud-enablement and adoption.

Organizations that are developing multi-cloud strategies need to consider the leverage of a Cloud management platform solution and its unique features. The characteristics to be taken into consideration include the depth and breadth of automation, monitoring, and analytics provided by the platform. Most multi-cloud environments encompass a range of vendors, services, application architectures, and middleware. Therefore, the effective Cloud management platforms need to ingest data from many sources, integrate and orchestrate workflows, and provide clear actionable insight.

The usability of reporting engines, visualization, query languages, and correlation analysis. Complex Cloud environments require robust discovery, dependency awareness, predictive analytics, and role-based insights. These Cloud environments need to provide rapid value out of the box but allow for deep inspection and custom queries. Organizations should consider the extent to which the platform will provide value to the business by enabling developers and line-of-business (LOB) analysts to access resources, support DevOps, and provide insight into business performance and productivity.

10.5   The Multi-cloud Management Solution Capabilities

Given the dynamic nature of today's digital and cloud-enabled architectures and applications, worldwide organizations find and feel that a unified Cloud management platform is highly relevant and capable of providing greater and sustainable business value than integrated Cloud management strategies that depend on best-of-breed point solutions or community-based open-source technologies. That is, rather than requiring a myriad of point-to-point integrations, business houses and behemoths need integrated Cloud management platforms that can ingest data from a variety of sources, normalize the data around a common data model, and then apply query, reporting, and analytics using a consistent set of interfaces. The unified platform comes with a growing family of interfaces for various capabilities such as performance and configuration management, log analysis, capacity planning, show back/chargeback, and provisioning and migration automation. Many platforms offer standard reporting and query templates out of the box and provide customizable role-based dashboards for IT operations, LOB analysts, and DevOps teams.

   Some of the most important capabilities that allow Cloud management platforms to contribute to business value are:

- Full-stack application and infrastructure automation using blueprints and templates to standardize and streamline application and infrastructure provisioning, configuration, and migration.
- Self-service catalogues and orchestration technology to enable both IT staff and end users to initiate and implement automation. This is particularly important for enabling developers to set up and tear down test, development, and staging resources as needed to keep up with continuous integration and delivery of DevOps programs.
- Proactive performance monitoring and predictive analytics allow IT teams to detect and remediate problems before they impact customers. Platforms must be able to ingest and analyze data from a wide range of sources and APIs and provide user-friendly graphics and visualizations to help IT staff quickly assess and respond to service-impacting events.
- Cross-cloud visibility spanning heterogeneous on-premises and public Cloud resource consumption and the ability to proactively predict when additional resources are required.
- Accurate, timely Cloud cost and capacity management, modeling, and forecasting to enable customers to optimize the cost of workload placement and Cloud resource utilization.
- The most dramatic benefits associated with Cloud management platforms are providing advanced automation with robust monitoring, capacity planning, cost management, and log analytics to ensure that infrastructure is available when development teams and end users need it.

By scaling infrastructure and applications rapidly, deploying new functionality as soon as it is ready, and keeping up with changing business requirements, Cloud management platforms can directly impact a company's ability to generate revenue and successfully engage with customers. IT staff and end-user productivity results come from the use of more standardized and consistent configuration and automation that reduce manual labor and downtime paired with proactive and predictive monitoring and analytics that detect emerging performance issues before they impact end users and help more rapidly to identify and remediate the root cause of performance problems. The functional capabilities of a CMP are as follows (based on the Gartner report)

- **Service Request Management**—This is the self-service interface, which is provided by CMPs, by which various Cloud services are being consumed with ease by consumers. Cloud service providers offer service catalogues with SLAs and cost details. Based on the published information, the CMP chooses the appropriate provider and services. The service requests can be routed through this interface to the CMP solution to automate most of the activities. Some users expect a service interface that serves as a pass-through to native capabilities within a public Cloud service. The service portal or marketplace is being continuously updated with fresh features, functionalities, and facilities to attain the edge or retain the edge earned. There are service and support management systems (ITSM) and other automation tools to readily fulfill the varying requests from users. There are operational team members owned by Cloud service providers or third-party teams teaming up together to fulfill service requests quickly.

- **Provisioning, Orchestration, and Automation**—This refers to the core capabilities of any CMP product. There is an arsenal of tools intrinsically enabling these vital features. Cloud orchestration, provisioning, and configuration tools are made available these days in plenty. There are industry-strength standards for service and Cloud infrastructure orchestration. Similarly, there are automation tools for job/task scheduling, load balancing, auto-scaling, resource allocation, etc. Further on, there are resource configuration management systems. Software deployment and delivery tools are also hitting the market. Precisely speaking, the Cloud operations are being meticulously automated in an end-to-end fashion.

- **Governance and Policy**—This is definitely a key capability within CMPs. Governance typically covers policy establishment and enforcement. Policies/rules and other knowledge bases emerge as the prime way for bringing forth the desired automation. For example, the auto-scaling policies are well-known and widely used.

- **Monitoring and Metering**—Monitoring, measurement, management, and metering are the basic requirements for any IT hardware and software packages. The service usage and resource consumption need to be accurately measured and metered. There are a bunch of tools for accomplishing these.

- **Multi-cloud Brokering**—Brokerage solutions and services are very important in the era of connected and federated Clouds. The interconnectivity, intermediation, and other enrichment and enablement capabilities are being performed through this Cloud service brokers. There are connectors, adapters, drivers, and other solutions in order to establish a seamless linkage between public and private Clouds. There are bridge solutions for establishing direct connectivity between public Clouds. Thus with multiple Clouds and services with different SLAs, the role and responsibility of Cloud brokers are bound to escalate in the days ahead. Advanced CMPs are being fitted with brokerage tools and engines.

- **Security and Identity**—As we all know, the security requirement is widely insisted for Cloud environments. As customer-facing applications and data (corporate, customer and confidential) are being stocked in Cloud environments, especially in public Clouds, the aspect of security is essential. User identification, authentication, authorization, and other accountability and auditability are being pronounced as the most critical and crucial one for the continued spread of the Cloud concept. The security and privacy of data while in transit, persistence, and usage are paramount for the intended success of the Cloud idea. Key-based encryption and decryption, key management, etc., are getting a lot of attention and attraction these days. Single sign-on (SSO) is indispensable for multi-cloud applications. United threat and vulnerability management solutions are becoming hot for Cloud environments

- **Service-Level Management**—Ensuring the service-level and operation-level contracts agreed between Cloud consumer and server is an important facet of the Cloud arena. Especially, the non-functional requirements (NFRs)/the quality of service (QoS) attributes are the key differentiators among all the participating service providers. The aspects of scalability, availability, fault tolerance, security, and dependability are the often repeated needs. The service resiliency, the application reliability, and the infrastructure versatility are given utmost importance for boosting the user confidence on the Cloud conundrum. There is a dazzling array of toolsets for facilitating these complex capabilities.

- **Cloud Migration and Disaster Recovery (DR)**—Personal and professional applications that were built several years back in the monolithic and legacy forms and are in the reckoning still are being consciously modernized and migrated to Cloud environments in order to reap all the originally envisaged Cloud benefits. Cloud migration may not be a straightforward task as this involves the Cloud readiness determination, discovery, lifting and shifting of workloads between and/or among on-premise and off-premise Cloud environments. The use cases involve both workloads being permanently migrated from one environment to another and workloads repositioned during DR testing or during an actual disaster. Thus, applications being moved to Cloud environments ought to be seamlessly managed by the CMP solutions. There are tools for risk-free automation of application modernization and migration to multiple Cloud environments. For ensuring disaster and data recovery and toward business continuity (BC), secondary Cloud centers are being set up and the CMP product is expected to work with primary and second Cloud centers.

- **Dynamic Capacity Planning and Resource Allocation**—This functionality allows for the efficient operational usage of the infrastructure footprint. It is often tied to orchestration and automation functionality. This is increasingly being combined with the cost transparency and optimization.

- **Cost Transparency and Optimization**—The functionality involves enabling tracking, budgeting, and optimization of the Cloud expenses.

Customer Delight—Cloud management platforms provide robust automation to standardize and streamline application and infrastructure provisioning, resulting in the more rapid availability of end-user services and more flexible scaling of resources as needed by changing business requirements. Proactive monitoring and predictive analytics allow IT teams to detect and remediate problems before they impact customers, which means service levels are more consistent and end-user satisfaction is higher.

Faster Time to Market—Cloud management platforms can monitor on-premises and public Cloud resource consumption and proactively predict when additional resources are required. Automated onboarding and application deployment and support for continuous DevOps integration and delivery combine to speed new services and applications to market. Particularly, for organizations that derive significant revenue from online services and mobile applications, this can have a significant impact on time to revenue.

Enhanced Resource Utilization—Digital transformation, DevOps, and Cloud technologies bring forth frequent and complex changes across corporate IT environments. Traditional manual processes are too slow and error-prone to support the rapid rate of change seen today. Cloud management platform automation, self-service engines, orchestration technologies, and blueprint design systems enable IT organizations to focus limited staff on getting the template design correct the first time and then rely on automation to manage deployments and changes consistently. Similarly, more sophisticated monitoring and analytics allow limited staff to find and remediate problems much more quickly than they could with traditional approaches, freeing staff to focus on more strategic initiatives. With higher application and infrastructure availability, developers and end users can focus on their jobs rather than waiting for resources.

Greater Business Flexibility and Extensibility—Cloud management platforms can monitor and detect changes in resource utilization and can pinpoint the best location for specific workloads based on cost, security, and performance. When paired with automated provisioning and migration capabilities, this type of analysis allows organizations to scale resources, react to rapid business changes, and maintain optimal cost and performance levels.

Affordability—With improved visibility into Cloud infrastructure costs, performance, and availability, IT organizations are in a better position to use and reclaim resources as needed, migrate workloads to the optimal resource, and focus staff on the highest-impact problems and end-user requests. The resulting improvements in staff productivity and reductions in the cost of infrastructure can be substantial for many organizations.

Turbonomic's hybrid Cloud management solution automates and augments multi-cloud management features.

1. Multi-cloud architectures put the foundation for elastic resources to increase resiliency, accelerate development and test efforts, access more geographic locations, and select best-of-breed providers. But managing such a distributed, complicated and multi-cloud environment without sacrificing performance, violating compliance constraints, wasting on-premises resources, or overspending in the Cloud is definitely not easy. This pioneering management platform simplifies the hybrid Cloud management by assuring high performance, lowering costs, and ensuring continuous compliance.

2. This solution determines which Cloud assets to migrate where and when. It assures application performance while lowering costs and maintaining compliance requirements across hybrid Cloud environments.

3. This also seamlessly extends to any on-premises environment to the public cloud. It understands the real-time workload consumption and performance characteristics and intelligently matches it to available resources in public Clouds. The platform automatically identifies the best placement and scaling across the hybrid environment while respecting compliance constraints.

4. Turbonomic continuously matches workload demand to AWS and Azure templates. It automatically presents scaling down options to reduce costs without impacting performance. This platform analyzes AWS and Azure expenses to track what is being spent and prevent unexpected bills. It aggregates bills across services, regions, accounts and lines a business and tracks them against a predefined budget. Individual workload costs accurately and comprehensively tracked and reported by regions, tags, or custom groups and include all associated costs (OS, IP, storage).

5. Turbonomic controls compute, storage, and database services across on-premises, AWS and Azure environments. Workload demand profiles are continuously matched with the right resources, whether those resources reside in the private data center, the public cloud, or a hybrid Cloud combination.

6. The platform automatically scales workloads across the hybrid environment. Without agents, Turbonomic connects to applications and uses met-

rics collected (e.g., connections, heap, threads, response times, transaction rates) to ensure applications get the resources they need when they need them to align with service levels on-premises or in the cloud.

7. Turbonomic seamlessly incorporates business policies. Most enterprises have compliance policies to adhere to whether it's PCI, HIPAA, data sovereignty, or resilience levels for mission-critical applications. Also, it enables to seamlessly incorporate pre-existing placement policies ensuring workload placement. And workload movement is limited to sanctioned Cloud provider regions or on-premises data centers and cluster. New policies are easily defined and incorporated into the Turbonomic decision engine.

8. With Turbonomic designated HA workloads are spread across multiple regions and availability zones or data center, cluster and hosts on-premises complying with risk management specifications for mission-critical applications.

9. Turbonomic offers a single pane of glass for resource consumption across on-premises data centers, AWS and Azure environments. Performance metrics of workloads in AWS and Azure environments are tracked, reported and trended, including compute and storage resources (CPU, memory, IOPS, and latency), across Cloud providers, regions, zones.

In hindsight, Cloud management platforms offer customers a range of integrated automation, monitoring, planning, and analytics to optimize workload performance, IT costs, and business agility across multiple Clouds. IT decision-makers emphasize that much of the power of Cloud management platforms comes from avoiding data and process silos that are common with point solutions and open-source tooling. The ability of platforms to normalize and correlate data and integrate process flows can enable enterprises to more effectively manage and optimize complex multi-cloud environments. Cloud management platforms must be proactive, predictive, and aware of workload performance and capacity demands across on-premises and public or hosted Cloud infrastructure. These platforms must integrate with existing management processes and tools and provide operations, development, and LOB analysts with user-friendly, role-based insight into service levels, availability, resource utilization, and control over provisioning and configuration.

There are several other functionalities emerging toward envisioning and establishing software-defined, workload-aware, shared, dynamic, and automated Cloud environments. Workload consolidation and optimization, resource (VMs and containers) allocation and placement, cloud orchestration and automation, service composition across disparate and distributed Clouds, centralized management of distributed resources and applications, and software deployment and deployment are the increasingly popular functionalities for the CMP tools. Cloud performance is another important area not to be sidestepped. When applications get moved to Cloud center, the same performance/throughput attained in the enterprise environment has to be guaranteed in the new environment through performance tuning tips. Cloud security and privacy are being taken care of through firewalls, intrusion detection and prevention systems, and other security solutions. Application performance management (APM) solutions are for ensuring the much-needed performance. An arsenal of Cloud connector, adaptor, and driver software solutions is being attached to CMP platform for an integrated management of Cloud resources and applications.

10.6 Multi-cloud Management Policies

Clouds typically represent IT industrialization, optimization, heightened resource utilization, and productivity. Clouds are also consolidated, centralized, even federated, virtualized, increasingly containerized, and shared. Several other optimizations through rationalization, convergence, organization, etc., are being done in order to present Clouds as the one-stop, futuristic, adaptive, and competent IT solution for business houses, individuals, innovators, and institutions. Professionals are working in unison to enhance the reliability of Cloud applications and infrastructures. With the accumulation and additional systems and solutions, the Cloud operation and management complexity are not bound to come down anytime soon. There are several complexity-mitigation and delegation techniques and tips.

As articulated above, policies are essential for running any complex environment of systems, networks, data sources, applications, and services in an automated fashion. With the flourishing of the Cloud idea everywhere, a proper nourishment has to be accentuated and provided in order to get the originally expressed success. The management aspect has to be handled with extra care. A proper strategy has to be in place followed by the well-defined execution plan. Now corporates are strategizing and embracing the famous hybrid Cloud option in order to flexible and extensible. Definitely managing multiple Clouds is not going to be easy and is beset with a number of challenges and concerns.

Enterprises become particularly concerned with security when highly sensitive and critical data lands on third-party storage appliances. There are other concerns such as the compute, network bandwidth, and storage costs and their unpredictability. Further on, public Clouds are under the total control of Cloud service providers (CSPs) and the typical worries include the site availability, performance, and reliability. The intervening network can also play the spoilsport. Therefore, a management strategy for hybrid Clouds has to clearly articulate and accentuate what needs to be done to manage the various components of a hybrid cloud. Generally, hybrid Clouds consist of a private Cloud and contracts with one or more public Cloud providers for additional capacity and capability. Hybrid Cloud administrators are therefore responsible for managing computing, networking, and storage resources in multiple and multi-faceted domains. The Cloud management policies have to be prepared and pressed into service for addressing the following topics.

- **Configuration and Installment Management Policies**—These should specify appropriate rules governing the creation, deployment, patching, and rebuilding of application images.
- **Access Control Policies**—This is for establishing and enforcing a variety of policies for controlling the access to various Cloud resources, applications, and data in Cloud environments.
- **Cost Management and Reporting Policies**—The Cloud usage charges vary based on different reasons and regions. Policies need to be formulated and firmed up so that any kind of cost deviation can be proactively captured and communicated to the application owner and users.

A multi-cloud infrastructure manifests in many different ways. In some enterprises, application teams adopt different Clouds independently to fit their needs. Developers use one Cloud for testing activity and a data center for running production workloads. The point is that every enterprise does multi-cloud differently and every enterprise has different constituencies with a wide variety of needs.

Scalr is built to operate on a massive scale. This is made possible by the hierarchical policy inheritance model. When enforcing policies at a large scale and offering self-service Cloud resources to thousands of users, it does not make sense to tie policies to each individual application. When policies are defined at the application level, introducing changes becomes difficult and the separation of responsibility becomes challenging.

Scalr, therefore, uses a tiered model to map the company's organizational structure. At each level, the relevant administrator can configure policies, catalogue items, and automation. The policies configured at a certain scope will be inherited by all lower scopes. Scalr layers policies on Cloud usage based on a user's identity and the environment she operates in. Policies adhere to Scalr's inheritance model, which means that a policy configured at a higher level will be propagated to all relevant environments. Once users with the proper permission log into these environments, RBAC policies can be applied based on their identity. Scalr policies generally fall into five categories:

- **Access Policies**—Resource access, security, and usage policies come under this category of policies.
- **Workload Placement Policies**—For optimally placing workloads, we need to worry about the number and configuration of server machines/virtual machines/containers. Besides, the network bandwidth and storage capacity play a vital role in accomplishing the workloads, capacity usage, and provisioning restrictions in Cloud environments.
- **Integration Policies**—Integration is the key. Several systems need to be integrated seamlessly in order to automate and orchestrate several things together in a concerted and cogent manner. Workflows typically com-

prise multiple co-located as well as remotely held systems. The prominent examples of integration policies include logging actions to CMDBs, leveraging configuration management tools such as Chef, Puppet, and Ansible.

- **Application Lifecycle Policies**—These policies are for automation that governs application life cycle from provisioning to termination. These also cover all aspects of application automation from bootstrapping servers with scripts, ongoing maintenance, and auto-scaling and scheduled application termination.
- **Financial Policies**—These are all related to cost reduction and cost metering. Financial policies include budgeting tools, notifications around budget consumption, showback/chargeback, and financial reports. Cost reduction policies tie into other Scalr policies such as reclamation of unused resources, application lifetime, ensuring usage of appropriate server sizes and more.

10.7   Multi-cloud Management: The Best Practices

The Cloud is evolving to meet changing business needs. Success is no longer about a quick, tactical Cloud implementation, but rather about finding the right Cloud solutions that strategically align with your business. This is pushing organizations to adopt a multi-cloud strategy. Market researchers and analysts forecast that around 85% of business is moving toward a multi-cloud strategy.

In this new era, we believe businesses need an IT infrastructure that allows them to develop the best insights from their data and turn them into action, regardless of where that data may sit. In a time when data is perhaps a business's most valuable resource, the ability to access, protect, and analyze information will play a critical role in an organization's overall multi-cloud strategy.

- **Business Innovation**—There are several new digital transformation and intelligence technologies and tools. Businesses have to carefully and consciously embrace those proven and potential technologies in order to be ahead of their competitors. Deeper and extreme connectivity pump a lot amount of data, and through the leverage of data science and cognitive computing technologies, real-time and actionable insights can be extricated out of exponentially growing data volumes. These insights empower enterprises to look ahead.
- **Data and Cloud Integration**—Customer-facing, Web-scale, and enterprise-class applications are being modernized using microservices architecture and moved to different Cloud environments in order to reap all the originally envisaged and expressed benefits. But at the same time, due to the security fear, customer, confidential, and corporate data are still being kept in highly secure traditional IT

environments and private Clouds. Thus, there is a need for seamless and smart synchronization between data and Cloud services in order to postulate newer applications and capabilities.

- **Data Management and Security Optimization**—For establishing and executing multi-cloud strategy, data collection, cleansing, and crunching aspects need to be looked into with all the intent. A successful multi-cloud strategy must safeguard critical data across all applications and platforms. Thus carefully and systematically collecting and securing data is the fundamental and foundational thing for the runaway success of multi-cloud strategy.
- **Legacy Modernization**—There are currently running IT infrastructures, platforms, applications, data sources and stores, middleware solutions, etc. For embracing the promising multi-cloud strategy, those investments and assets need to be methodically refurbished and reused for the digital era too. The number of fresh investments can be radically reduced through the smart leverage of all the current and conventional IT resources and artifacts.

It is all about building, managing, and governing the entire Cloud ecosystem while retaining control of the existing IT environment. Also, it is about sending non-mission-critical workloads to the public Cloud to take advantage of its flexibility and scalability.

- Accelerate and improve service delivery with solutions that deploy and manage workloads across all Cloud models.
- Manage multiple Cloud providers from a single console.
- Manage budgets across multiple providers and users who access images running in multiple Clouds.
- Govern and secure hybrid Cloud usage across the enterprise, including industry regulatory and organizational requirements.

Managing Multi-Clouds—We can achieve greater flexibility and choice for enterprise IT when deploying and managing a multi-cloudenvironment, by using self-service capabilities and governance to avoid vendor lock-in.

- Automate multi-cloud services management and delivery.
- Monitor usage, performance, and costs across multi-cloud environments.
- Track Cloud services (SaaS, IaaS), costs, and billing in multi-cloud environments.
- Aggregate services across multiple Cloud domains.

Managing Roles and Privileges—We need to control access to Cloud services, and proactively define and enforce enterprise-wide access policies and privileges. Apply automated authentication and authorization policies for both privileges and end-user access.

- Enable users to perform specific operations based on assigned roles and permissions.
- Define who receives elevated privileges, and when, how, and from where these privileges are granted.

- Control which commands can be executed by privileged users, and audit privileged activity.
- Centrally manage and enforce role-based authorization and authentication policies.
- Automatically provision and de-provision user accounts and access rights across diverse servers, including the propagated blocking of AD users.

Unified Billing for all Cloud Services—We need to consolidate our Cloud spend with a single point of billing. Also, it is to optimize Cloud setup with unified Cloud resource usage, metering, and billing, which works seamlessly across single and hybrid Cloud deployments.

- Empower IT users to compare, order, manage, access, and consolidate billing across Cloud services (public, private, and hybrid).
- Track Cloud services usage costs incurred by internal cost centers and departments.
- Monitor and govern resource utilization and cost across all of IT infrastructure.
- Maintain flexibility in how we use Cloud resources by defining a budget that can be used across multiple providers.

Open Standards Architecture—**We need to** develop, deploy, and deliver services on various Cloud environments using an open standards architecture. Enterprise IT can now manage and deliver Cloud services ranging from infrastructure to applications.

- Adopt a multi-cloud strategy easily using standard architectures
- Build and deliver enterprise Cloud services across hybrid Cloud environments.
- Increase the speed of enterprise IT delivery by leveraging various Cloud services.
- Create a foundation for an abstraction layer that normalizes interfaces across disparate IaaS providers and API services.

Thus, setting up and sustaining multi-cloud environments are essential for bringing forth a dazzling array of business innovations. There are ways and means being widely accentuated and articulated. It is to start with a flexible and futuristic multi-cloud formation strategy, a detailed planning and insights-driven execution.

---

vRealize Operations—This will bring together all management functions—performance management, capacity, log analytics, cost analytics, planning, topology analysis, troubleshooting, and automated workload balancing—in one integrated, highly intuitive, scalable, and extensible platform. VMware vRealize Operations integrated with vRealize Log Insight and vRealize Business for Cloud delivers core capabilities around.

- **Application-aware SDDC and multi-cloud monitoring** to help customers accelerate adoption of SDDC and integrate public Clouds. Native

SDDC integrations such as with VMware vSAN and VMware Cloud Foundation, redesigned intuitive user interface, unified visibility from applications to infrastructure and actionable insights combining metrics and logs deliver quick time to value. Customers get unified operations view into applications and infrastructure health, visualize key performance indicators, and infrastructure components dependencies. Predictive analytics and smart alerts enable proactive remediation of performance problems. Simple actionable out-of-the-box persona-based dashboards, metrics and logs side-by-side, custom dashboards, reports, and views enable role-based access and smarter troubleshooting.

- **Automated and proactive performance management** helps customers simplify operations, avoid disruption, and free up time for more strategic tasks. The new capabilities in vRealize Operations include fully automated workload balancing across hosts, clusters, and data stores supporting both VMotion and Storage VMotion. It also offers full Distributed Resource Scheduler (DRS) management and predictive DRS. Predictive DRS combines predictive analytics from vRealize Operations with DRS capabilities to inform DRS of an expected spike in load so that DRS can move VMs before contention occurs. Anomalies and issues can be proactively detected and automatically remediated before end users are impacted.

- **Cloud Planning, capacity optimization, and compliance**—Upcoming vRealize Operations includes tight integration with vRealize Business for Cloud which appears as "Business Management" tab within the vRealize Operations UI. Now vRealize Operations can correlate operational metrics with cost insights to understand how capacity utilization drives cost optimization. Fine-grained cost analysis for private Cloud and ability to compare costs across private and multiple public Clouds accelerate Cloud planning, budgeting and procurement decisions, control costs and reduce risk. Customers can optimize cost and resource usage through capacity management, reclamation, and right-sizing and improve planning and forecasting. Also included are new SDDC health dashboards and hardening across the entire SDDC stack including NSX and VSAN.

10.8 Managing Multi-cloud Environments Through Predictive Analytics

IT organizations not only will be asked to provide business users and developers with unified access to multiple Cloud services but will also be expected to manage contracts, optimize spending, ensure service -level agreements (SLAs), and maintain regulatory compliance. As the operational complexity of multi-cloud environments grows, business and IT decision-makers will find a great value in management processes and automated tools that can vastly simplify operations, maintain end-to-end service levels, and ensure that resources adapt seamlessly to dynamic changes in workload, processing, storage, and network requirements. For achieving digital transformation, an effective management of complex multi-cloud environments is critical. Cloud management platforms typically offer an option for unified automation, monitoring, and analytics across multiple Clouds.

The Contributions of Predictive Analytics—As Cloud computing gets more complicated, the advanced analytics such as predictive analytics can help in predicting resource consumption rates, costs, and availability. Due to various reasons, software applications and data sources are being deployed on a variety of Clouds. Predictive analytics is a class of analytics that projects and forecasts future events based on historical and real-time data patterns and trends. Predictive analytics are used today in myriad ways, including predicting and managing the cost of Amazon Web Services (AWS) Spot instances, preventing server and network failures, and managing customer experiences. The key to getting the most out of predictive analytics in a multi-cloud environment is in first understanding that data is at the center of everything. It is the gravity that holds all the business applications together. Data is the driver of every business decision. It is the center spindle on which all analytics turn.

Use of these analytics capabilities can help in pre-emptively and proactively managing IT resources and capabilities. It ensures meeting the licensing and service-level agreement requirements and predicts bottlenecks and process entanglements. For that reason, accessible and flexible data storage and a refined overall data strategy are essential to making the whole of business analytics work. Busting every data silo residing inside each Cloud is certainly essential to making a collection of Cloud services work holistically for the sake of the business.

Morpheus Data, which prides itself on being an infrastructure-agnostic Cloud application management and orchestration platform, has added the capability of predictive analytics to Cloud management. This platform enables something that used to be impossible: an end-to-end application lifecycle management in multi-cloud Hybrid IT environments.

Morpheus has updated its Unified Ops Orchestration platform with machine learning algorithms to lower Cloud costs and provide new third-party integrations to speed application deployments. Unified Ops provides a systematic solution to optimize resources, enable governance, accelerate workflows and modernize applications. The solution was architected to be 100% infrastructure agnostic across bare metal, virtual machine and containerized deployments spanning on-premises, hosted and public Clouds.

Much of the current growth in enterprise Cloud services spending comes from application teams trying to emulate best-in-class DevOps organizations, where time to deployment is measured in minutes, not days. At the same time, enterprise IT teams are signaling adoption of multi-cloud strategies rather than standardizing on a single provider. Unfortunately, fragmented Cloud management has been a roadblock to deployment, and rouge development has led to expensive Cloud sprawl.

To help organizations improve efficiency and establish visibility of complex multi-cloud infrastructure, Morpheus provides cross-platform discovery to identify what applications, VMs, and containers have been deployed and gather data on capacity, memory use, performance and power consumption. Using machine learning, Morpheus' new Guided Remediation feature enables customers to phase out unused instances, move workloads to lower cost Clouds, adjust memory or capacity allocation, and even setup power schedules to tightly control costs. Unlike pure-play VM analytics tools, Morpheus will find and fix issues in both VMs and containers across a wide number of on-premise and off-premise Clouds. Additionally, customers can take advantage of robust policy management and Cloud brokerage tools to set, compare and control costs at the time of provisioning to prevent future issues.

Some users are interested in using analytics to do dynamic tuning of application scaling, deployment zone usage or multi-cloud usage. This demands a quick condition-response cycle that is more consistent with complex event processing than with traditional analytics. There's also an option for many public Cloud providers to build scaling and resiliency triggers into our Cloud hosting using parameters. If this is the case, then use analytics and configuration testing to create different Cloud hosting models, and test their cost/performance. Then, enforce the specific configuration using the Cloud provider tools.

Cloud analytics and management tools, like Microsoft Operations Management Suite or Amazon CloudWatch, will combine analytics and at least basic remedial steps into a single approach that doesn't rely on external tools or coupling with operations processes via DevOps. Where tools will generate alerts, these can be used to trigger things like scaling. Cloud analytics ultimately gains value by creating actionable insights. There are many Cloud trends that are linked to real-time events, both at the application level and for Cloud management. As these event-driven concepts mature, they'll impact both the requirements applications impose on the Cloud and the mechanisms we have available to turn Cloud performance and status information into action.

10.9 Application Modernization and Migration: The Approaches and Architectures

When organizations decide to shift their workloads, data and processes across multiple on-premises, hosted, private, and public Cloud services, there will be a need for a new approach. This new approach leads to hybrid multi-cloud Cloud management. But this approach requires uniform solutions in terms of billing and provisioning, access control, cost control, and performance analysis and capacity management.

A hybrid multi-cloud architecture is emerging within nearly all enterprises. IT organizations are no longer limited to managing data centers and a few hosted and managed services providers. Needy lines-of-business teams and impatient IT developers have procured SaaS, IaaS, and PaaS Cloud services to overcome resource constraints. Now many enterprises' IT structures are composed of multi-Clouds.

In the IT industry, the tools and technologies needed to craft and manage hybrid multi-Clouds architecture are fragmented. Multi-Clouds and hybrid Clouds bring workload and infrastructure challenges that will drive the development of new Cloud management technology. In addition to having to manage resource utilization, performance and costs of various public and private Cloud services, Cloud management platforms must also be aware of the integrations and processes that transcend on-premises and Cloud execution venues and interoperate in some way with the new multi-purpose hybrid iPaaS that connects them, to assure business continuity.

According to the above challenges, the author of this article (https://www.simform.com/multi-cloud-architecture/) has introduced two hybrid multi-cloud architectures for migrating on-premise environment to a hybrid multi-cloud environment. There are many multi-cloud architectures, namely re-deployment, cloudification, relocation, refactoring, rebinding, replacement, and modernization for organizations to for adopt multi-cloud environments.

1. **Multi-application Rebinding**

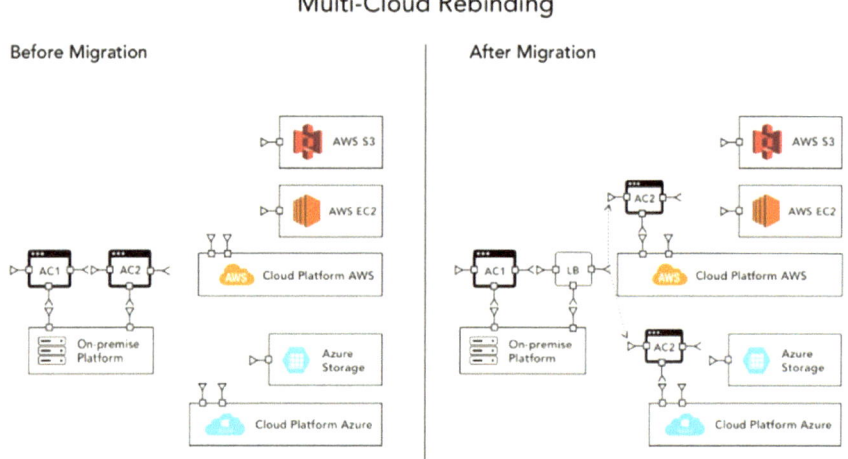

In the above hybrid multi-cloud architecture, a re-architected application is deployed partially on multiple Cloud environments. This architecture can be used for the systems that route users to the nearest data center when the primary or on-premise data center fails. In particular, they can be configured to monitor the status of the service to which they are directing the users. If any service is not available, all the traffic will be routed to another healthy instance. This architecture uses an on-premise Cloud adapter (e.g., service bus or elastic load balancer) to provide an integration of components in different Cloud platforms. The main benefits of using this architecture are the application's response rate increases to the maximum level and unhealthy services become healthy again.

2. **Multi-application Modernization**

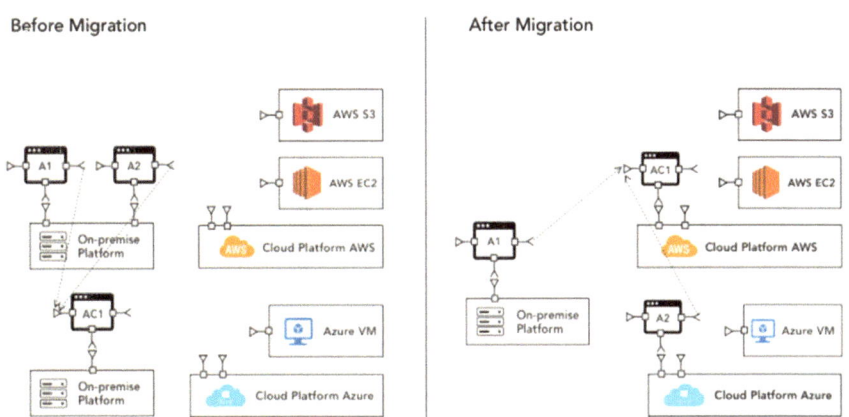

In this architecture, on-premise applications are re-architected as a portfolio and deployed in the Cloud environment. This architecture overcomes the problem where re-architecting an on-premise application does not remove duplicated functionality and inconsistencies. Multi-Application Modernization analyzes an application as a portfolio to identify opportunities for consolidation and sharing. The separation of workloads enables the identification of components that are shared by more than one solution. This architecture provides a consistent performance and reduces operational tasks and maintenance costs for shared components.

10.10   Conclusion

Multi-cloud architectures provide an environment where businesses can build secure and powerful Cloud environments outside the traditional infrastructure. Maximizing the impact of multi-cloud, however, means tackling a number of challenges including application sprawl, unique portals, compliance, migration, and security head-on. We need automated tools, integrated platforms, best practices, design metrics, key guidelines, architectural considerations, security, governance and middleware solutions in order to embark on multi-cloud environments. Above all, we need multi-cloud management platform in order to moderate the multi-cloud complexity that gets introduced and increased due to heightened heterogeneity and multiplicity of technologies and tools. This chapter has clearly laid down the right and relevant details for enterprises and executives to smoothly embrace the multi-cloud phenomenon in a risk-free and rewarding manner.

Appendix

The CMP Architecture and Functionality by Gartner

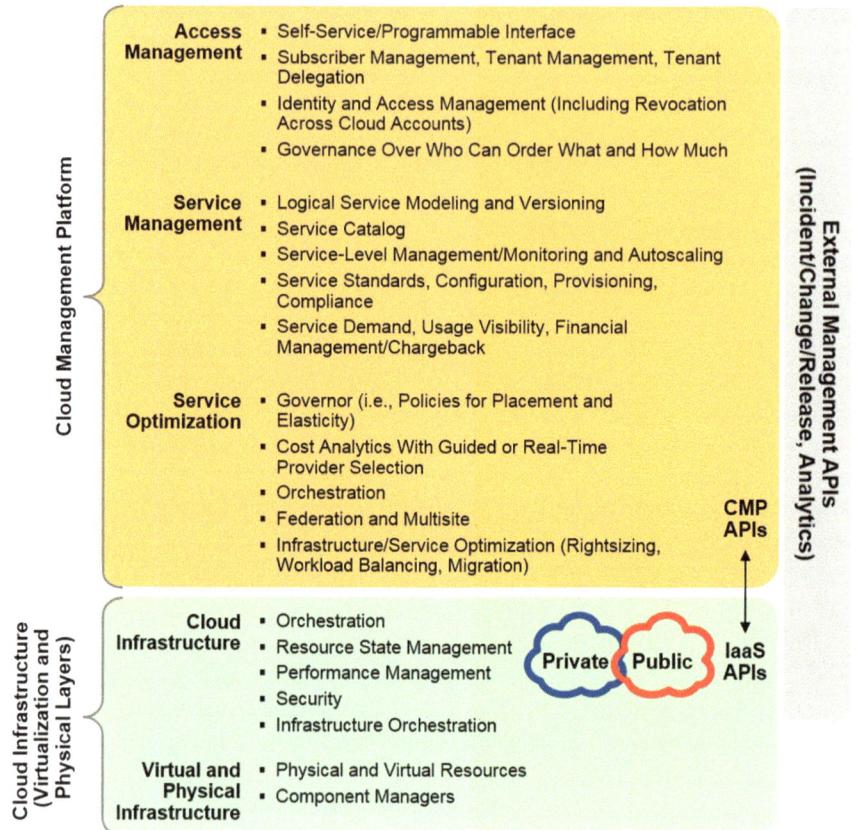

Index